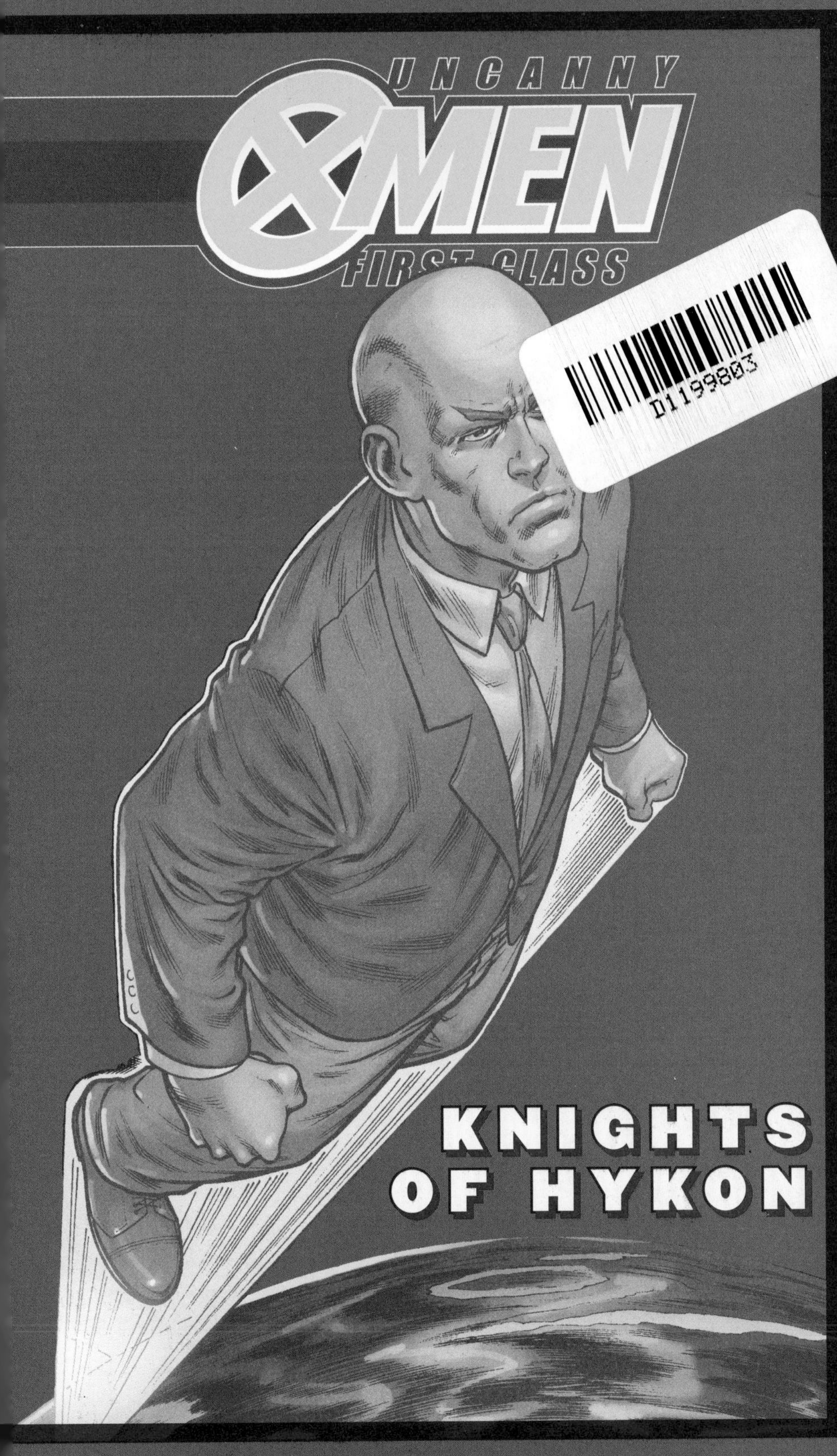
UNCANNY
X-MEN
FIRST CLASS
KNIGHTS OF HYKON

UNCANNY X-MEN FIRST CLASS

KNIGHTS OF HYKON

Writer: **SCOTT GRAY**

Art: **SCOTT KOBLISH & NELSON DECASTRO AND FERNANDO BLANCO (issue #8)**

Colors: **VAL STAPLES & FERNANDO BLANCO (issue #8)**

Letters: **BLAMBOT'S NATE PIEKOS**

Cover Art: **ROGER CRUZ & CHRIS SOTOMAYOR, PAUL PELLETIER, REILLY BROWN AND CAMERON STEWART**

Editor: **JORDAN D. WHITE**

Supervising Editor: **NATHAN COSBY**

X-Men #102-103

Writer: **CHRIS CLAREMONT**

Penciler: **DAVE COCKRUM**

Inker: **SAM GRAINGER**

Letterer: **JOHN COSTANZA**

Colorists: **BONNIE WILFORD & JANICE COHEN**

Collection Editor: **ALEX STARBUCK** · Associate Editor: **JOHN DENNING**
Editors, Special Projects: **JENNIFER GRÜNWALD & MARK D. BEAZLEY**
Senior Editor, Special Projects: **JEFF YOUNGQUIST** · Book Design: **SPRING HOTELING**
Senior Vice President of Sales: **DAVID GABRIEL**

Editor in Chief: **JOE QUESADA** · Publisher: **DAN BUCKLEY**
Executive Producer: **ALAN FINE**

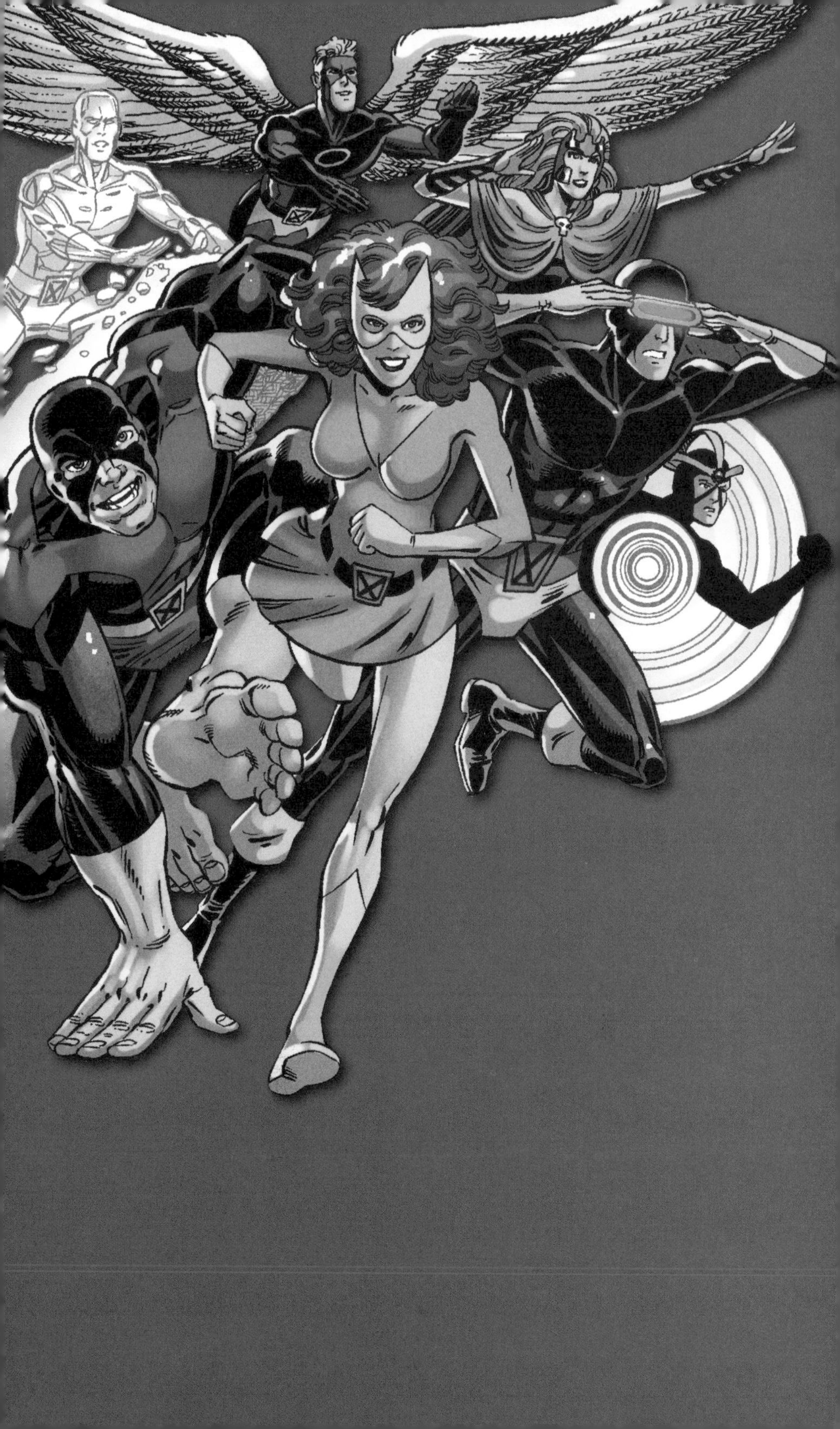

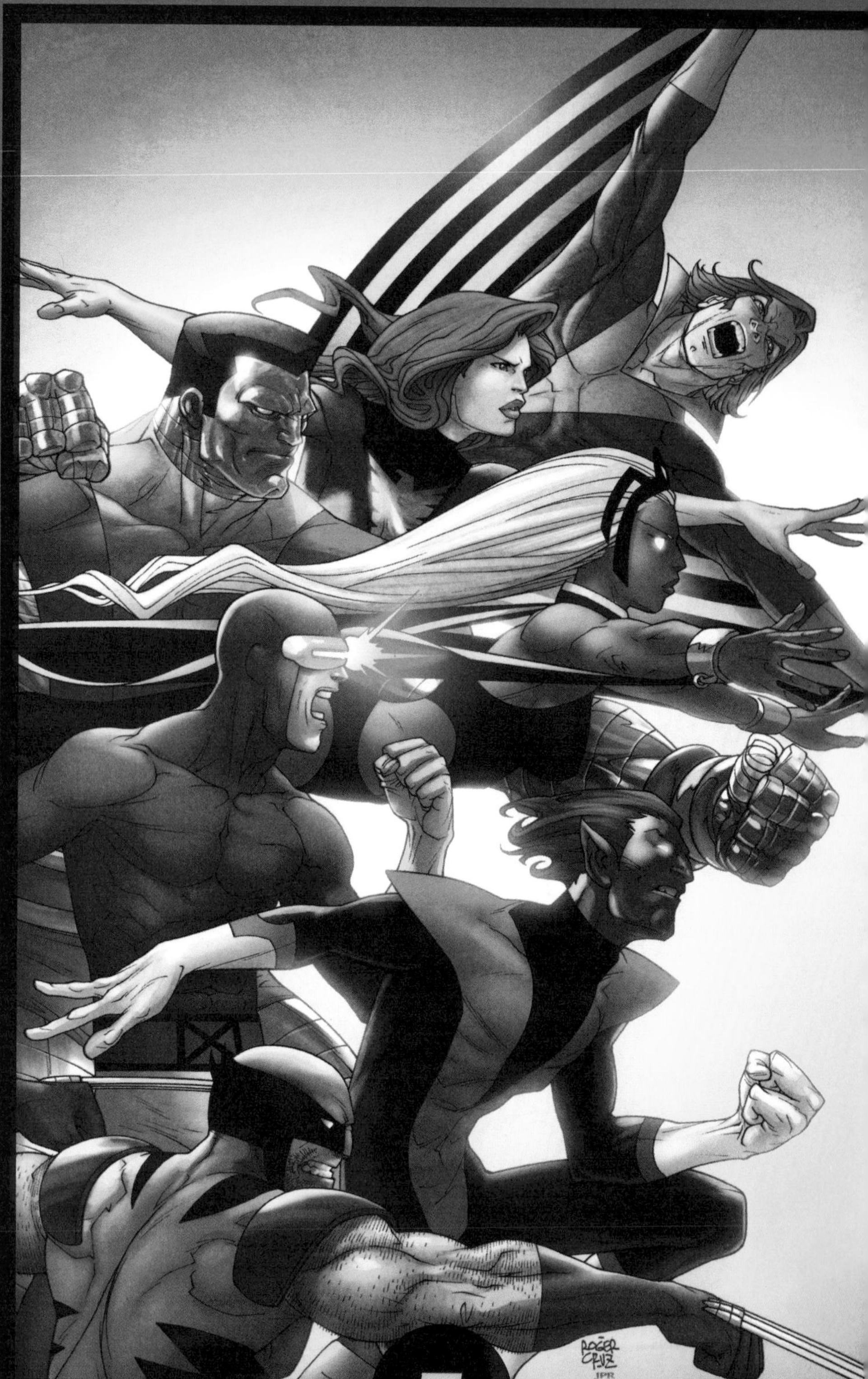
ROGER CRUZ
JPR

5

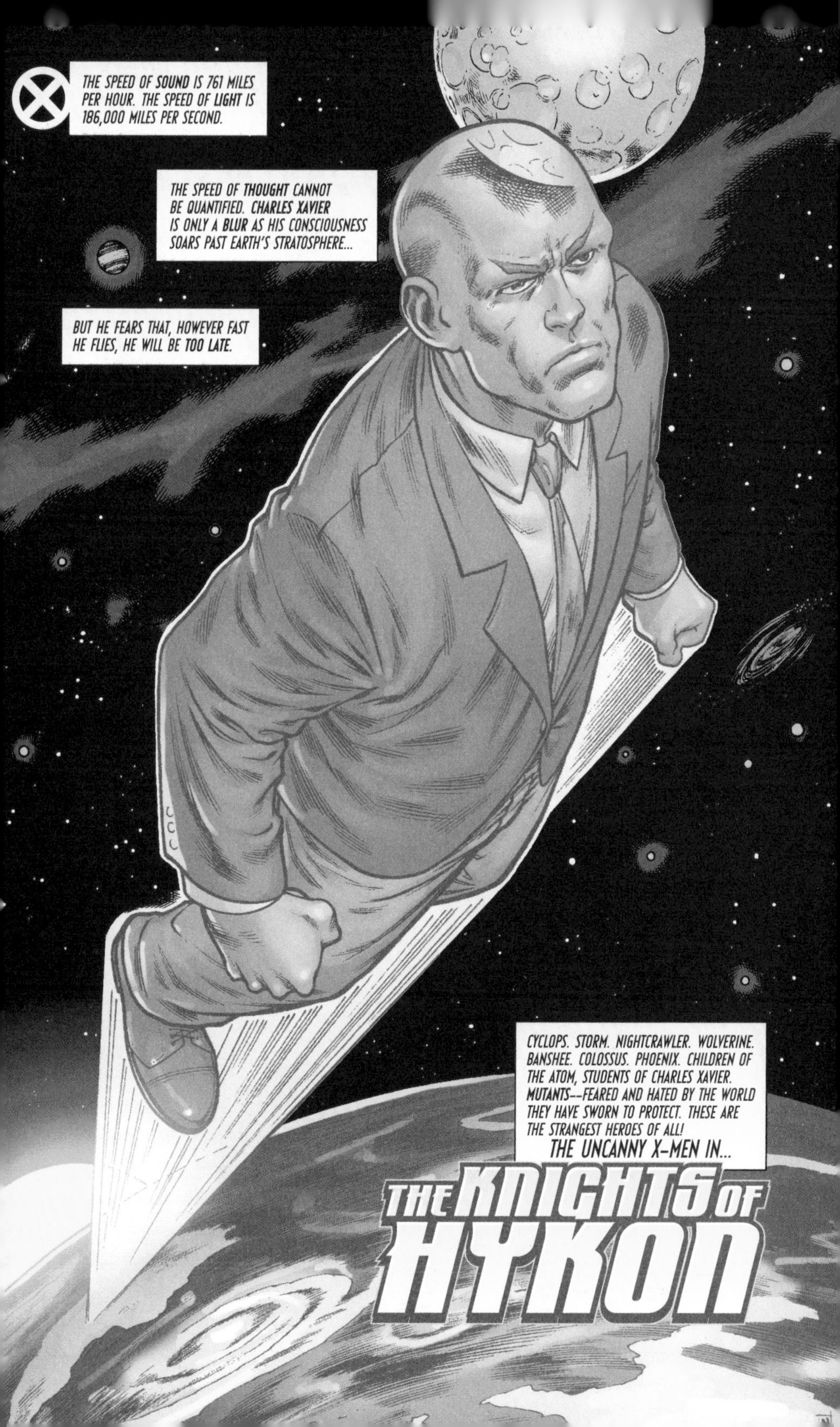
THE SPEED OF SOUND IS 761 MILES PER HOUR. THE SPEED OF LIGHT IS 186,000 MILES PER SECOND.
THE SPEED OF THOUGHT CANNOT BE QUANTIFIED. CHARLES XAVIER IS ONLY A BLUR AS HIS CONSCIOUSNESS SOARS PAST EARTH'S STRATOSPHERE...
BUT HE FEARS THAT, HOWEVER FAST HE FLIES, HE WILL BE TOO LATE.
CYCLOPS. STORM. NIGHTCRAWLER. WOLVERINE. BANSHEE. COLOSSUS. PHOENIX. CHILDREN OF THE ATOM, STUDENTS OF CHARLES XAVIER. MUTANTS--FEARED AND HATED BY THE WORLD THEY HAVE SWORN TO PROTECT. THESE ARE THE STRANGEST HEROES OF ALL!
THE UNCANNY X-MEN IN...
THE KNIGHTS OF HYKON

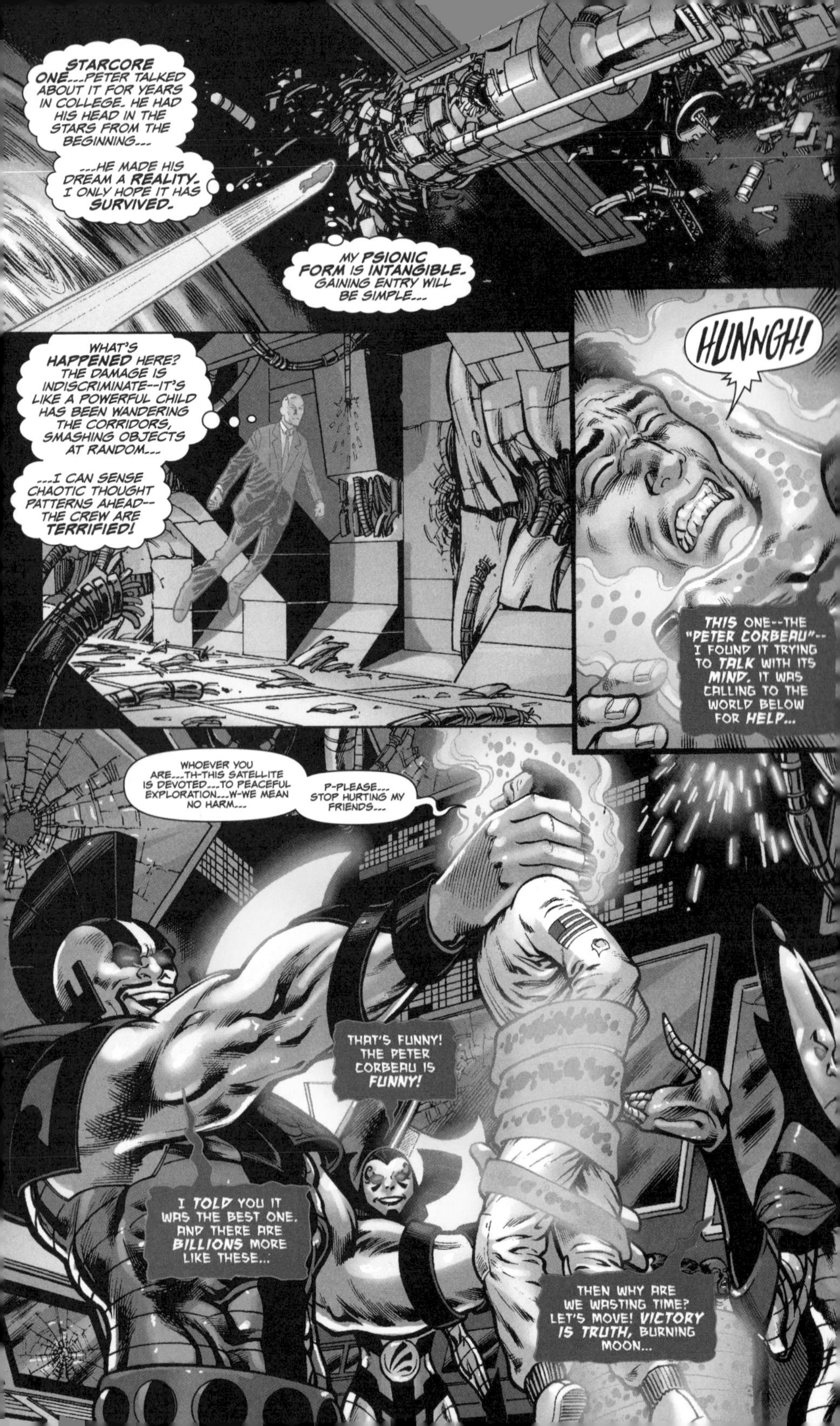
STARCORE ONE---PETER TALKED ABOUT IT FOR YEARS IN COLLEGE. HE HAD HIS HEAD IN THE STARS FROM THE BEGINNING---
---HE MADE HIS DREAM A REALITY. I ONLY HOPE IT HAS SURVIVED.
MY PSIONIC FORM IS INTANGIBLE. GAINING ENTRY WILL BE SIMPLE---
WHAT'S HAPPENED HERE? THE DAMAGE IS INDISCRIMINATE--IT'S LIKE A POWERFUL CHILD HAS BEEN WANDERING THE CORRIDORS, SMASHING OBJECTS AT RANDOM---
---I CAN SENSE CHAOTIC THOUGHT PATTERNS AHEAD--THE CREW ARE TERRIFIED!
HUNNGH!
THIS ONE--THE "PETER CORBEAU"--I FOUND IT TRYING TO TALK WITH ITS MIND. IT WAS CALLING TO THE WORLD BELOW FOR HELP...
WHOEVER YOU ARE---TH-THIS SATELLITE IS DEVOTED---TO PEACEFUL EXPLORATION---W-WE MEAN NO HARM---
P-PLEASE--- STOP HURTING MY FRIENDS---
THAT'S FUNNY! THE PETER CORBEAU IS FUNNY!
I TOLD YOU IT WAS THE BEST ONE. AND THERE ARE BILLIONS MORE LIKE THESE...
THEN WHY ARE WE WASTING TIME? LET'S MOVE! VICTORY IS TRUTH, BURNING MOON...

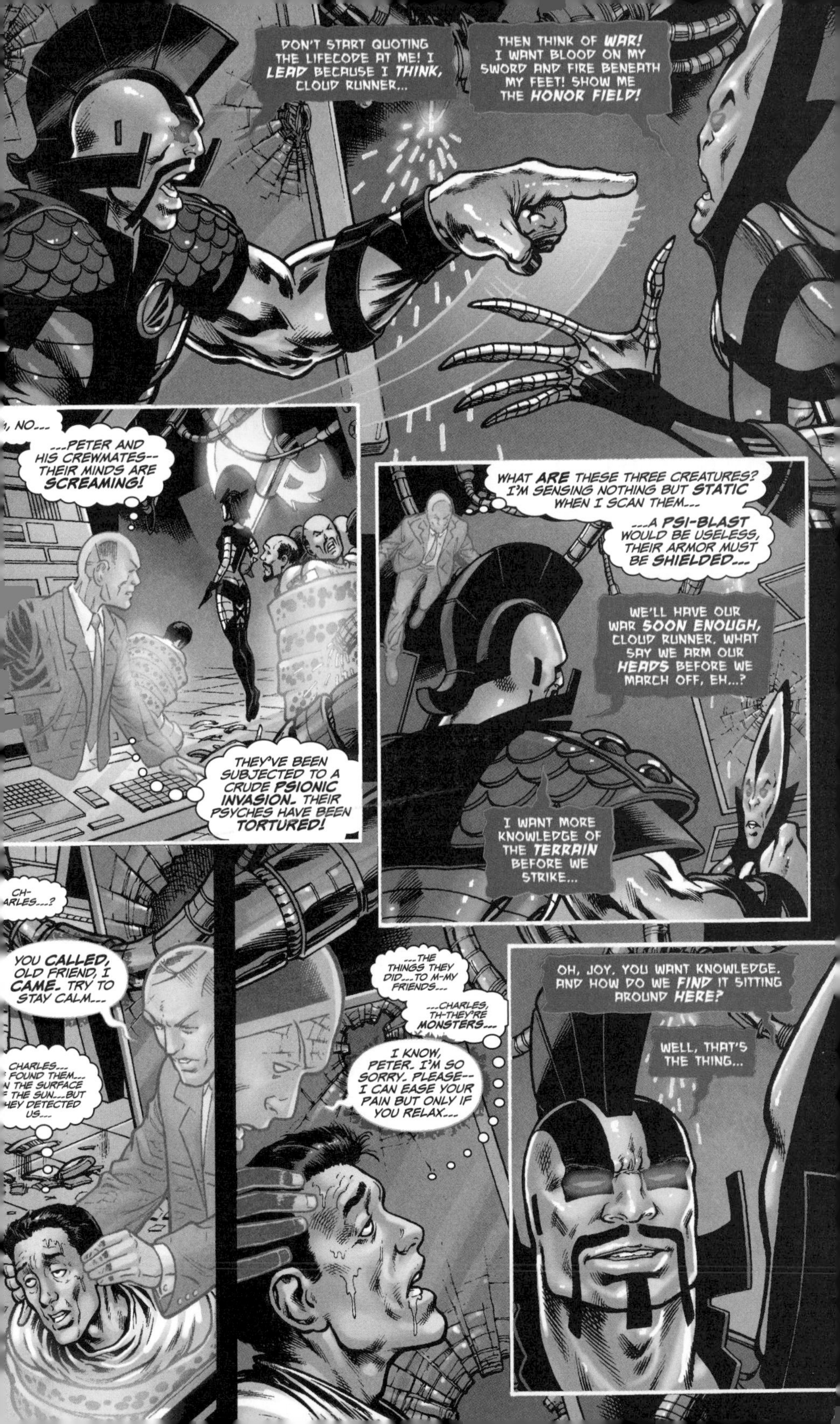
DON'T START QUOTING THE LIFECODE AT ME! I LEAD BECAUSE I THINK, CLOUD RUNNER...
THEN THINK OF WAR! I WANT BLOOD ON MY SWORD AND FIRE BENEATH MY FEET! SHOW ME THE HONOR FIELD!
, NO---
---PETER AND HIS CREWMATES-- THEIR MINDS ARE SCREAMING!
THEY'VE BEEN SUBJECTED TO A CRUDE PSIONIC INVASION. THEIR PSYCHES HAVE BEEN TORTURED!
WHAT ARE THESE THREE CREATURES? I'M SENSING NOTHING BUT STATIC WHEN I SCAN THEM---
---A PSI-BLAST WOULD BE USELESS, THEIR ARMOR MUST BE SHIELDED---
WE'LL HAVE OUR WAR SOON ENOUGH, CLOUD RUNNER. WHAT SAY WE ARM OUR HEADS BEFORE WE MARCH OFF, EH...?
I WANT MORE KNOWLEDGE OF THE TERRAIN BEFORE WE STRIKE...
CH- ARLES---?
YOU CALLED, OLD FRIEND, I CAME. TRY TO STAY CALM---
CHARLES--- FOUND THEM--- N THE SURFACE THE SUN---BUT HEY DETECTED US---
---THE THINGS THEY DID---TO M-MY FRIENDS---
---CHARLES, TH-THEY'RE MONSTERS---
I KNOW, PETER. I'M SO SORRY. PLEASE-- I CAN EASE YOUR PAIN BUT ONLY IF YOU RELAX---
OH, JOY. YOU WANT KNOWLEDGE. AND HOW DO WE FIND IT SITTING AROUND HERE?
WELL, THAT'S THE THING...

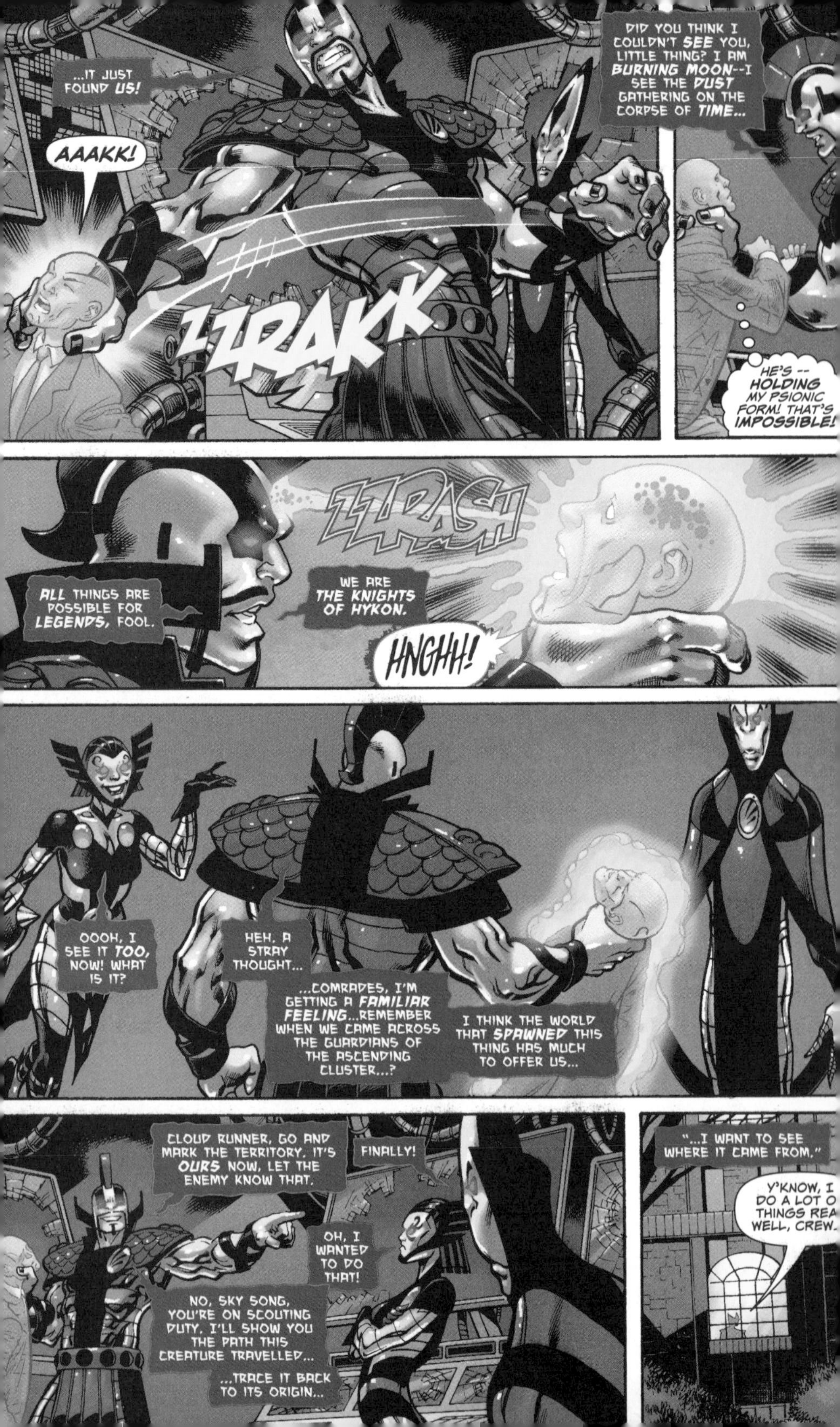

...IT JUST FOUND *US!*
AAAKK!
DID YOU THINK I COULDN'T *SEE* YOU, LITTLE THING? I AM *BURNING MOON*--I SEE THE *DUST* GATHERING ON THE CORPSE OF *TIME*...
ZZRAKK
HE'S -- *HOLDING* MY PSIONIC FORM! THAT'S *IMPOSSIBLE!*
ZZRASH
ALL THINGS ARE POSSIBLE FOR *LEGENDS,* FOOL.
WE ARE *THE KNIGHTS OF HYKON.*
HNGHH!
OOOH, I SEE IT *TOO,* NOW! WHAT IS IT?
HEH. A STRAY THOUGHT...
...COMRADES, I'M GETTING A *FAMILIAR FEELING*...REMEMBER WHEN WE CAME ACROSS THE GUARDIANS OF THE ASCENDING CLUSTER...?
I THINK THE WORLD THAT *SPAWNED* THIS THING HAS MUCH TO OFFER US...
CLOUD RUNNER, GO AND MARK THE TERRITORY. IT'S *OURS* NOW. LET THE ENEMY KNOW THAT.
FINALLY!
OH, I WANTED TO DO THAT!
NO, SKY SONG, YOU'RE ON SCOUTING DUTY. I'LL SHOW YOU THE PATH THIS CREATURE TRAVELLED...
...TRACE IT BACK TO ITS ORIGIN...
"...I WANT TO SEE WHERE IT CAME FROM."
Y'KNOW, I DO A LOT O THINGS REA WELL, CREW.

...BUT *WAITIN'* AIN'T ONE OF THEM. WHY ARE WE LETTIN' SUMMERS AND CO. TREAT US LIKE A PACK O' GRUNTS?

PATIENCE, BOYO. I'M THINKIN' WE'LL GET OUR TURN AT THE WHEEL SOON ENOUGH...

EVEN SO, PROFESSOR XAVIER SUMMONED THE OTHERS OVER AN *HOUR* AGO. IT WOULD BE POLITE TO KEEP US *INFORMED*...

THEY WILL CALL US WHEN WE ARE *NEEDED*, KURT...

...RE A REGULAR TIN ...ER, AIN'TCHA, PETEY? ...BET CHARLEY GIVES ...N EXTRA GOLD STAR ...R REPORT CARD ...MONTH...

THANK YOU, *TOVARISCH*, BUT THE PROFESSOR DOES NOT...

...WAIT. THIS IS SARCASM?

IF HIS LIPS ARE MOVING, PETER, THEN YES...

E-FLAMIN'-*NUFF!* YOU BOYS WANNA PLAY IN THE NURSERY WHILE THE GROWN-UPS TALK, *FINE*--I'M GETTIN' SOME *AIR*...

WE WERE ASKED TO STAY INSIDE, WOLVERINE.

IF I CATCH A *CHILL* I'LL SCREAM FOR *HELP*, IRISH...

...T MAN'S A *POWDER KEG* ...BE SURE. ONE DAY HE'S ...IN' TO *BLOW*, AN' HEAVEN ...P ANYONE STANDIN' ...IS WAY...

ACH, I HATE TO ADMIT IT, BUT I KNOW HOW HE FEELS.

THERE IS A... *WRONGNESS* ABROAD TONIGHT, SEAN. CAN'T YOU SENSE IT? WE ARE ON THE EDGE OF SOMETHING *HUGE.* SOMETHING *TERRIBLE*...

EASY NOW, LAD, DON'T LET YER IMAGINATION CARRY YOU AWAY. ALL *I'M* SENSIN' IS A CAFFEINE OVERLOAD...

...I'LL JUST POKE ME HEAD AROUND THE DOOR AN' SEE WHAT'S WHAT...

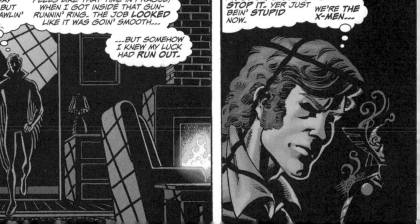

DIDN'T WANT TO SAY ANYTHIN' TO KURT, BUT ...Y SKIN'S BEEN CRAWLING ALL NIGHT TOO.

FEELS LIKE THAT TIME IN PRAGUE, WHEN I GOT INSIDE THAT GUN-RUNNIN' RING. THE JOB *LOOKED* LIKE IT WAS GOIN' SMOOTH...

...BUT SOMEHOW I KNEW MY LUCK HAD *RUN OUT.*

AH, C'MON, CASSIDY, *STOP IT.* YER JUST BEIN' *STUPID* NOW.

WE'RE *THE X-MEN*...

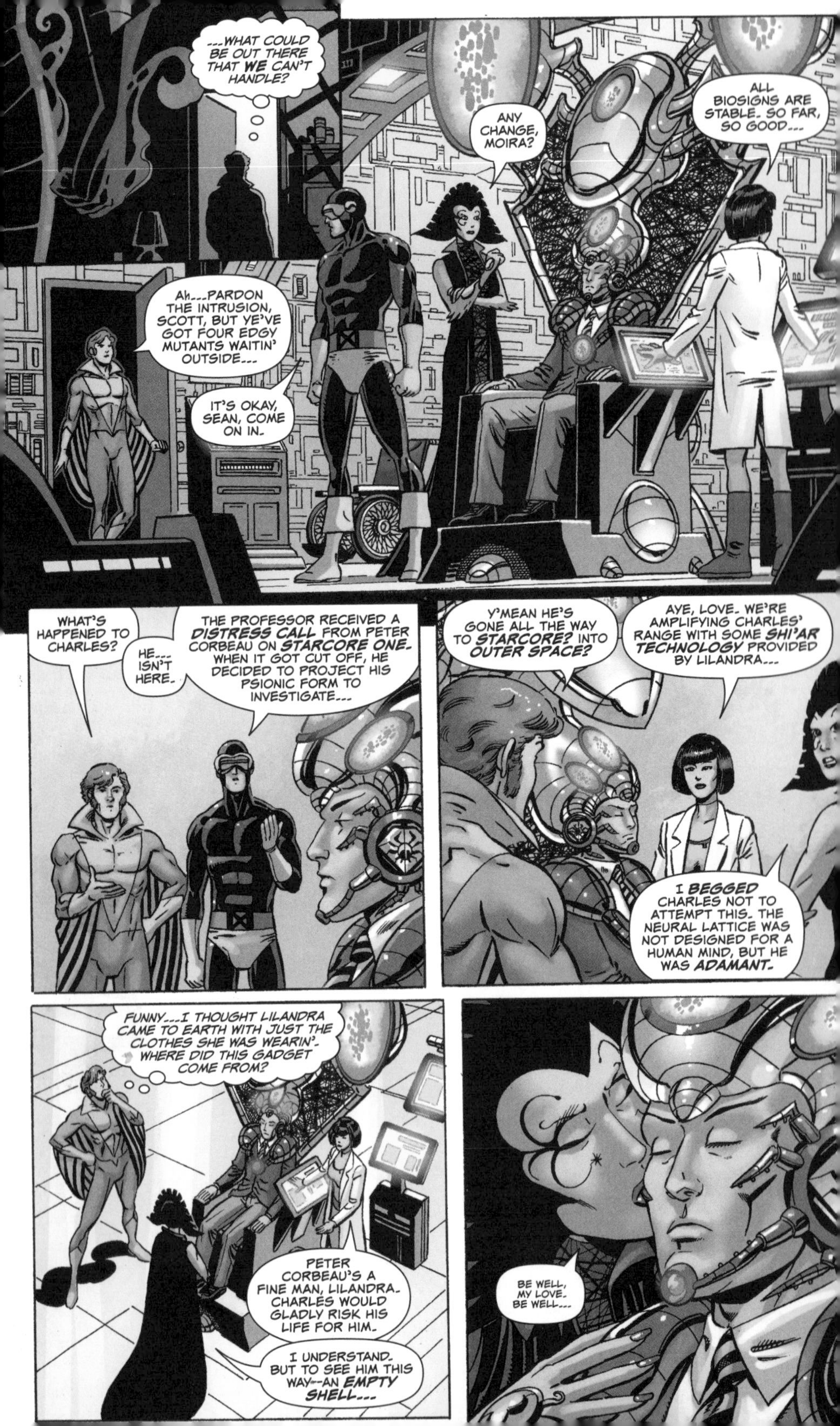
...WHAT COULD BE OUT THERE THAT WE CAN'T HANDLE?
ANY CHANGE, MOIRA?
ALL BIOSIGNS ARE STABLE. SO FAR, SO GOOD...
AH...PARDON THE INTRUSION, SCOTT, BUT YE'VE GOT FOUR EDGY MUTANTS WAITIN' OUTSIDE...
IT'S OKAY, SEAN, COME ON IN.
WHAT'S HAPPENED TO CHARLES?
HE... ISN'T HERE.
THE PROFESSOR RECEIVED A DISTRESS CALL FROM PETER CORBEAU ON STARCORE ONE. WHEN IT GOT CUT OFF, HE DECIDED TO PROJECT HIS PSIONIC FORM TO INVESTIGATE...
Y'MEAN HE'S GONE ALL THE WAY TO STARCORE? INTO OUTER SPACE?
AYE, LOVE. WE'RE AMPLIFYING CHARLES' RANGE WITH SOME SHI'AR TECHNOLOGY PROVIDED BY LILANDRA...
I BEGGED CHARLES NOT TO ATTEMPT THIS. THE NEURAL LATTICE WAS NOT DESIGNED FOR A HUMAN MIND, BUT HE WAS ADAMANT.
FUNNY...I THOUGHT LILANDRA CAME TO EARTH WITH JUST THE CLOTHES SHE WAS WEARIN'. WHERE DID THIS GADGET COME FROM?
PETER CORBEAU'S A FINE MAN, LILANDRA. CHARLES WOULD GLADLY RISK HIS LIFE FOR HIM.
I UNDERSTAND. BUT TO SEE HIM THIS WAY--AN EMPTY SHELL...
BE WELL, MY LOVE. BE WELL...

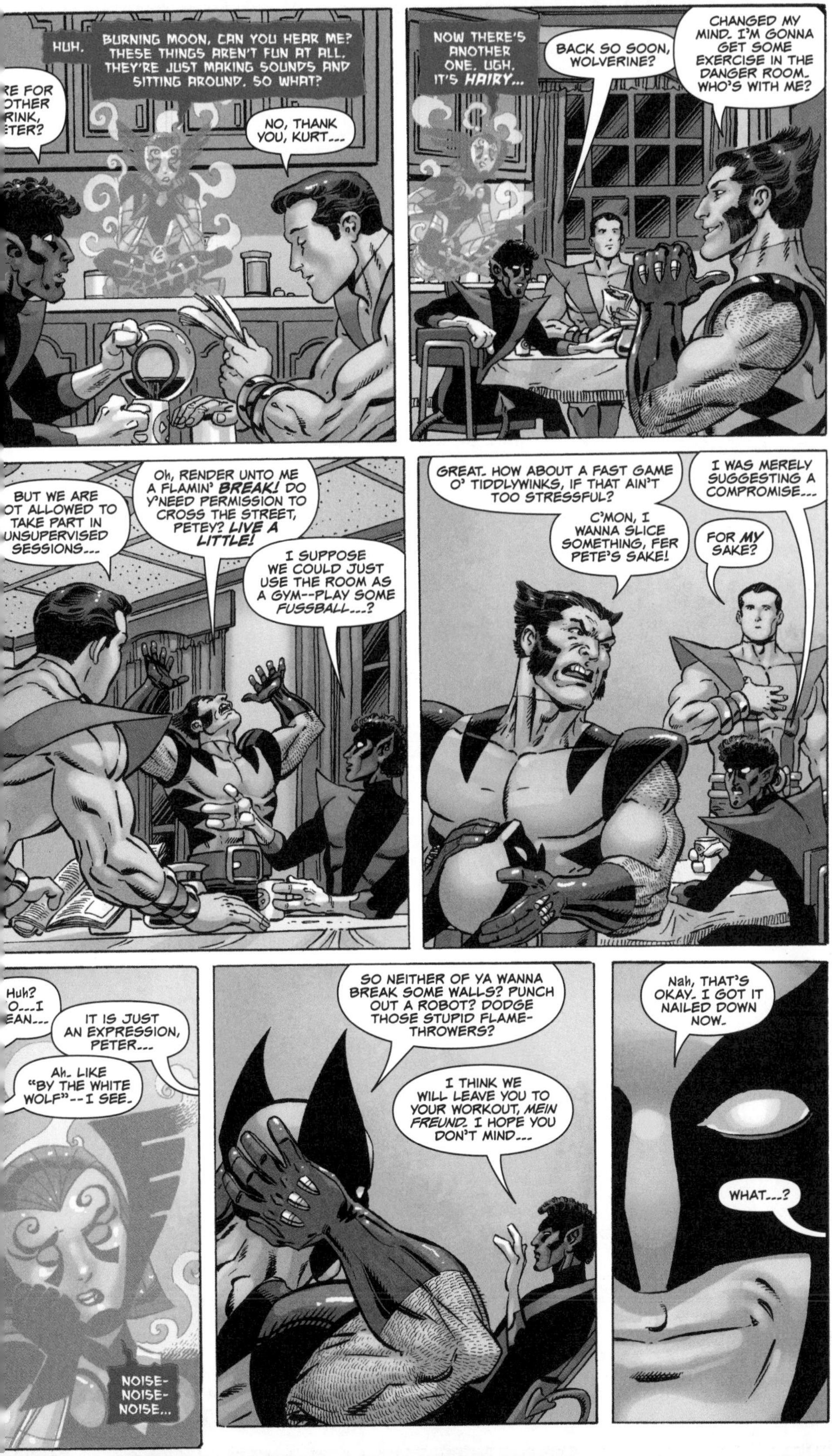
HUH.
BURNING MOON, CAN YOU HEAR ME? THESE THINGS AREN'T FUN AT ALL. THEY'RE JUST MAKING SOUNDS AND SITTING AROUND. SO WHAT?
RE FOR OTHER RINK, ETER?
NO, THANK YOU, KURT...
NOW THERE'S ANOTHER ONE. UGH. IT'S *HAIRY*...
BACK SO SOON, WOLVERINE?
CHANGED MY MIND. I'M GONNA GET SOME EXERCISE IN THE DANGER ROOM. WHO'S WITH ME?
BUT WE ARE OT ALLOWED TO TAKE PART IN UNSUPERVISED SESSIONS...
Oh, RENDER UNTO ME A FLAMIN' *BREAK!* DO Y'NEED PERMISSION TO CROSS THE STREET, PETEY? *LIVE A LITTLE!*
I SUPPOSE WE COULD JUST USE THE ROOM AS A GYM--PLAY SOME *FUSSBALL*...?
GREAT. HOW ABOUT A FAST GAME O' TIDDLYWINKS, IF THAT AIN'T TOO STRESSFUL?
C'MON, I WANNA SLICE SOMETHING, FER PETE'S SAKE!
I WAS MERELY SUGGESTING A COMPROMISE...
FOR *MY* SAKE?
Huh? O...I EAN...
IT IS JUST AN EXPRESSION, PETER...
Ah. LIKE "BY THE WHITE WOLF"--I SEE.
NOISE-NOISE-NOISE...
SO NEITHER OF YA WANNA BREAK SOME WALLS? PUNCH OUT A ROBOT? DODGE THOSE STUPID FLAME-THROWERS?
I THINK WE WILL LEAVE YOU TO YOUR WORKOUT, *MEIN FREUND.* I HOPE YOU DON'T MIND...
Nah, THAT'S OKAY. I GOT IT NAILED DOWN NOW.
WHAT...?

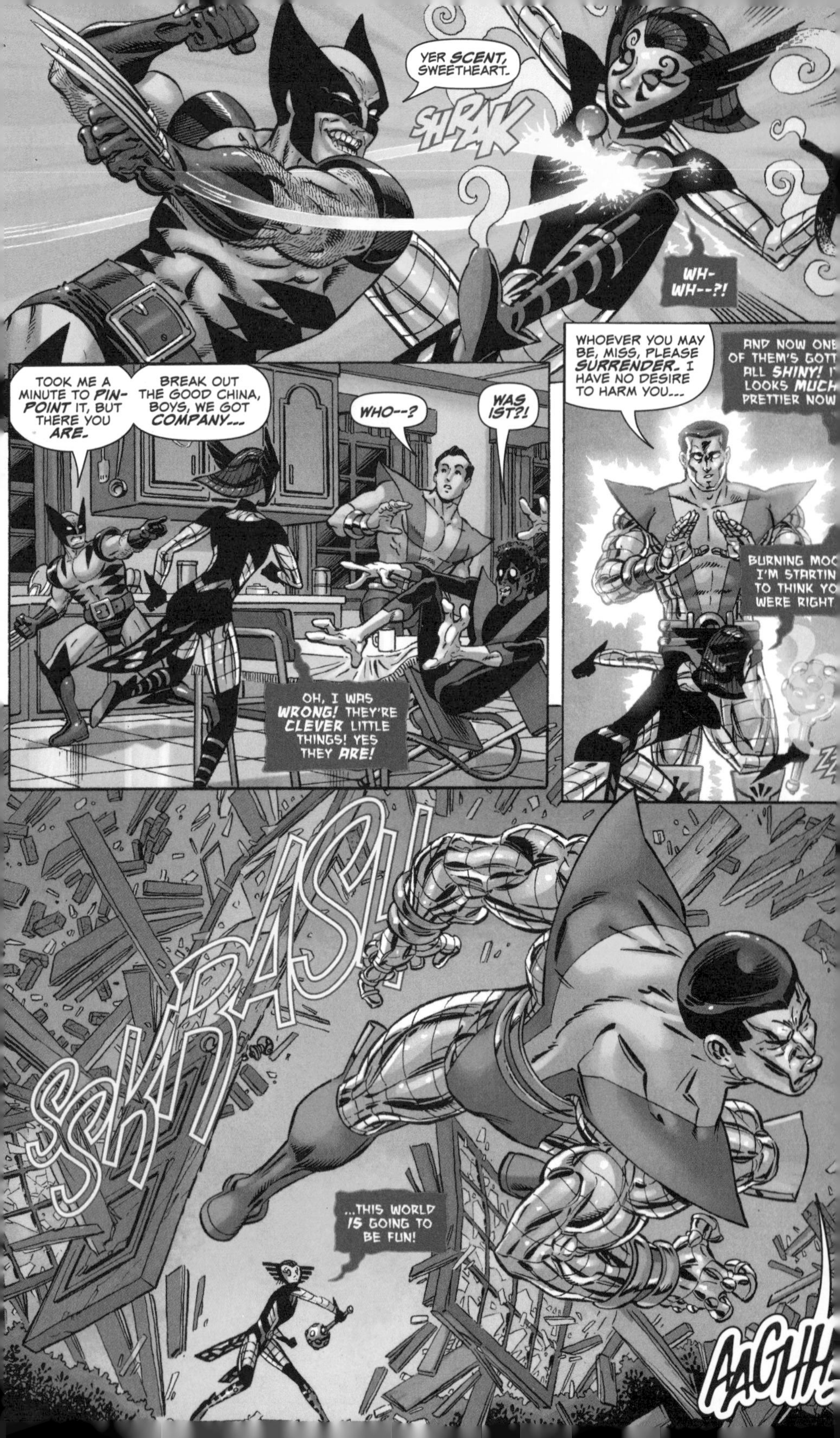
YER SCENT, SWEETHEART.
SHRAK
WH- WH--?!
TOOK ME A MINUTE TO PIN-POINT IT, BUT THERE YOU ARE.
BREAK OUT THE GOOD CHINA, BOYS, WE GOT COMPANY...
WHO--?
WAS IST?!
OH, I WAS WRONG! THEY'RE CLEVER LITTLE THINGS! YES THEY ARE!
WHOEVER YOU MAY BE, MISS, PLEASE SURRENDER. I HAVE NO DESIRE TO HARM YOU...
AND NOW ONE OF THEM'S GOTT ALL SHINY! I LOOKS MUCH PRETTIER NOW
BURNING MOO I'M STARTIN TO THINK YO WERE RIGHT
SSKRASH
...THIS WORLD IS GOING TO BE FUN!
AAGHH

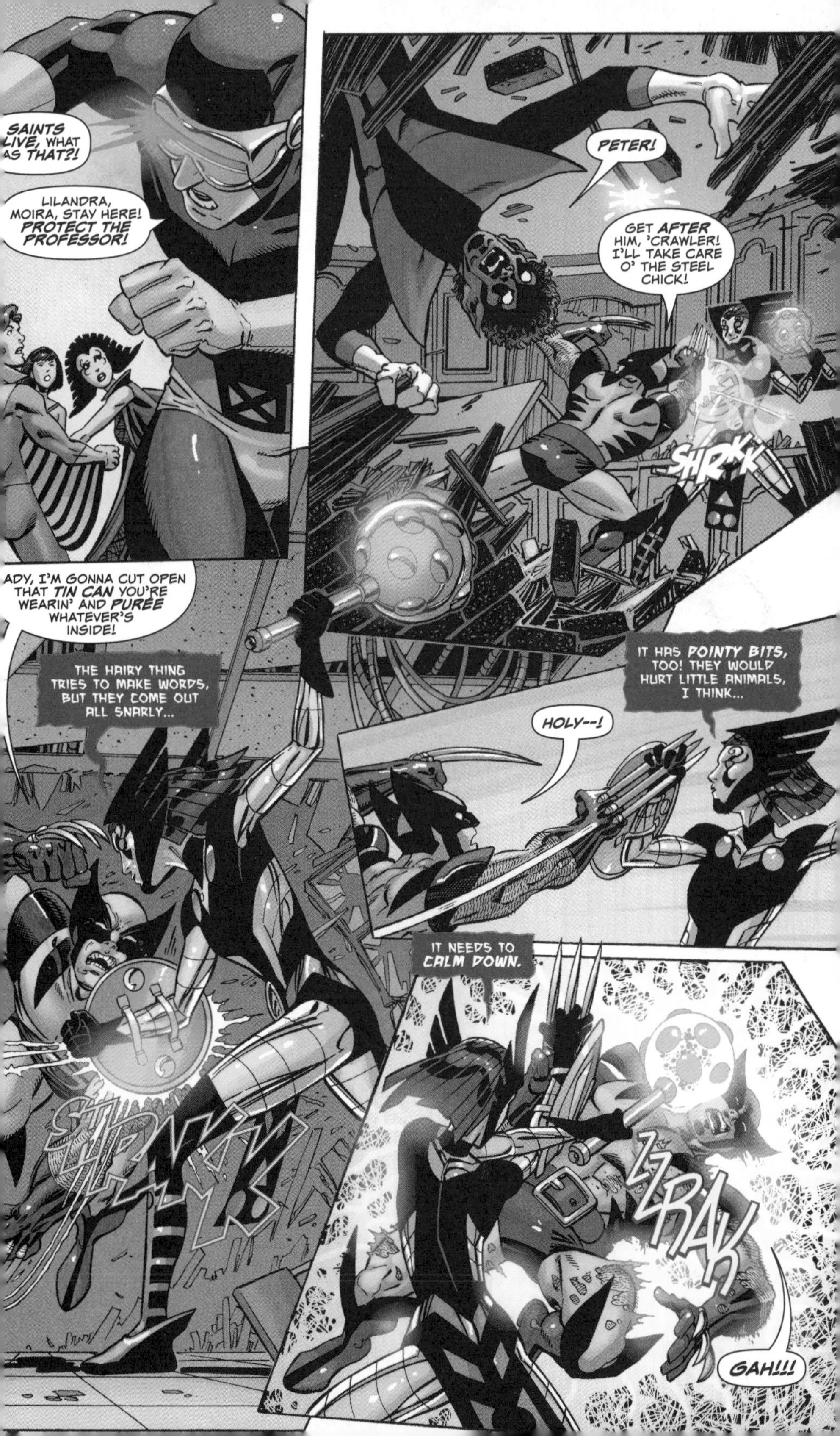

SAINTS LIVE, WHAT AS THAT?!
LILANDRA, MOIRA, STAY HERE! PROTECT THE PROFESSOR!
PETER!
GET AFTER HIM, 'CRAWLER! I'LL TAKE CARE O' THE STEEL CHICK!
SHRKKK
ADY, I'M GONNA CUT OPEN THAT TIN CAN YOU'RE WEARIN' AND PUREE WHATEVER'S INSIDE!
THE HAIRY THING TRIES TO MAKE WORDS, BUT THEY COME OUT ALL SNARLY...
IT HAS POINTY BITS, TOO! THEY WOULD HURT LITTLE ANIMALS, I THINK...
HOLY--!
IT NEEDS TO CALM DOWN.
ZZRAK
GAH!!!

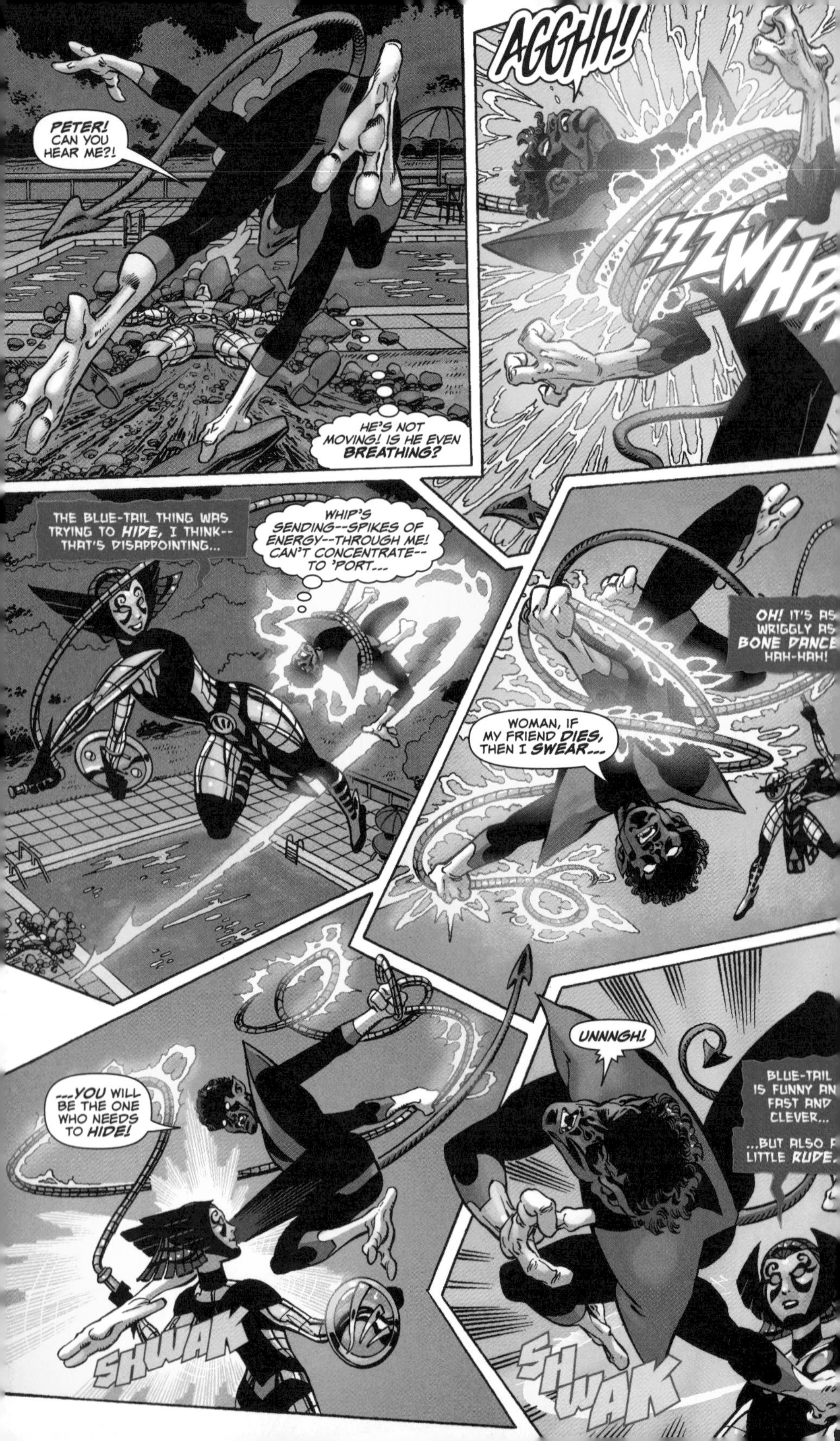
PETER! CAN YOU HEAR ME?!
HE'S NOT MOVING! IS HE EVEN BREATHING?
AGGHH!
ZZZWHPP
THE BLUE-TAIL THING WAS TRYING TO HIDE, I THINK-- THAT'S DISAPPOINTING...
WHIP'S SENDING--SPIKES OF ENERGY--THROUGH ME! CAN'T CONCENTRATE-- TO 'PORT...
OH! IT'S AS WRIGGLY AS BONE DANCE HAH-HAH!
WOMAN, IF MY FRIEND DIES, THEN I SWEAR...
...YOU WILL BE THE ONE WHO NEEDS TO HIDE!
SHWAK
UNNNGH!
BLUE-TAIL IS FUNNY AN FAST AND CLEVER...
...BUT ALSO A LITTLE RUDE.
SHWAK

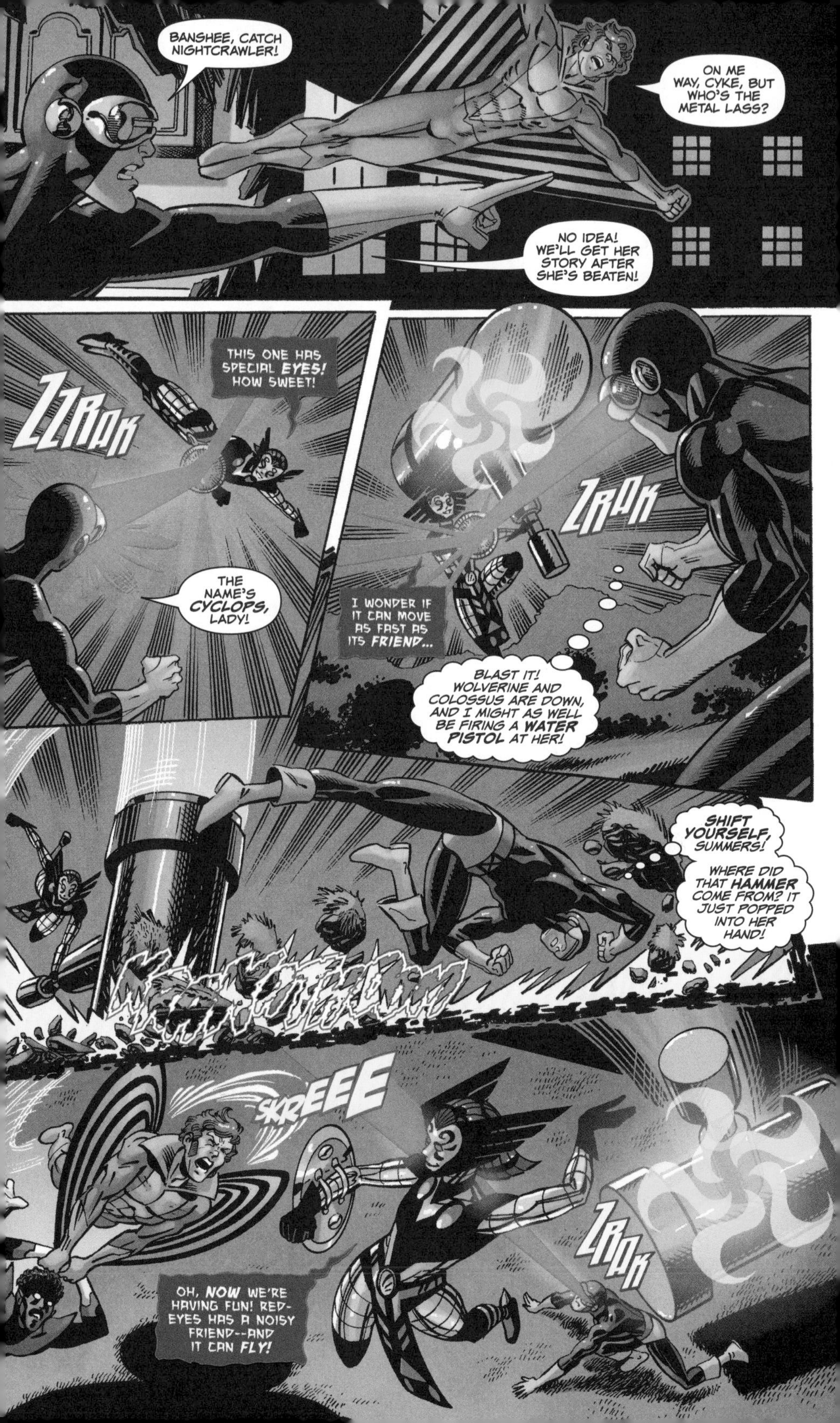

BANSHEE, CATCH NIGHTCRAWLER!
ON ME WAY, CYKE, BUT WHO'S THE METAL LASS?
NO IDEA! WE'LL GET HER STORY AFTER SHE'S BEATEN!
ZZRAK
THIS ONE HAS SPECIAL EYES! HOW SWEET!
THE NAME'S CYCLOPS, LADY!
ZRAK
I WONDER IF IT CAN MOVE AS FAST AS ITS FRIEND...
BLAST IT! WOLVERINE AND COLOSSUS ARE DOWN, AND I MIGHT AS WELL BE FIRING A WATER PISTOL AT HER!
SHIFT YOURSELF, SUMMERS!
WHERE DID THAT HAMMER COME FROM? IT JUST POPPED INTO HER HAND!
SKREEEE
ZRAK
OH, NOW WE'RE HAVING FUN! RED-EYES HAS A NOISY FRIEND--AND IT CAN FLY!

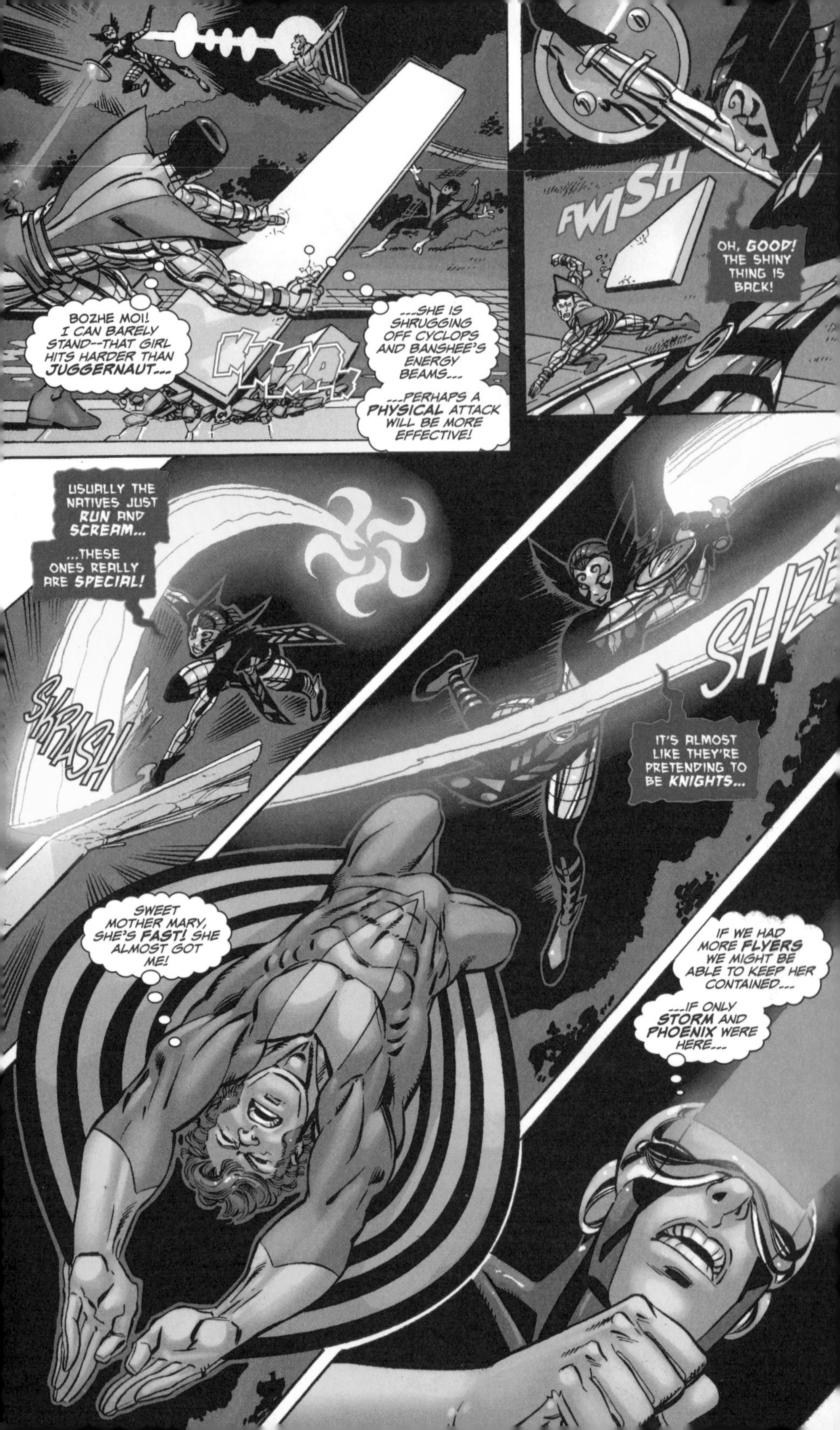
BOZHE MOI! I CAN BARELY STAND--THAT GIRL HITS HARDER THAN JUGGERNAUT---
KRAK
---SHE IS SHRUGGING OFF CYCLOPS AND BANSHEE'S ENERGY BEAMS---
---PERHAPS A PHYSICAL ATTACK WILL BE MORE EFFECTIVE!
FWISH
OH, GOOD! THE SHINY THING IS BACK!
USUALLY THE NATIVES JUST RUN AND SCREAM...
...THESE ONES REALLY ARE SPECIAL!
SKRASH
SHIZE
IT'S ALMOST LIKE THEY'RE PRETENDING TO BE KNIGHTS...
SWEET MOTHER MARY, SHE'S FAST! SHE ALMOST GOT ME!
IF WE HAD MORE FLYERS WE MIGHT BE ABLE TO KEEP HER CONTAINED---
---IF ONLY STORM AND PHOENIX WERE HERE---

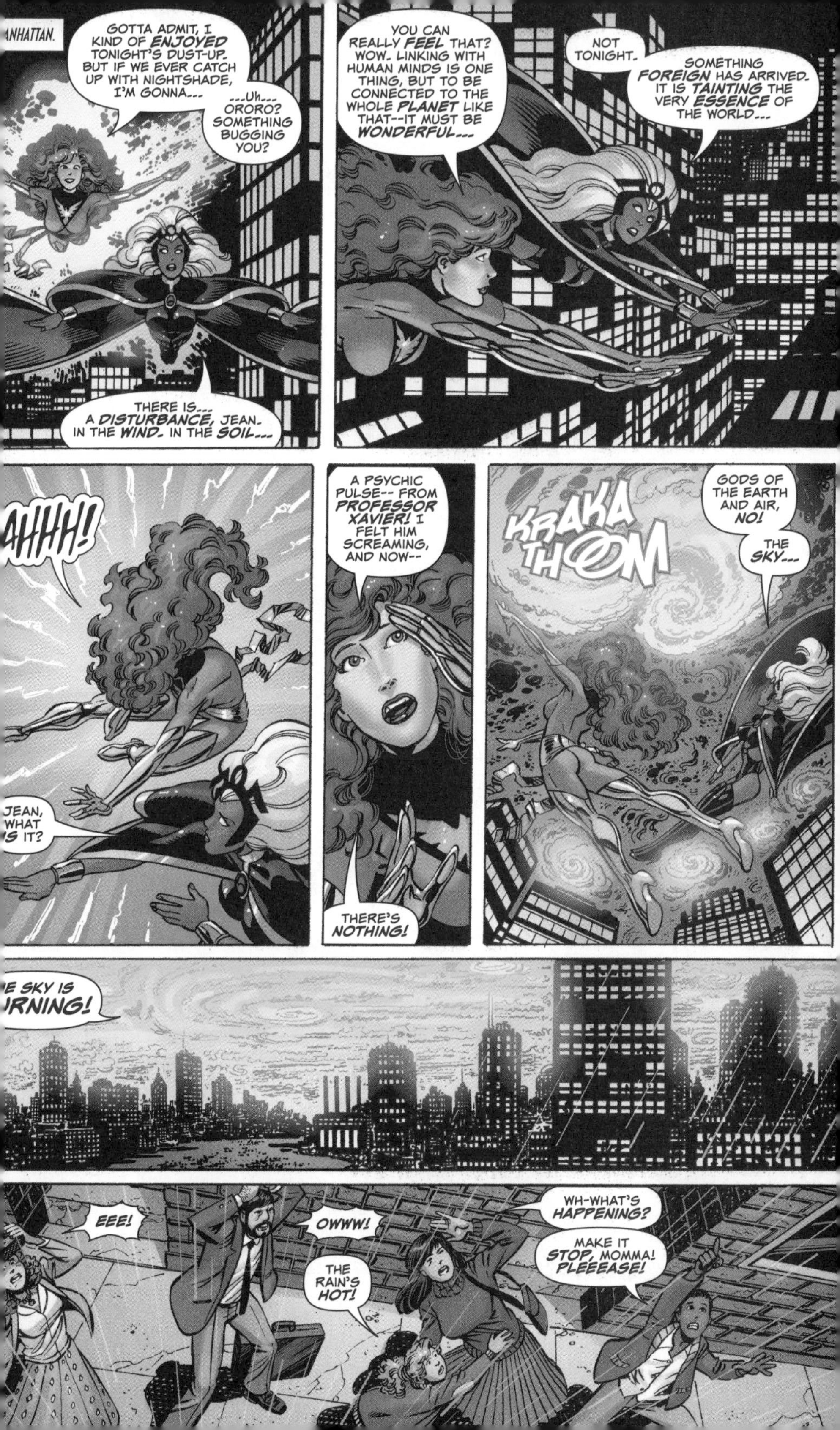

ANHATTAN.
GOTTA ADMIT, I KIND OF ENJOYED TONIGHT'S DUST-UP. BUT IF WE EVER CATCH UP WITH NIGHTSHADE, I'M GONNA...
...UH... ORORO? SOMETHING BUGGING YOU?
THERE IS... A DISTURBANCE, JEAN. IN THE WIND. IN THE SOIL...
YOU CAN REALLY FEEL THAT? WOW. LINKING WITH HUMAN MINDS IS ONE THING, BUT TO BE CONNECTED TO THE WHOLE PLANET LIKE THAT--IT MUST BE WONDERFUL...
NOT TONIGHT.
SOMETHING FOREIGN HAS ARRIVED. IT IS TAINTING THE VERY ESSENCE OF THE WORLD...
AHHHH!
JEAN, WHAT IS IT?
A PSYCHIC PULSE-- FROM PROFESSOR XAVIER! I FELT HIM SCREAMING, AND NOW--
THERE'S NOTHING!
KRAKATHOOM
GODS OF THE EARTH AND AIR, NO!
THE SKY...
E SKY IS RNING!
EEE!
OWWW!
THE RAIN'S HOT!
WH-WHAT'S HAPPENING?
MAKE IT STOP, MOMMA! PLEEEASE!

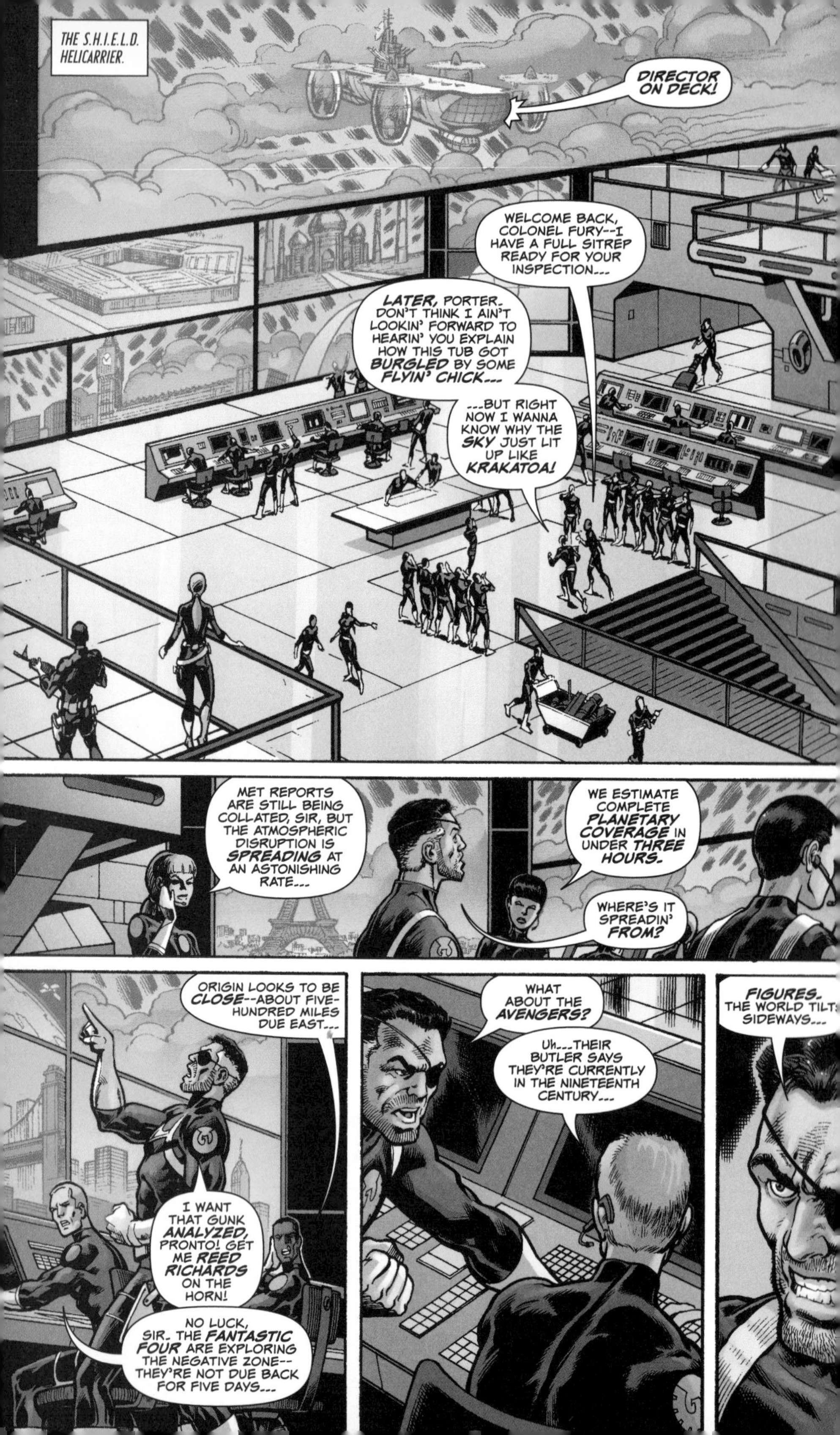
THE S.H.I.E.L.D. HELICARRIER.
DIRECTOR ON DECK!
WELCOME BACK, COLONEL FURY--I HAVE A FULL SITREP READY FOR YOUR INSPECTION...
LATER, PORTER. DON'T THINK I AIN'T LOOKIN' FORWARD TO HEARIN' YOU EXPLAIN HOW THIS TUB GOT BURGLED BY SOME FLYIN' CHICK...
...BUT RIGHT NOW I WANNA KNOW WHY THE SKY JUST LIT UP LIKE KRAKATOA!
MET REPORTS ARE STILL BEING COLLATED, SIR, BUT THE ATMOSPHERIC DISRUPTION IS SPREADING AT AN ASTONISHING RATE...
WE ESTIMATE COMPLETE PLANETARY COVERAGE IN UNDER THREE HOURS.
WHERE'S IT SPREADIN' FROM?
ORIGIN LOOKS TO BE CLOSE--ABOUT FIVE-HUNDRED MILES DUE EAST...
I WANT THAT GUNK ANALYZED, PRONTO! GET ME REED RICHARDS ON THE HORN!
NO LUCK, SIR. THE FANTASTIC FOUR ARE EXPLORING THE NEGATIVE ZONE--THEY'RE NOT DUE BACK FOR FIVE DAYS...
WHAT ABOUT THE AVENGERS?
Uh...THEIR BUTLER SAYS THEY'RE CURRENTLY IN THE NINETEENTH CENTURY...
FIGURES. THE WORLD TILTS SIDEWAYS...

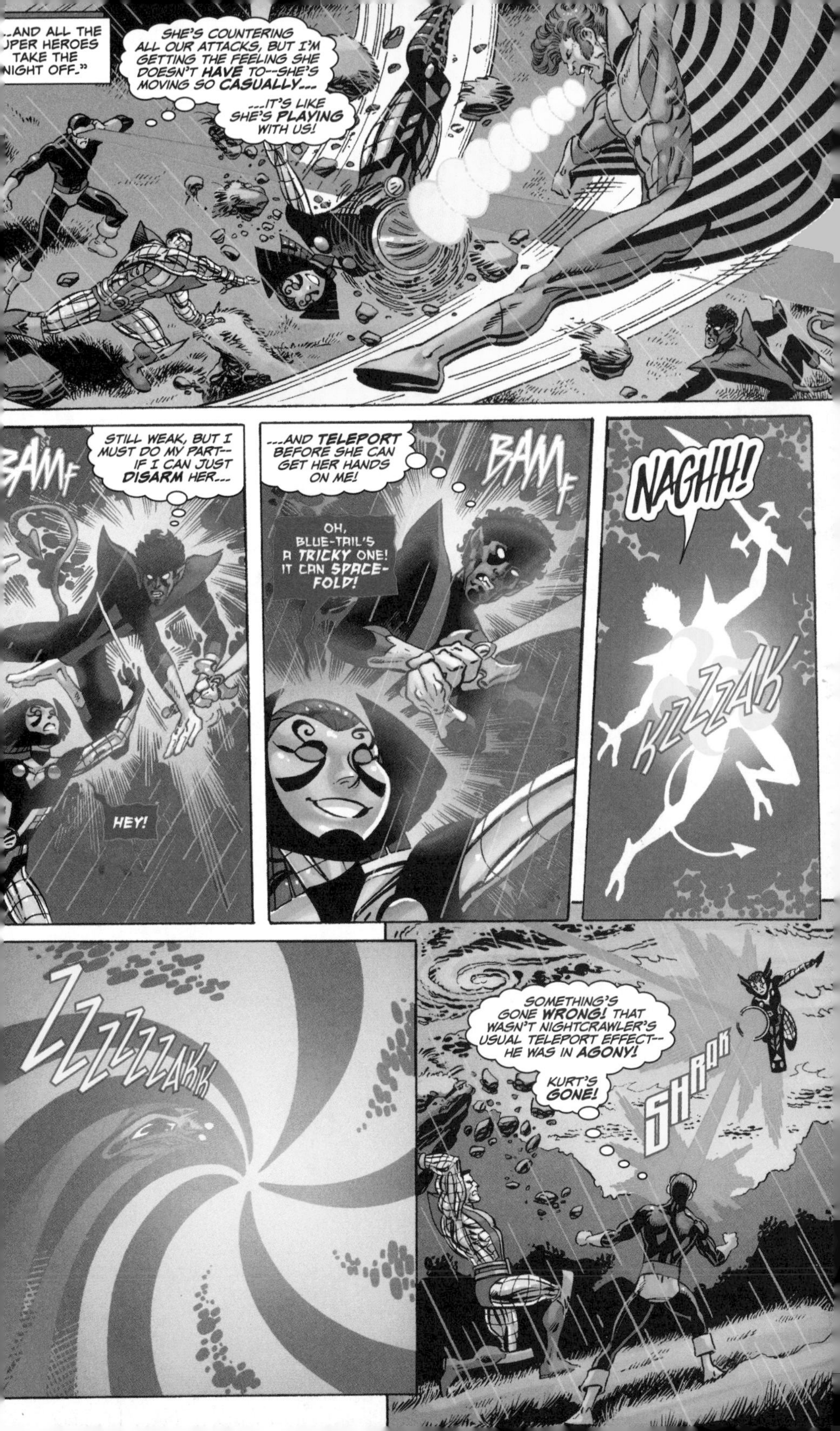
...AND ALL THE SUPER HEROES TAKE THE NIGHT OFF."
SHE'S COUNTERING ALL OUR ATTACKS, BUT I'M GETTING THE FEELING SHE DOESN'T HAVE TO--SHE'S MOVING SO CASUALLY...
...IT'S LIKE SHE'S PLAYING WITH US!
BAMF
STILL WEAK, BUT I MUST DO MY PART-- IF I CAN JUST DISARM HER...
HEY!
...AND TELEPORT BEFORE SHE CAN GET HER HANDS ON ME!
BAMF
OH, BLUE-TAIL'S A TRICKY ONE! IT CAN SPACE-FOLD!
NAGHH!
KZZZZAK
ZZZZZZAKK
SOMETHING'S GONE WRONG! THAT WASN'T NIGHTCRAWLER'S USUAL TELEPORT EFFECT--HE WAS IN AGONY!
KURT'S GONE!
SHRAK

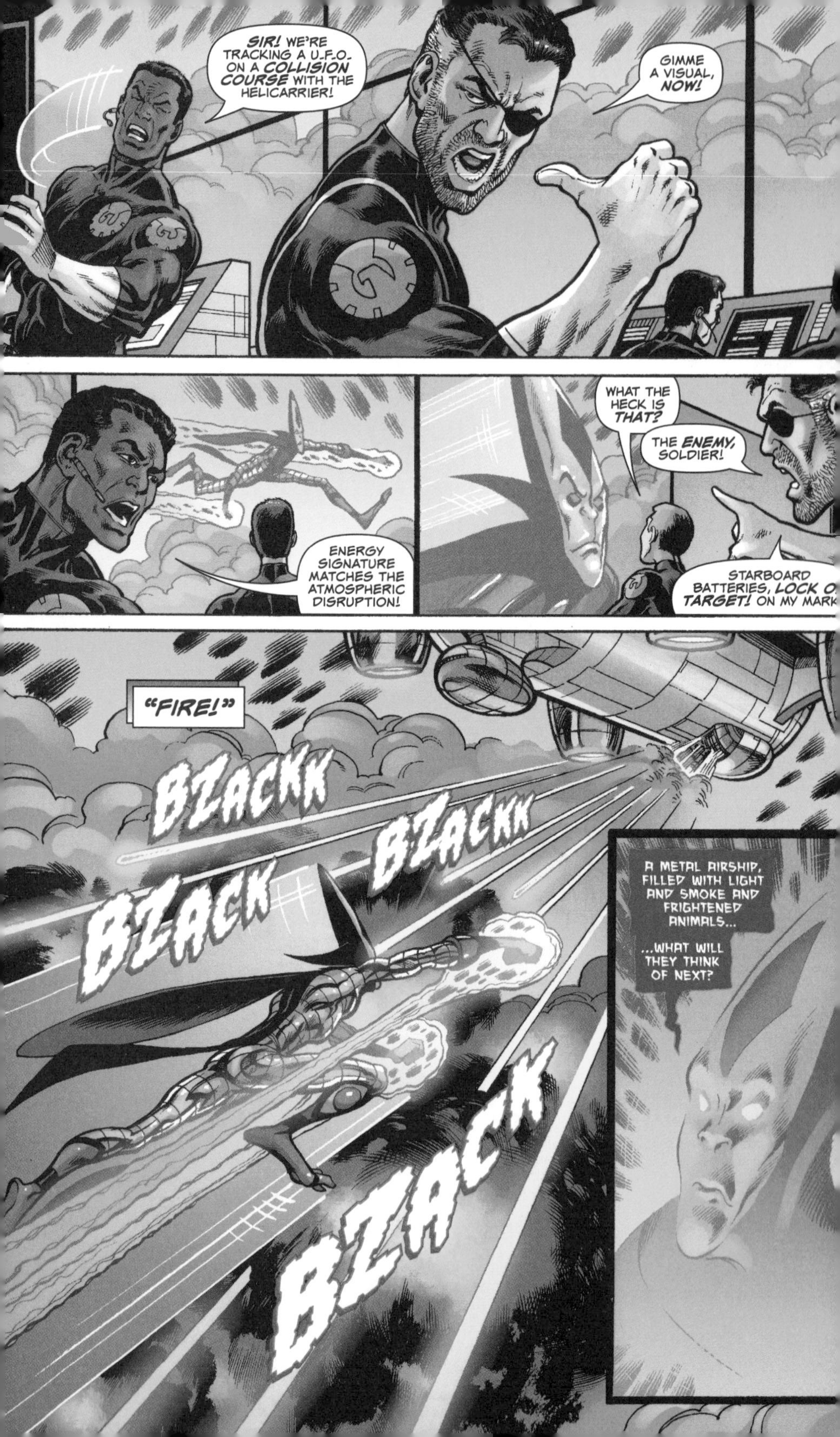
SIR! WE'RE TRACKING A U.F.O. ON A COLLISION COURSE WITH THE HELICARRIER!
GIMME A VISUAL, NOW!
ENERGY SIGNATURE MATCHES THE ATMOSPHERIC DISRUPTION!
WHAT THE HECK IS THAT?
THE ENEMY, SOLDIER!
STARBOARD BATTERIES, LOCK O TARGET! ON MY MARK
"FIRE!"
BZACKK
BZACKK
BZACK
BZACK
A METAL AIRSHIP, FILLED WITH LIGHT AND SMOKE AND FRIGHTENED ANIMALS...
...WHAT WILL THEY THINK OF NEXT?

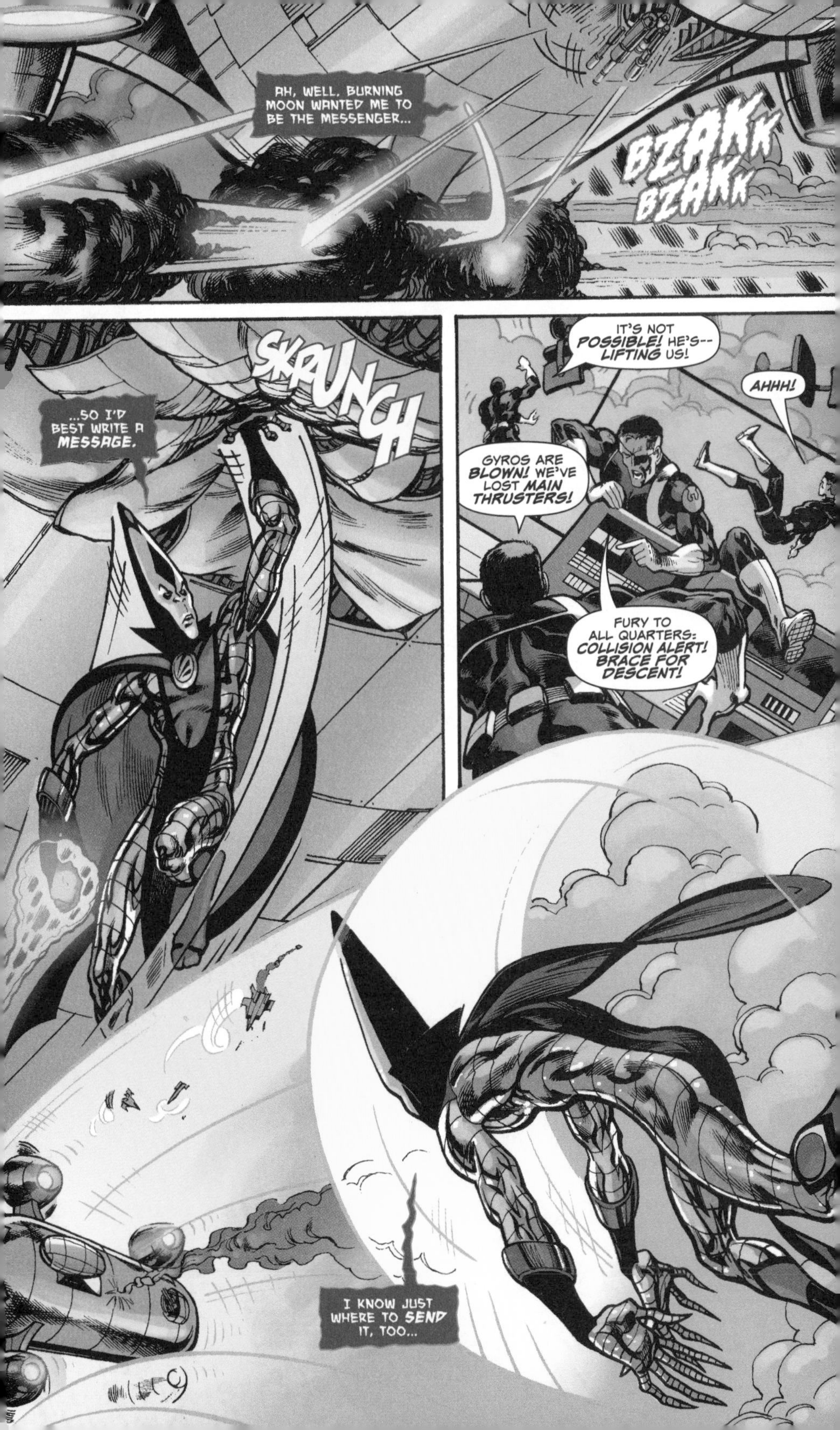
AH, WELL. BURNING MOON WANTED ME TO BE THE MESSENGER...
BZAKK
BZAKK
SKRUNCH
...SO I'D BEST WRITE A MESSAGE.
IT'S NOT POSSIBLE! HE'S-- LIFTING US!
AHHH!
GYROS ARE BLOWN! WE'VE LOST MAIN THRUSTERS!
FURY TO ALL QUARTERS: COLLISION ALERT! BRACE FOR DESCENT!
I KNOW JUST WHERE TO SEND IT, TOO...

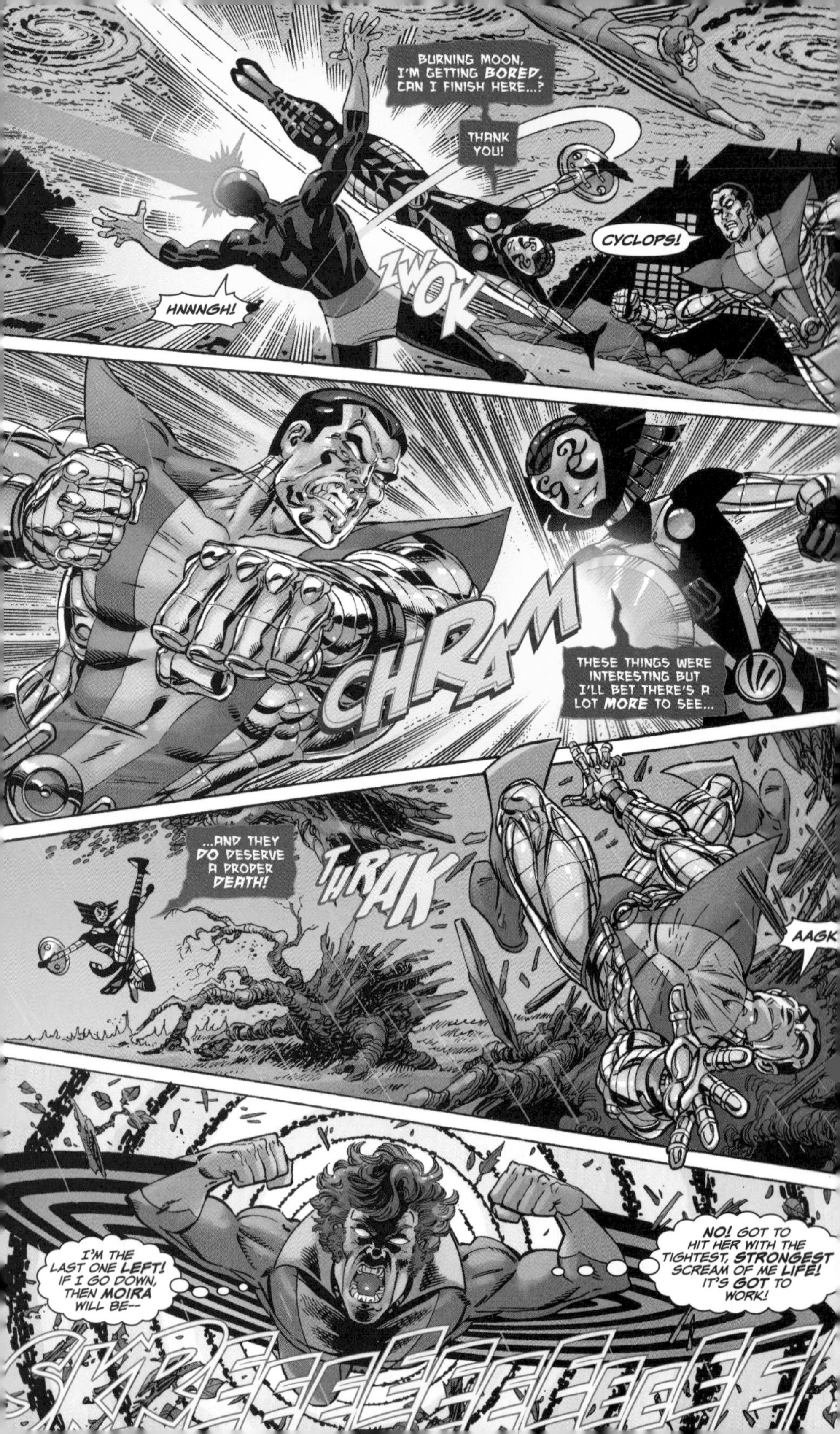
BURNING MOON, I'M GETTING BORED. CAN I FINISH HERE...?
THANK YOU!
CYCLOPS!
HNNNGH!
ZWOK
CHRAM
THESE THINGS WERE INTERESTING BUT I'LL BET THERE'S A LOT MORE TO SEE...
...AND THEY DO DESERVE A PROPER DEATH!
THRAK
AAGK
I'M THE LAST ONE LEFT! IF I GO DOWN, THEN MOIRA WILL BE--
NO! GOT TO HIT HER WITH THE TIGHTEST, STRONGEST SCREAM OF ME LIFE! IT'S GOT TO WORK!

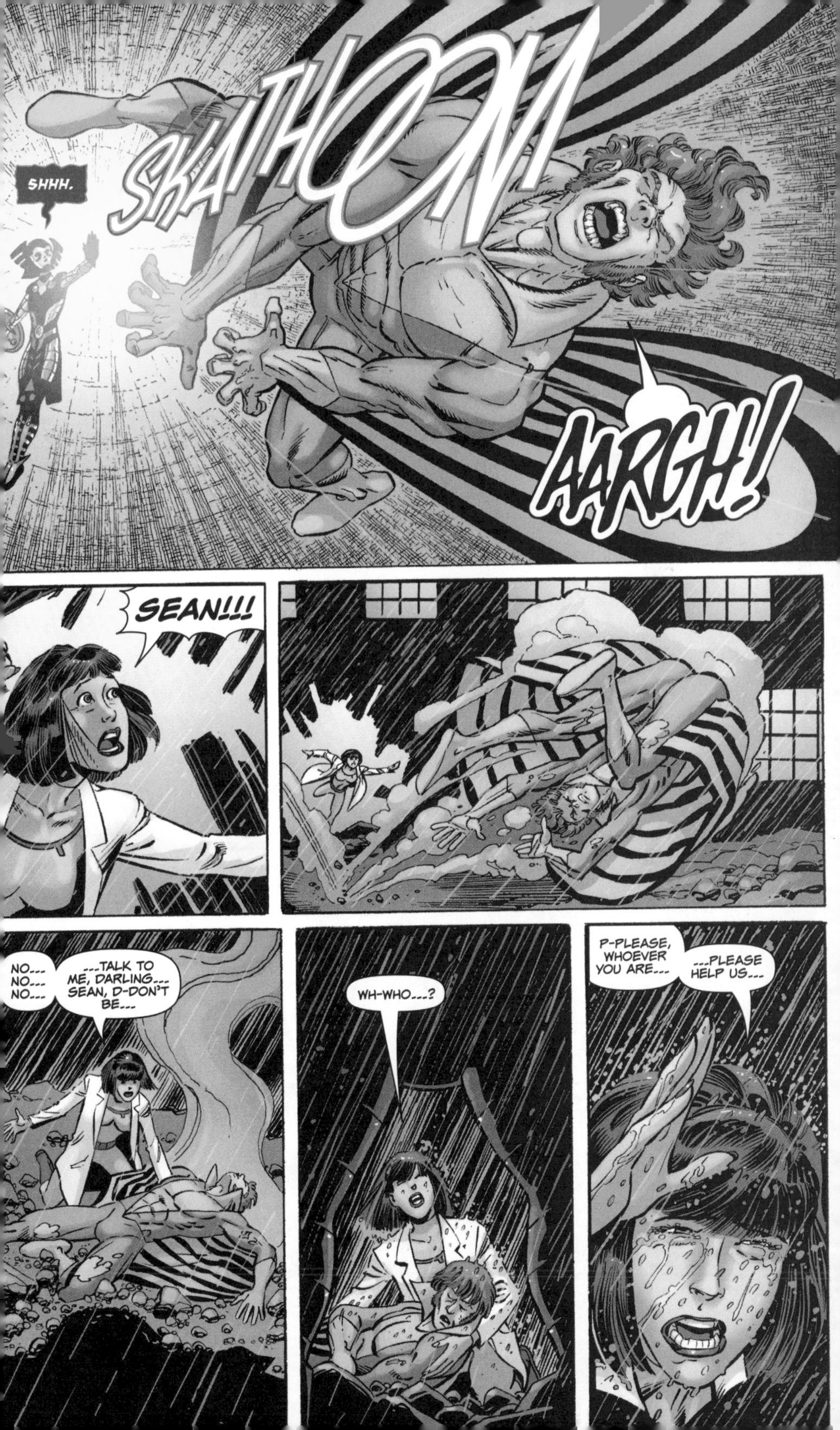

SHHH.
SKATHOOM
AARGH!
SEAN!!!
NO---
NO---
NO---
---TALK TO ME, DARLING--- SEAN, D-DON'T BE---
WH-WHO---?
P-PLEASE, WHOEVER YOU ARE---
---PLEASE HELP US---

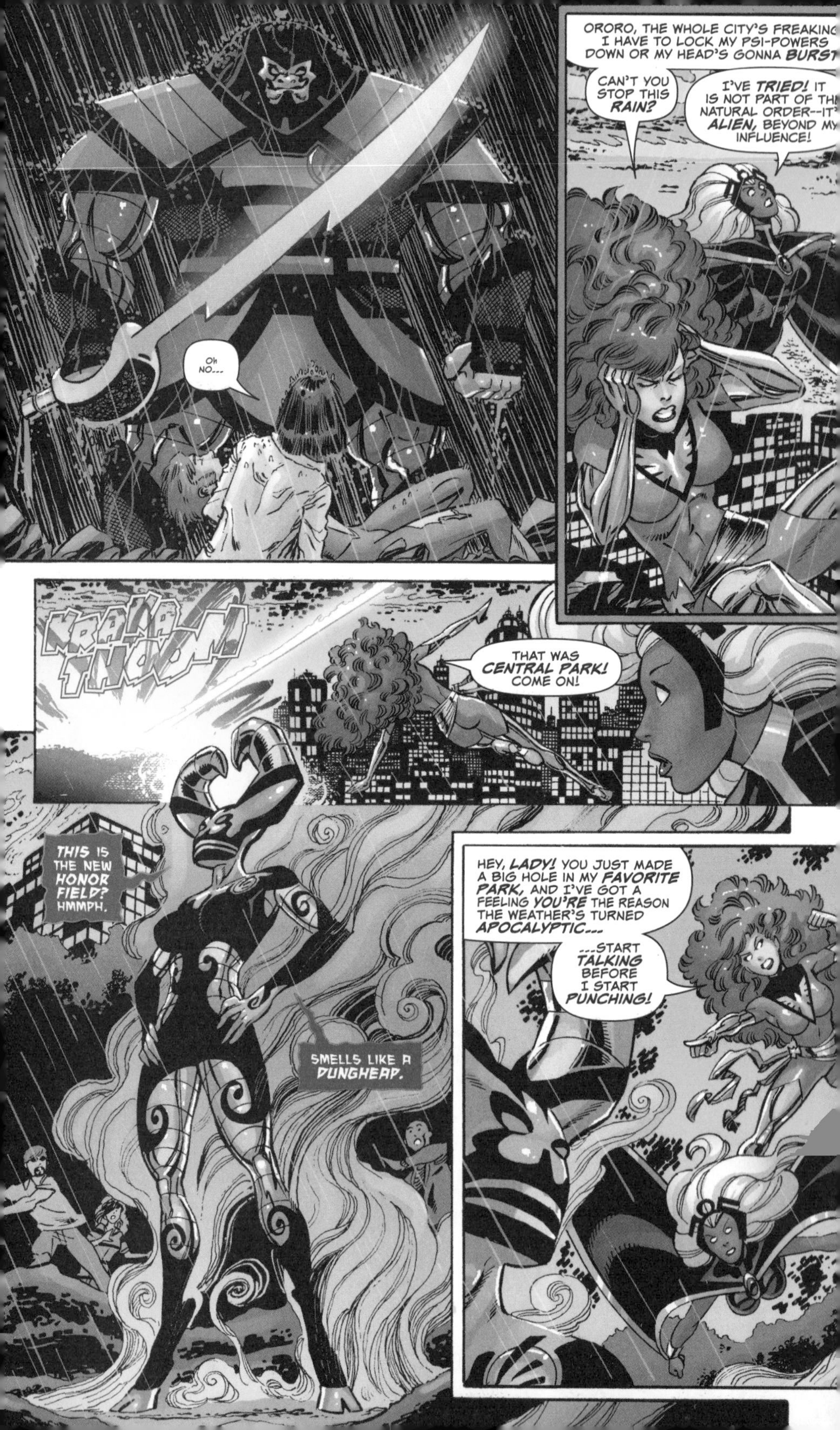
Oh NO---
ORORO, THE WHOLE CITY'S FREAKING. I HAVE TO LOCK MY PSI-POWERS DOWN OR MY HEAD'S GONNA BURST!
CAN'T YOU STOP THIS RAIN?
I'VE TRIED! IT IS NOT PART OF THE NATURAL ORDER--IT'S ALIEN, BEYOND MY INFLUENCE!
THAT WAS CENTRAL PARK! COME ON!
THIS IS THE NEW HONOR FIELD? HMMPH.
SMELLS LIKE A DUNGHEAP.
HEY, LADY! YOU JUST MADE A BIG HOLE IN MY FAVORITE PARK, AND I'VE GOT A FEELING YOU'RE THE REASON THE WEATHER'S TURNED APOCALYPTIC---
---START TALKING BEFORE I START PUNCHING!

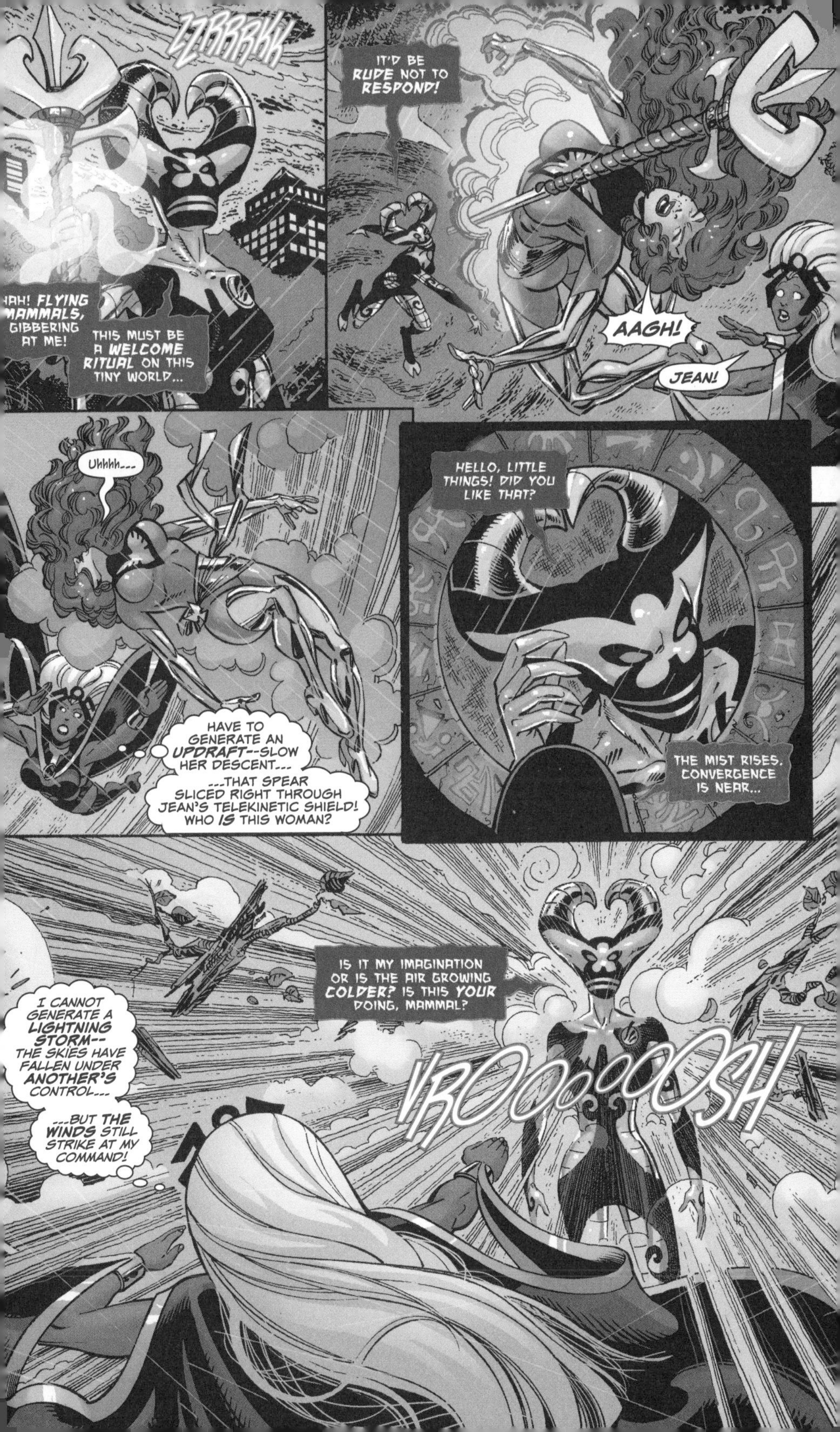
ZZRRRKK
HAH! FLYING MAMMALS, GIBBERING AT ME!
THIS MUST BE A WELCOME RITUAL ON THIS TINY WORLD...
IT'D BE RUDE NOT TO RESPOND!
AAGH!
JEAN!
Uhhhh---
HAVE TO GENERATE AN UPDRAFT--SLOW HER DESCENT---
---THAT SPEAR SLICED RIGHT THROUGH JEAN'S TELEKINETIC SHIELD! WHO IS THIS WOMAN?
HELLO, LITTLE THINGS! DID YOU LIKE THAT?
THE MIST RISES. CONVERGENCE IS NEAR...
I CANNOT GENERATE A LIGHTNING STORM-- THE SKIES HAVE FALLEN UNDER ANOTHER'S CONTROL---
---BUT THE WINDS STILL STRIKE AT MY COMMAND!
IS IT MY IMAGINATION OR IS THE AIR GROWING COLDER? IS THIS YOUR DOING, MAMMAL?
VROOOOOOSH

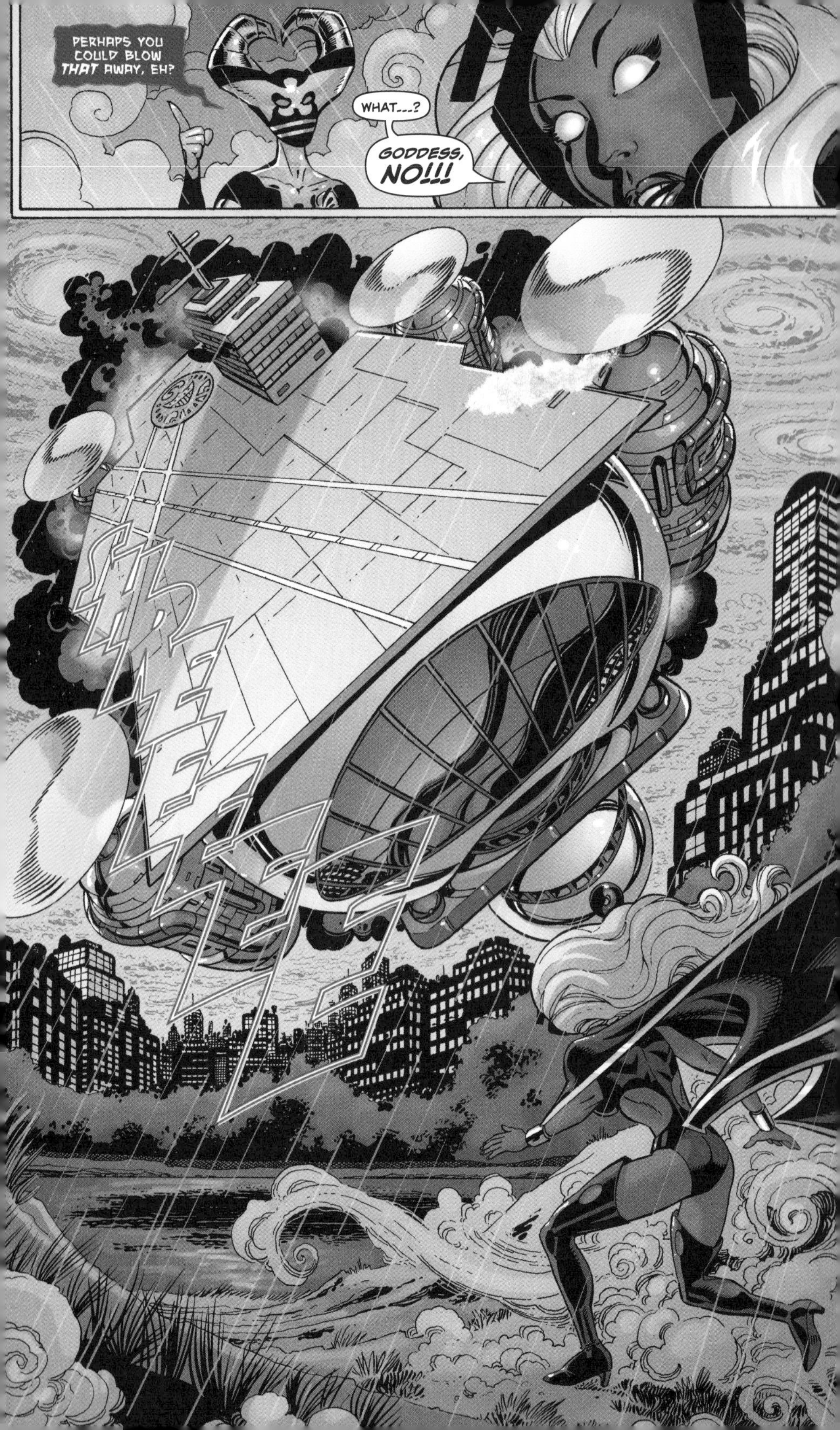
PERHAPS YOU COULD BLOW *THAT* AWAY, EH?
WHAT---?
GODDESS, NO!!!

UNCANNY X-MEN FIRST CLASS

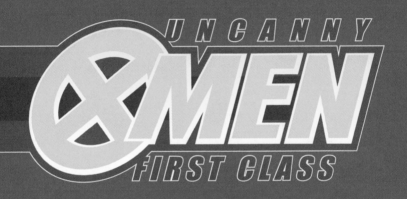

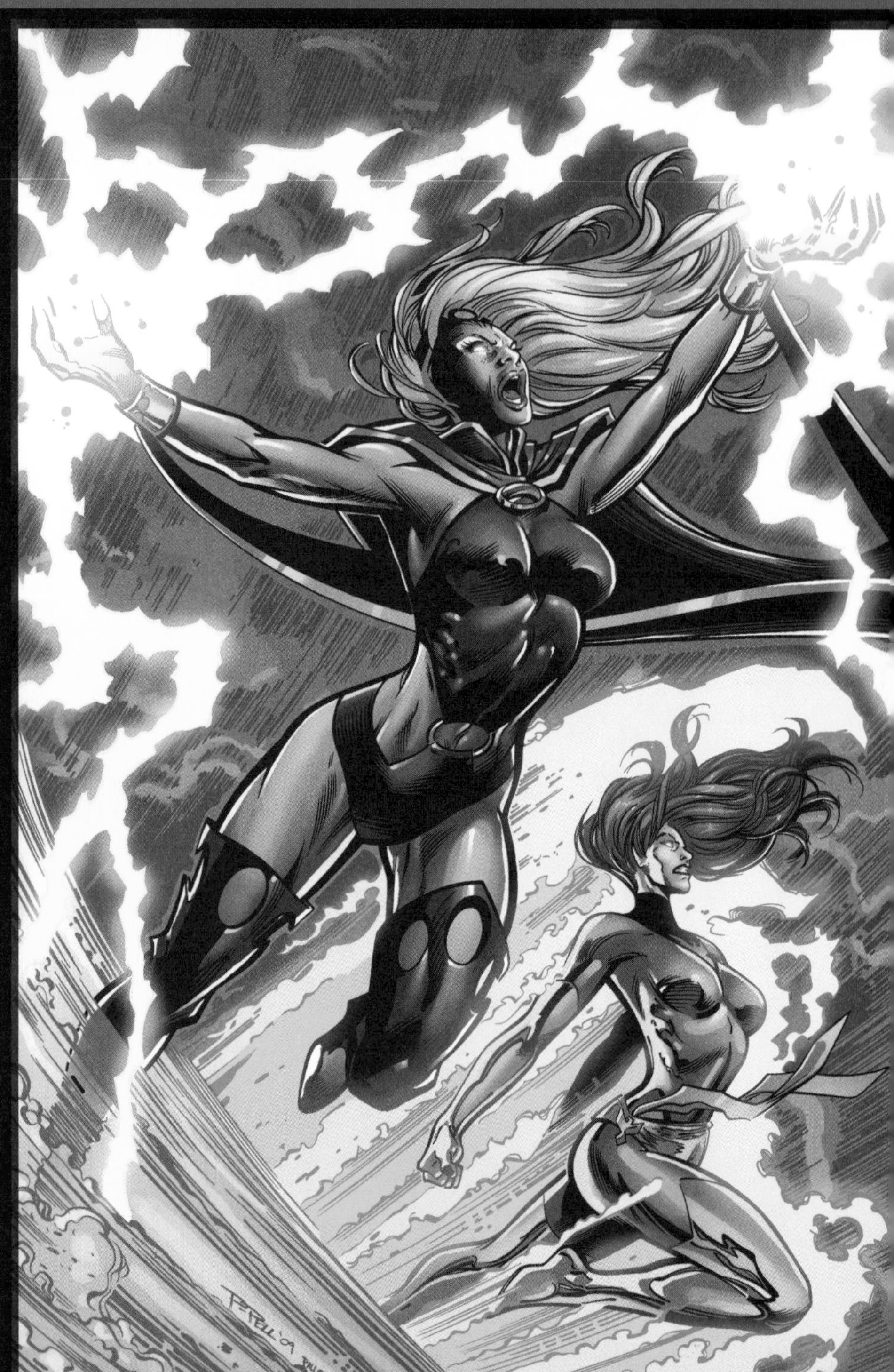

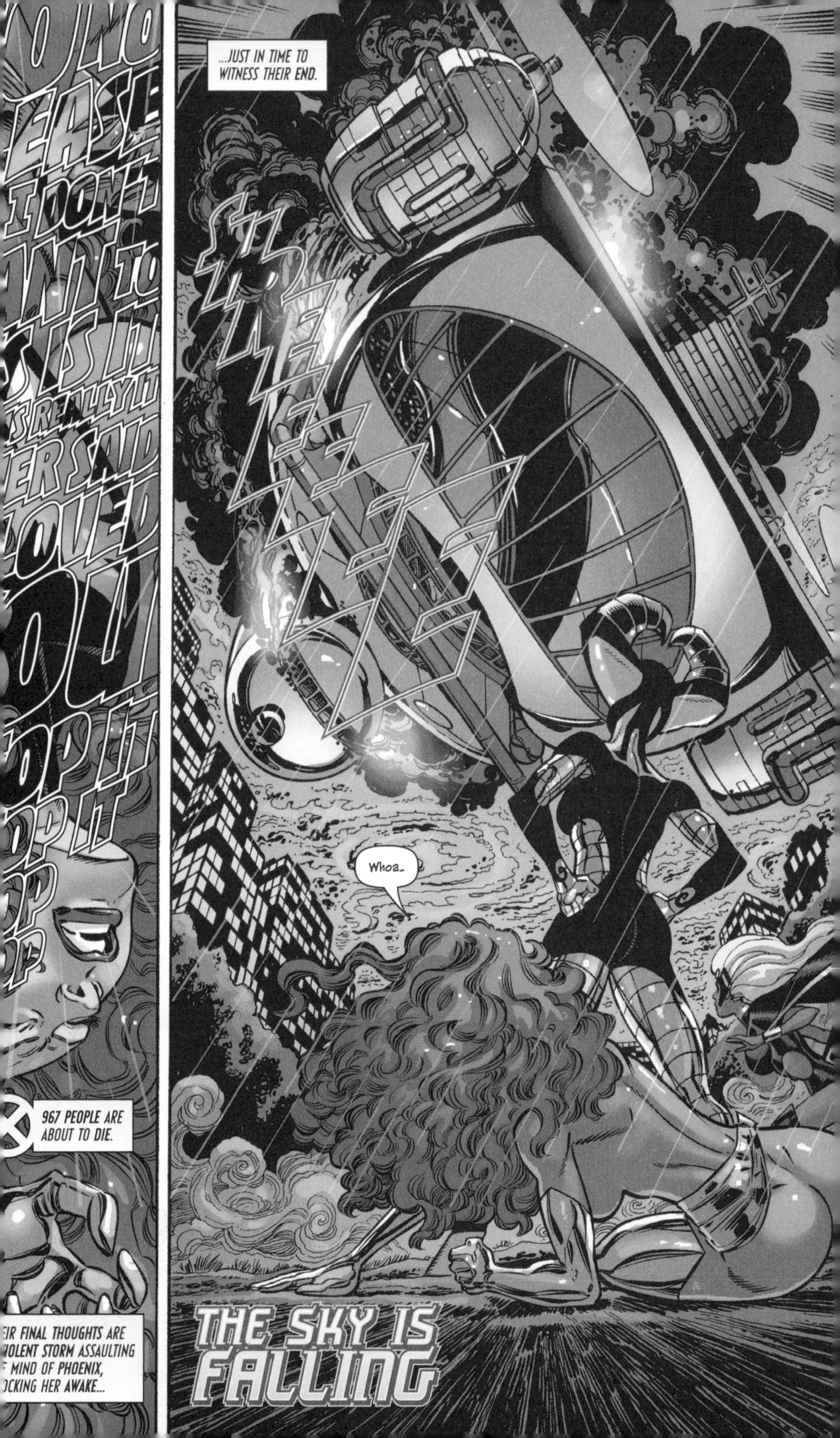

I DON'T
967 PEOPLE ARE ABOUT TO DIE.
EIR FINAL THOUGHTS ARE
OLENT STORM ASSAULTING
MIND OF PHOENIX,
OCKING HER AWAKE...
...JUST IN TIME TO WITNESS THEIR END.
Whoa_
THE SKY IS FALLING

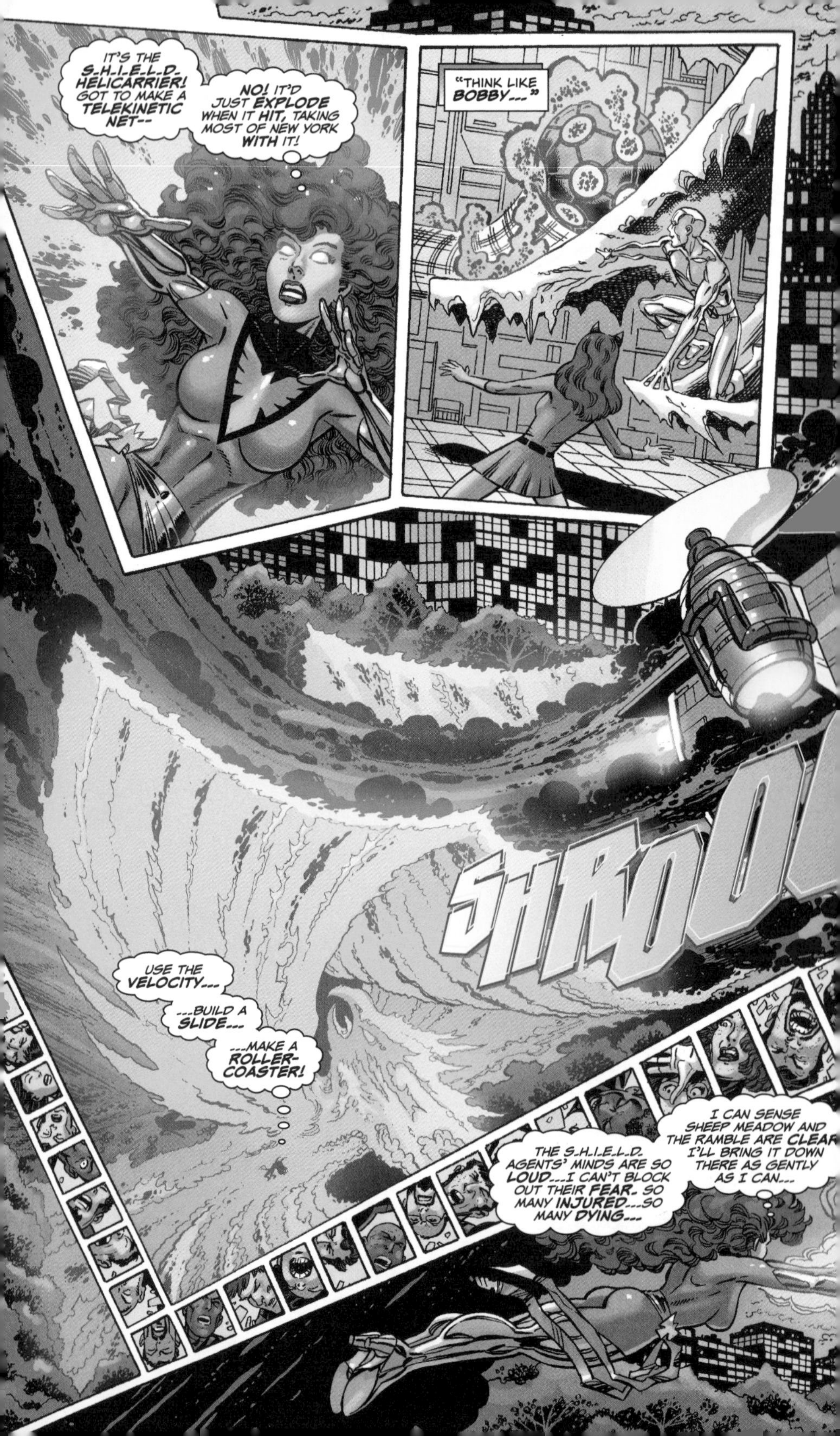

IT'S THE S.H.I.E.L.D. HELICARRIER! GOT TO MAKE A TELEKINETIC NET--
NO! IT'D JUST EXPLODE WHEN IT HIT, TAKING MOST OF NEW YORK WITH IT!
"THINK LIKE BOBBY..."
SHROO
USE THE VELOCITY...
...BUILD A SLIDE...
...MAKE A ROLLER-COASTER!
THE S.H.I.E.L.D. AGENTS' MINDS ARE SO LOUD...I CAN'T BLOCK OUT THEIR FEAR. SO MANY INJURED...SO MANY DYING...
I CAN SENSE SHEEP MEADOW AND THE RAMBLE ARE CLEAR. I'LL BRING IT DOWN THERE AS GENTLY AS I CAN...

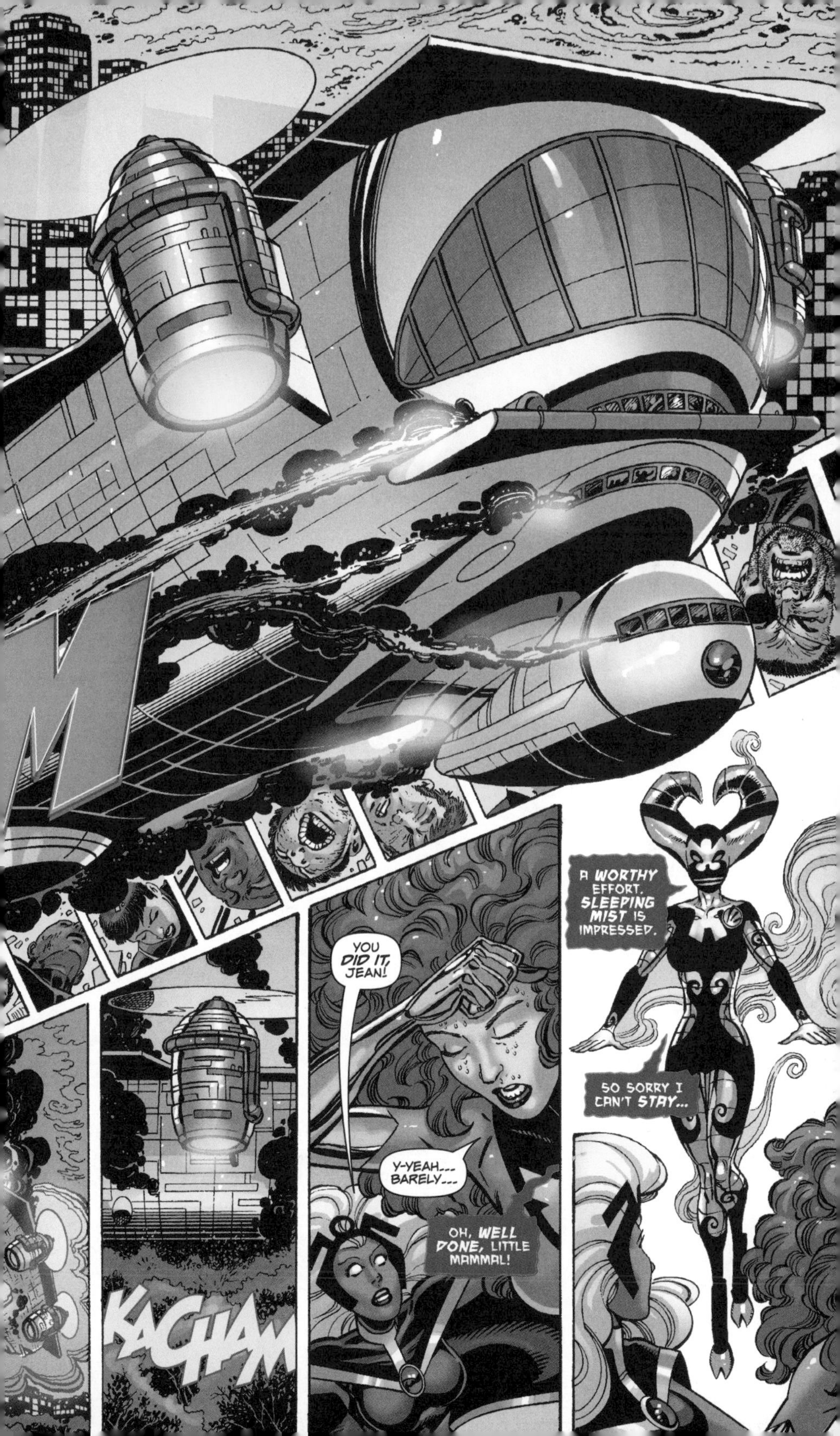
YOU DID IT, JEAN!
Y-YEAH... BARELY...
OH, WELL DONE, LITTLE MAMMAL!
A WORTHY EFFORT. SLEEPING MIST IS IMPRESSED.
SO SORRY I CAN'T STAY...
KACHAM

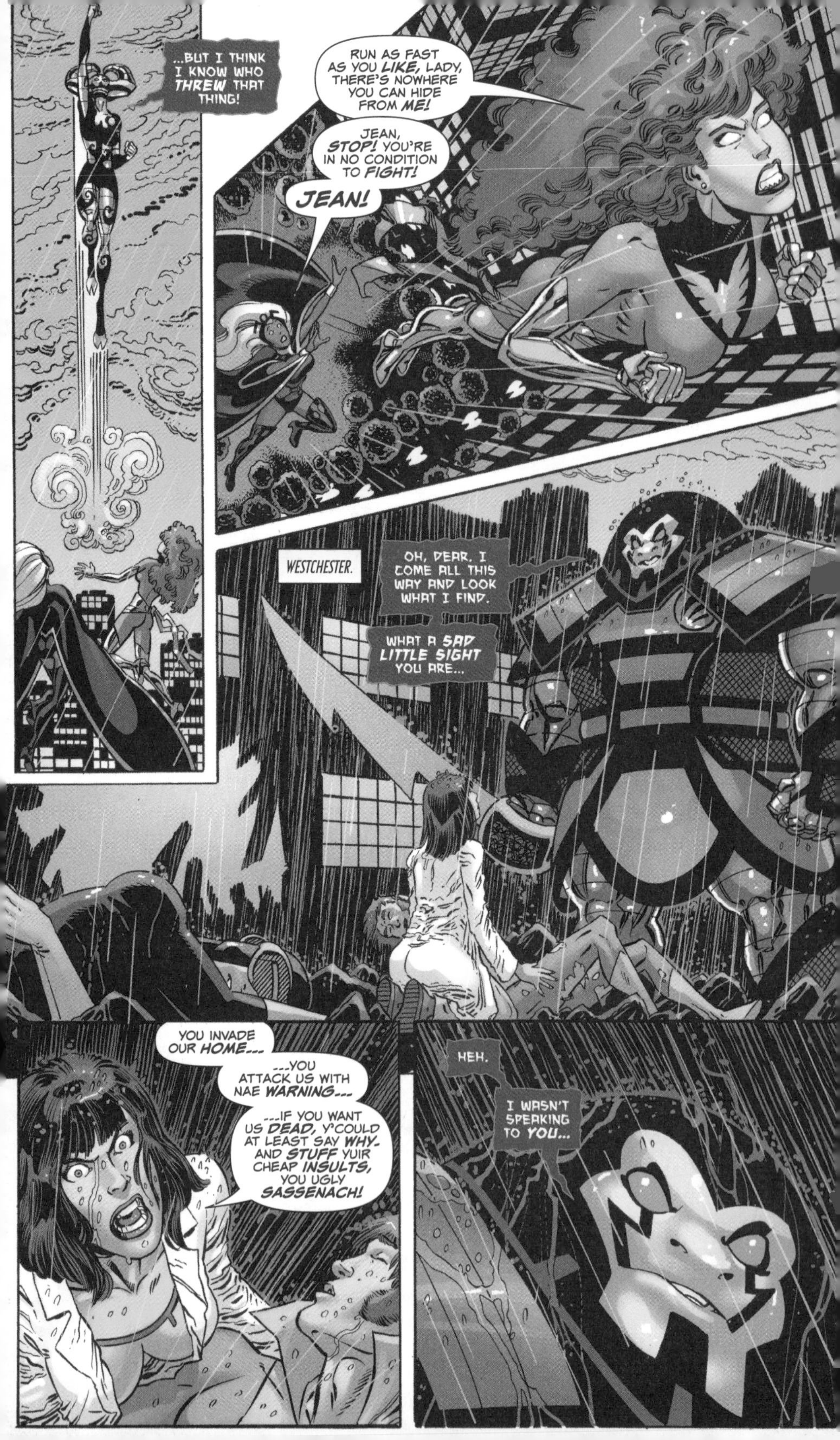

...BUT I THINK I KNOW WHO THREW THAT THING!
RUN AS FAST AS YOU LIKE, LADY, THERE'S NOWHERE YOU CAN HIDE FROM ME!
JEAN, STOP! YOU'RE IN NO CONDITION TO FIGHT!
JEAN!
WESTCHESTER.
OH, DEAR. I COME ALL THIS WAY AND LOOK WHAT I FIND.
WHAT A SAD LITTLE SIGHT YOU ARE...
YOU INVADE OUR HOME---
---YOU ATTACK US WITH NAE WARNING---
---IF YOU WANT US DEAD, Y'COULD AT LEAST SAY WHY-AND STUFF YUIR CHEAP INSULTS, YOU UGLY SASSENACH!
HEH.
I WASN'T SPEAKING TO YOU...

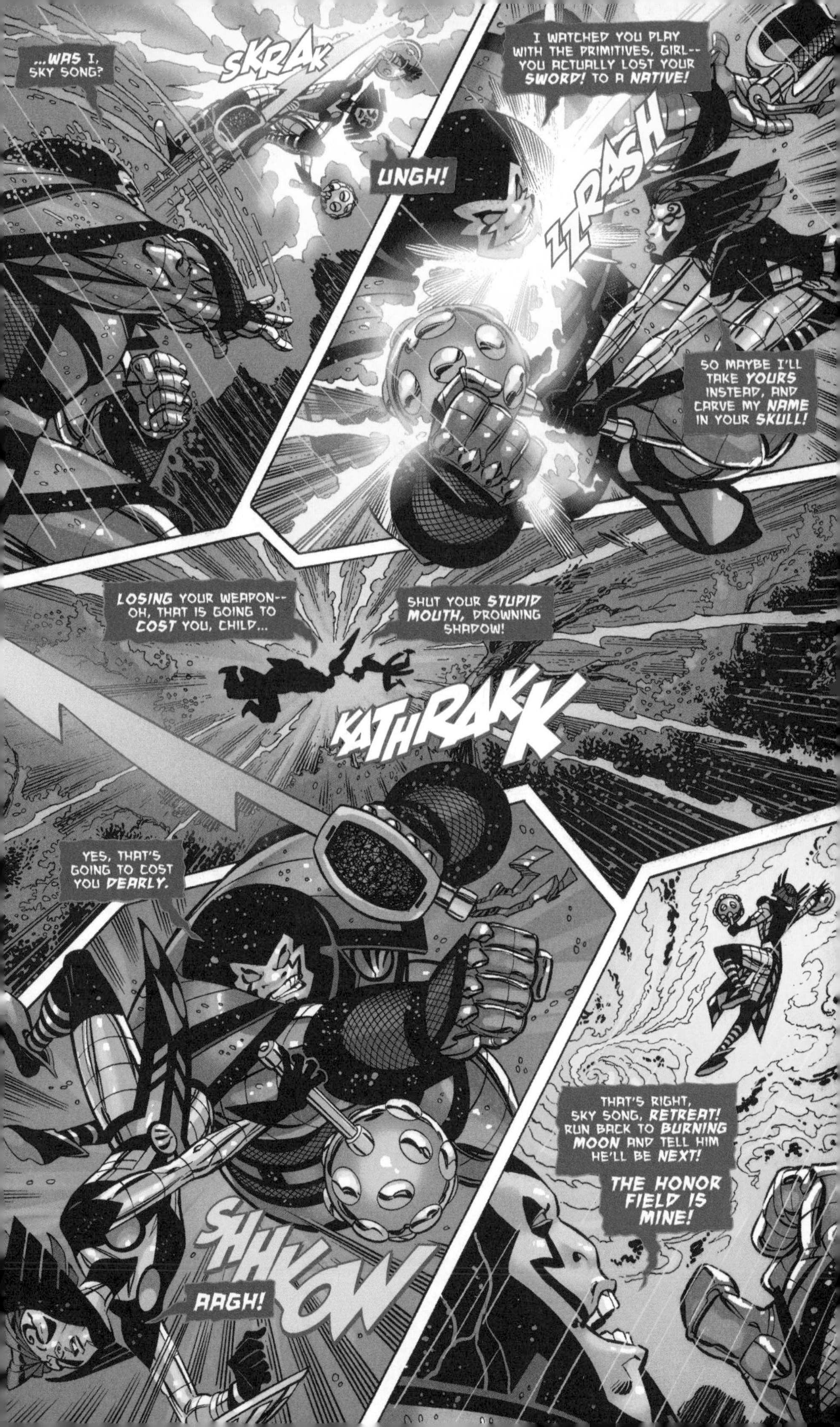
...WAS I, SKY SONG?
SKRAK
I WATCHED YOU PLAY WITH THE PRIMITIVES, GIRL-- YOU ACTUALLY LOST YOUR SWORD! TO A NATIVE!
UNGH!
ZZRASH
SO MAYBE I'LL TAKE YOURS INSTEAD, AND CARVE MY NAME IN YOUR SKULL!
LOSING YOUR WEAPON-- OH, THAT IS GOING TO COST YOU, CHILD...
SHUT YOUR STUPID MOUTH, DROWNING SHADOW!
KATHRAKK
YES, THAT'S GOING TO COST YOU DEARLY.
SHHVOOM
AAGH!
THAT'S RIGHT, SKY SONG, RETREAT! RUN BACK TO BURNING MOON AND TELL HIM HE'LL BE NEXT!
THE HONOR FIELD IS MINE!

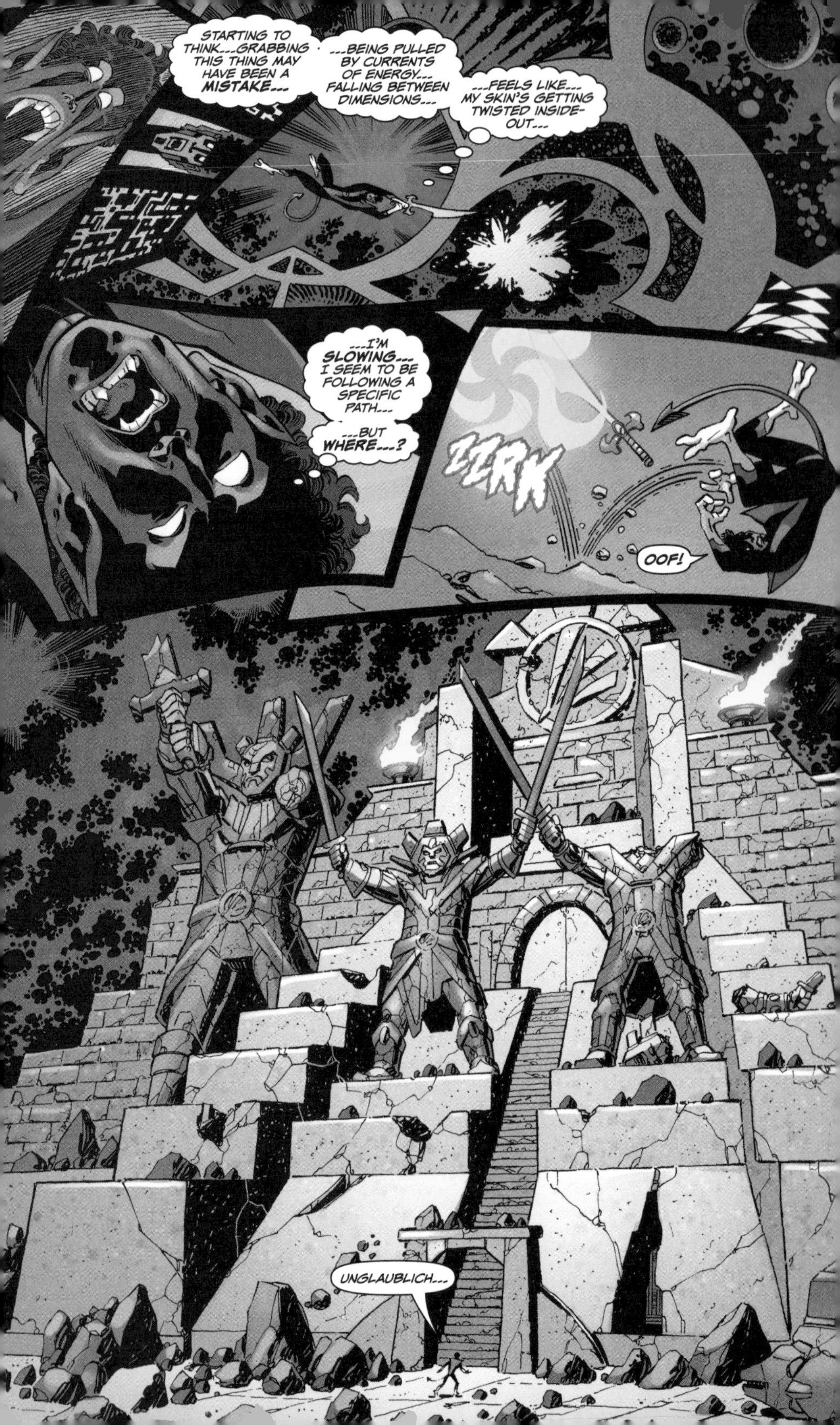

STARTING TO THINK...GRABBING THIS THING MAY HAVE BEEN A **MISTAKE**...
...BEING PULLED BY CURRENTS OF ENERGY... FALLING BETWEEN DIMENSIONS...
...FEELS LIKE... MY SKIN'S GETTING TWISTED INSIDE-OUT...
...I'M **SLOWING**... I SEEM TO BE FOLLOWING A SPECIFIC PATH...
...BUT **WHERE**...?
ZZRK
OOF!
UNGLAUBLICH...

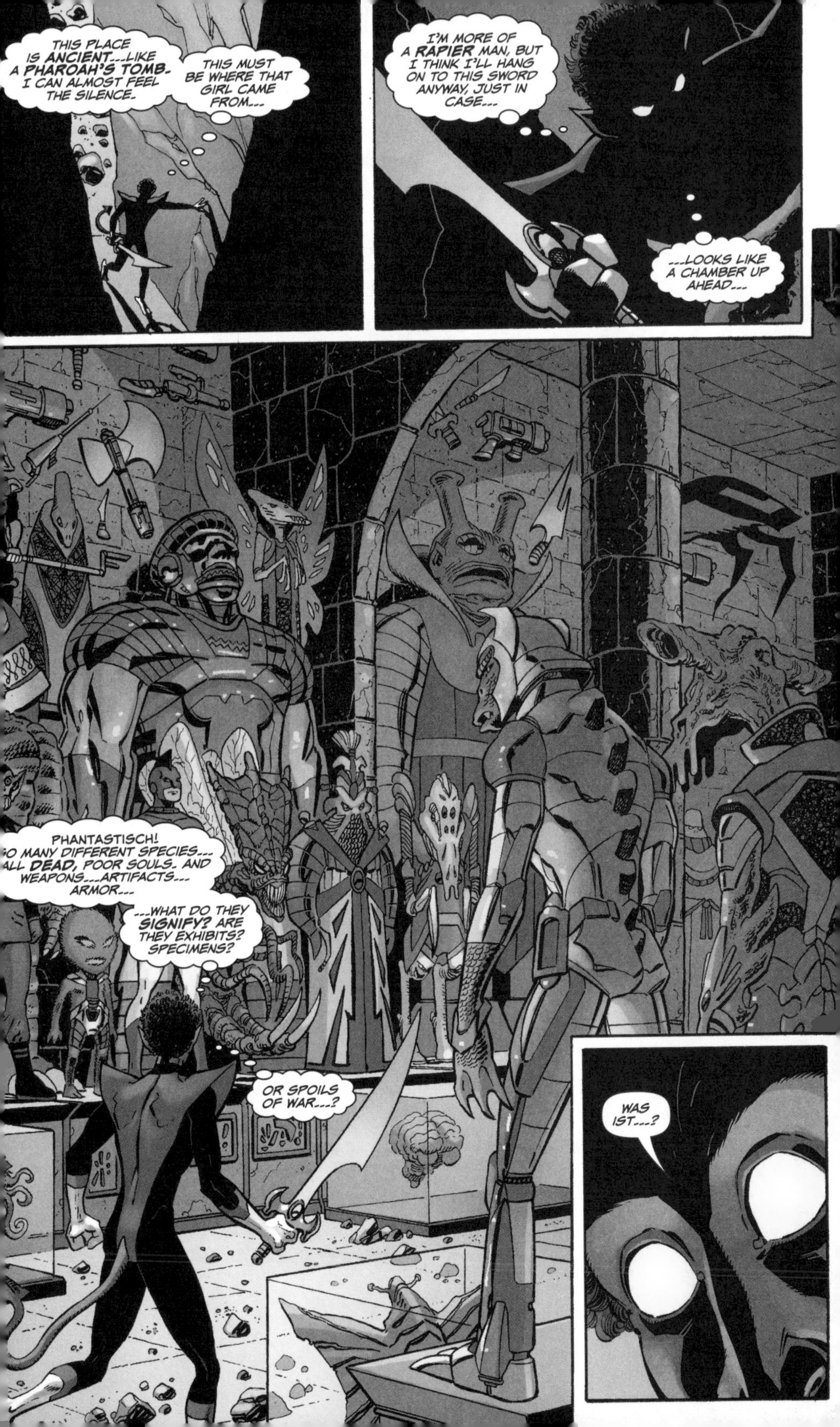

THIS PLACE IS ANCIENT---LIKE A PHAROAH'S TOMB. I CAN ALMOST FEEL THE SILENCE.
THIS MUST BE WHERE THAT GIRL CAME FROM---
I'M MORE OF A RAPIER MAN, BUT I THINK I'LL HANG ON TO THIS SWORD ANYWAY, JUST IN CASE---
---LOOKS LIKE A CHAMBER UP AHEAD---
PHANTASTISCH! SO MANY DIFFERENT SPECIES--- ALL DEAD, POOR SOULS. AND WEAPONS---ARTIFACTS--- ARMOR---
---WHAT DO THEY SIGNIFY? ARE THEY EXHIBITS? SPECIMENS?
OR SPOILS OF WAR---?
WAS IST---?

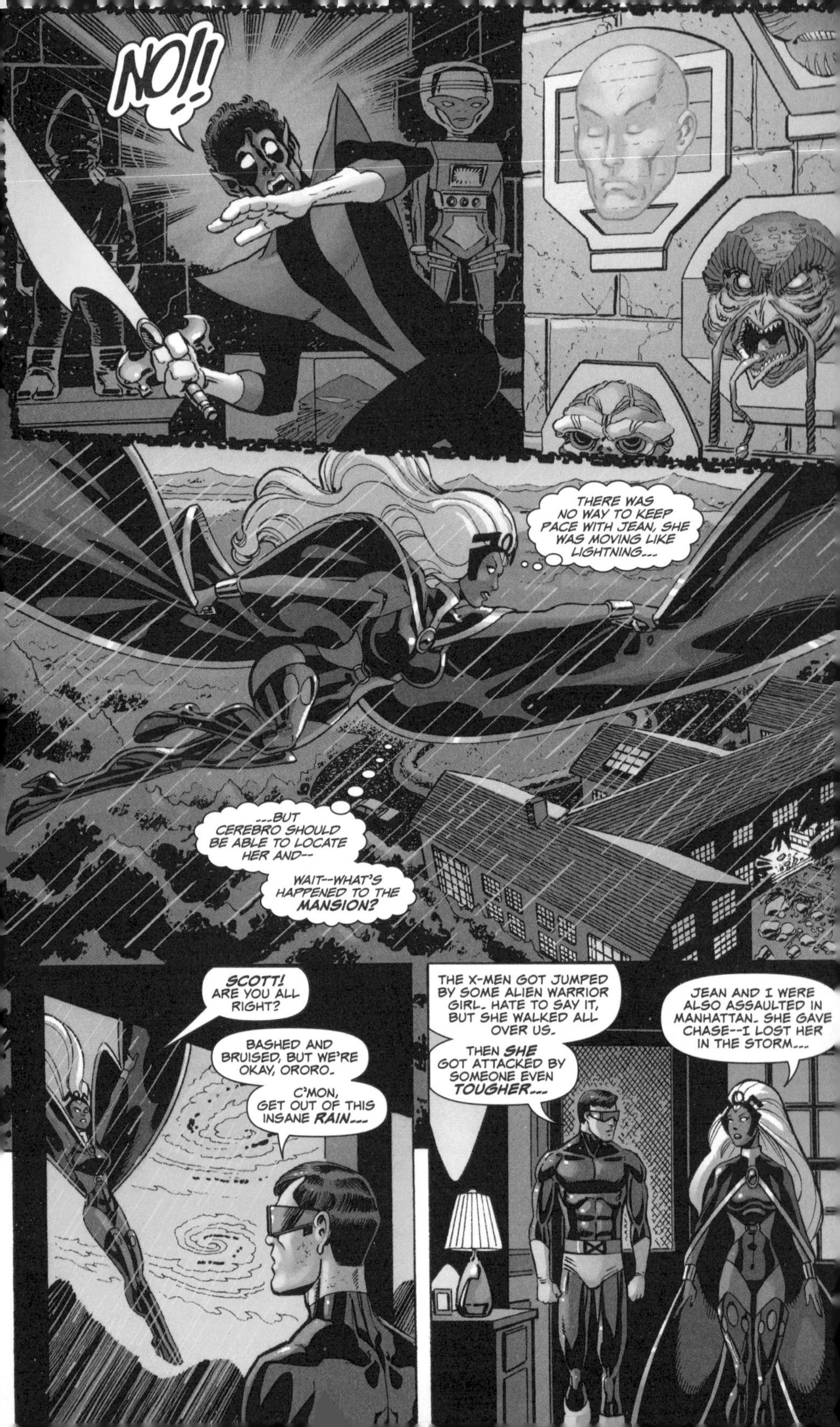
NO!!
THERE WAS NO WAY TO KEEP PACE WITH JEAN, SHE WAS MOVING LIKE LIGHTNING...
...BUT CEREBRO SHOULD BE ABLE TO LOCATE HER AND--
WAIT--WHAT'S HAPPENED TO THE MANSION?
SCOTT! ARE YOU ALL RIGHT?
BASHED AND BRUISED, BUT WE'RE OKAY, ORORO.
C'MON, GET OUT OF THIS INSANE RAIN...
THE X-MEN GOT JUMPED BY SOME ALIEN WARRIOR GIRL. HATE TO SAY IT, BUT SHE WALKED ALL OVER US.
THEN SHE GOT ATTACKED BY SOMEONE EVEN TOUGHER...
JEAN AND I WERE ALSO ASSAULTED IN MANHATTAN. SHE GAVE CHASE--I LOST HER IN THE STORM...

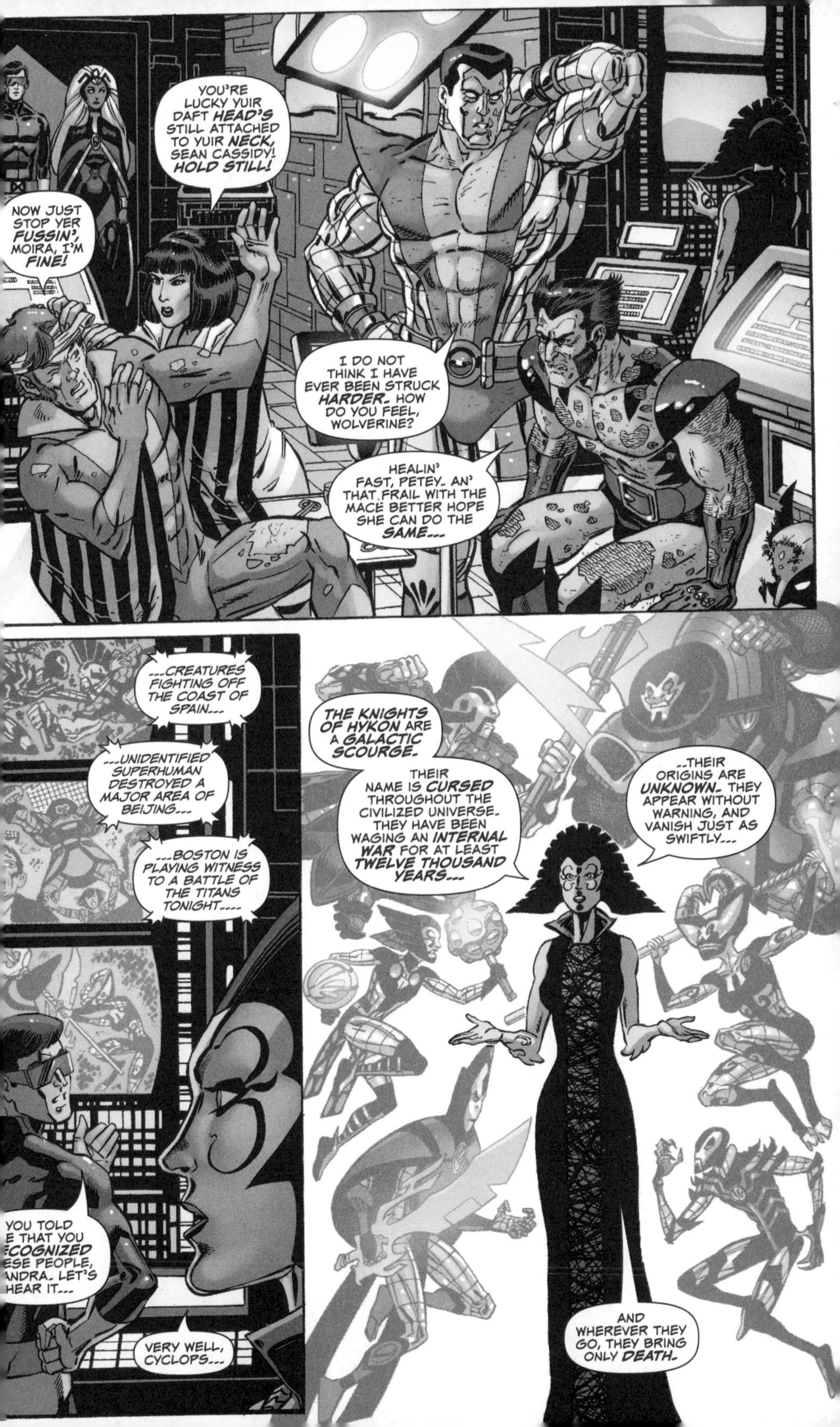
YOU'RE LUCKY YUIR DAFT HEAD'S STILL ATTACHED TO YUIR NECK, SEAN CASSIDY! HOLD STILL!
NOW JUST STOP YER FUSSIN', MOIRA, I'M FINE!
I DO NOT THINK I HAVE EVER BEEN STRUCK HARDER. HOW DO YOU FEEL, WOLVERINE?
HEALIN' FAST, PETEY. AN' THAT FRAIL WITH THE MACE BETTER HOPE SHE CAN DO THE SAME...
...CREATURES FIGHTING OFF THE COAST OF SPAIN...
...UNIDENTIFIED SUPERHUMAN DESTROYED A MAJOR AREA OF BEIJING...
...BOSTON IS PLAYING WITNESS TO A BATTLE OF THE TITANS TONIGHT....
YOU TOLD E THAT YOU ECOGNIZED ESE PEOPLE, ANDRA. LET'S HEAR IT...
VERY WELL, CYCLOPS...
THE KNIGHTS OF HYKON ARE A GALACTIC SCOURGE.
THEIR NAME IS CURSED THROUGHOUT THE CIVILIZED UNIVERSE. THEY HAVE BEEN WAGING AN INTERNAL WAR FOR AT LEAST TWELVE THOUSAND YEARS...
..THEIR ORIGINS ARE UNKNOWN. THEY APPEAR WITHOUT WARNING, AND VANISH JUST AS SWIFTLY...
AND WHEREVER THEY GO, THEY BRING ONLY DEATH.

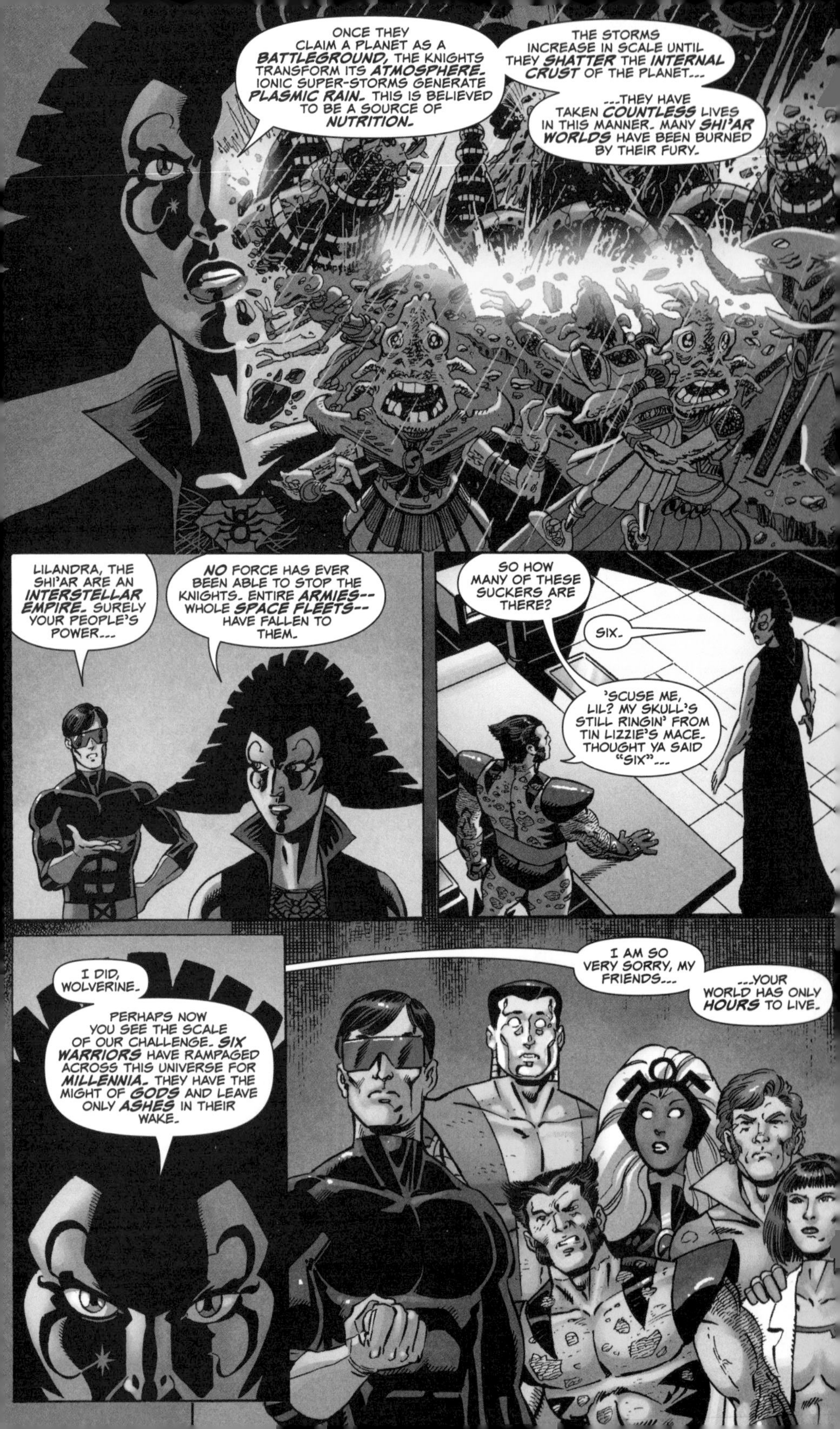
ONCE THEY CLAIM A PLANET AS A BATTLEGROUND, THE KNIGHTS TRANSFORM ITS ATMOSPHERE. IONIC SUPER-STORMS GENERATE PLASMIC RAIN. THIS IS BELIEVED TO BE A SOURCE OF NUTRITION.
THE STORMS INCREASE IN SCALE UNTIL THEY SHATTER THE INTERNAL CRUST OF THE PLANET...
...THEY HAVE TAKEN COUNTLESS LIVES IN THIS MANNER. MANY SHI'AR WORLDS HAVE BEEN BURNED BY THEIR FURY.
LILANDRA, THE SHI'AR ARE AN INTERSTELLAR EMPIRE. SURELY YOUR PEOPLE'S POWER...
NO FORCE HAS EVER BEEN ABLE TO STOP THE KNIGHTS. ENTIRE ARMIES-- WHOLE SPACE FLEETS-- HAVE FALLEN TO THEM.
SO HOW MANY OF THESE SUCKERS ARE THERE?
SIX.
'SCUSE ME, LIL? MY SKULL'S STILL RINGIN' FROM TIN LIZZIE'S MACE. THOUGHT YA SAID "SIX"...
I DID, WOLVERINE.
PERHAPS NOW YOU SEE THE SCALE OF OUR CHALLENGE. SIX WARRIORS HAVE RAMPAGED ACROSS THIS UNIVERSE FOR MILLENNIA. THEY HAVE THE MIGHT OF GODS AND LEAVE ONLY ASHES IN THEIR WAKE.
I AM SO VERY SORRY, MY FRIENDS...
...YOUR WORLD HAS ONLY HOURS TO LIVE.

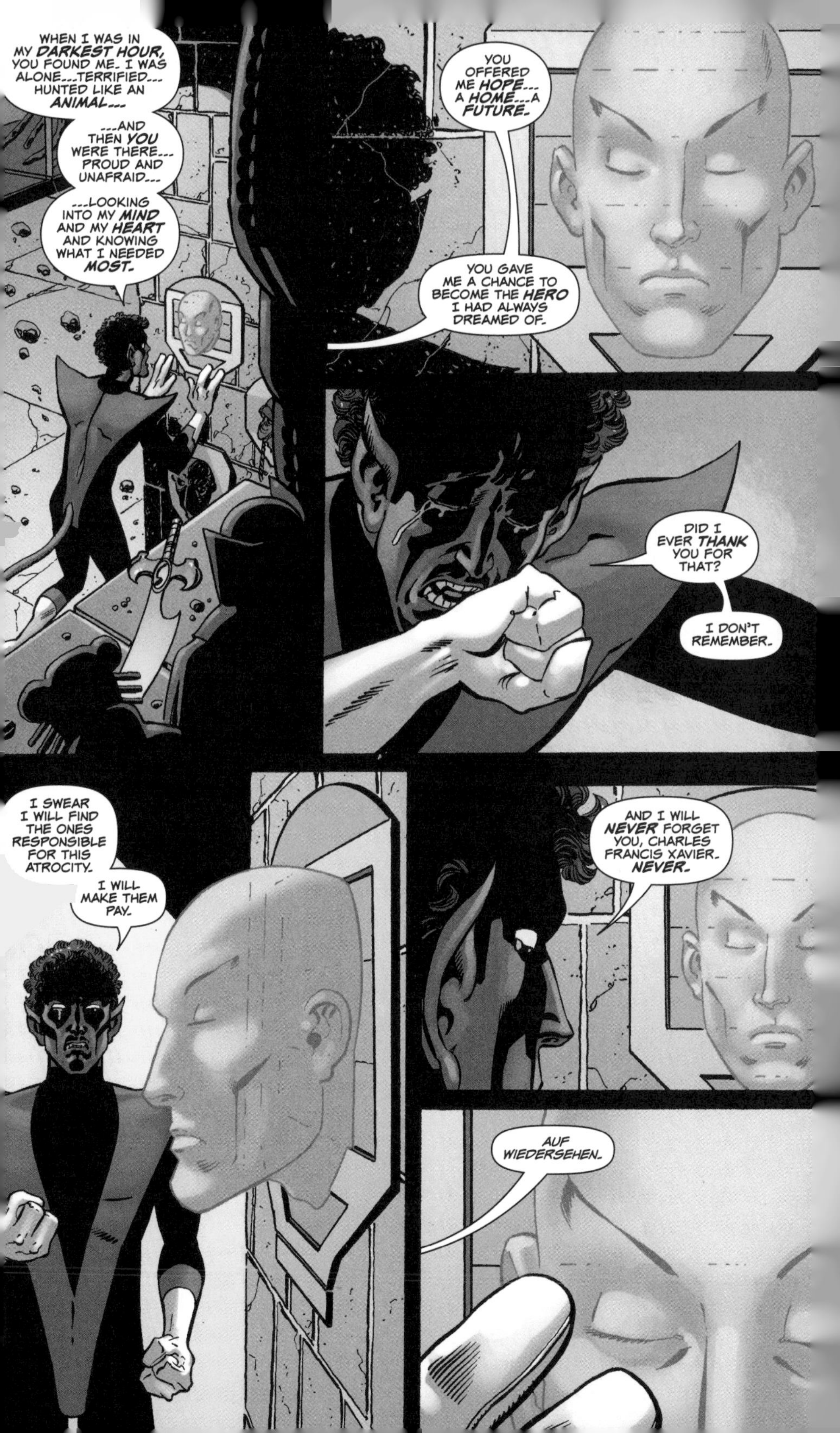
WHEN I WAS IN MY DARKEST HOUR, YOU FOUND ME. I WAS ALONE... TERRIFIED... HUNTED LIKE AN ANIMAL...
...AND THEN YOU WERE THERE... PROUD AND UNAFRAID...
...LOOKING INTO MY MIND AND MY HEART AND KNOWING WHAT I NEEDED MOST.
YOU OFFERED ME HOPE... A HOME... A FUTURE.
YOU GAVE ME A CHANCE TO BECOME THE HERO I HAD ALWAYS DREAMED OF.
DID I EVER THANK YOU FOR THAT?
I DON'T REMEMBER.
I SWEAR I WILL FIND THE ONES RESPONSIBLE FOR THIS ATROCITY.
I WILL MAKE THEM PAY.
AND I WILL NEVER FORGET YOU, CHARLES FRANCIS XAVIER. NEVER.
AUF WIEDERSEHEN.

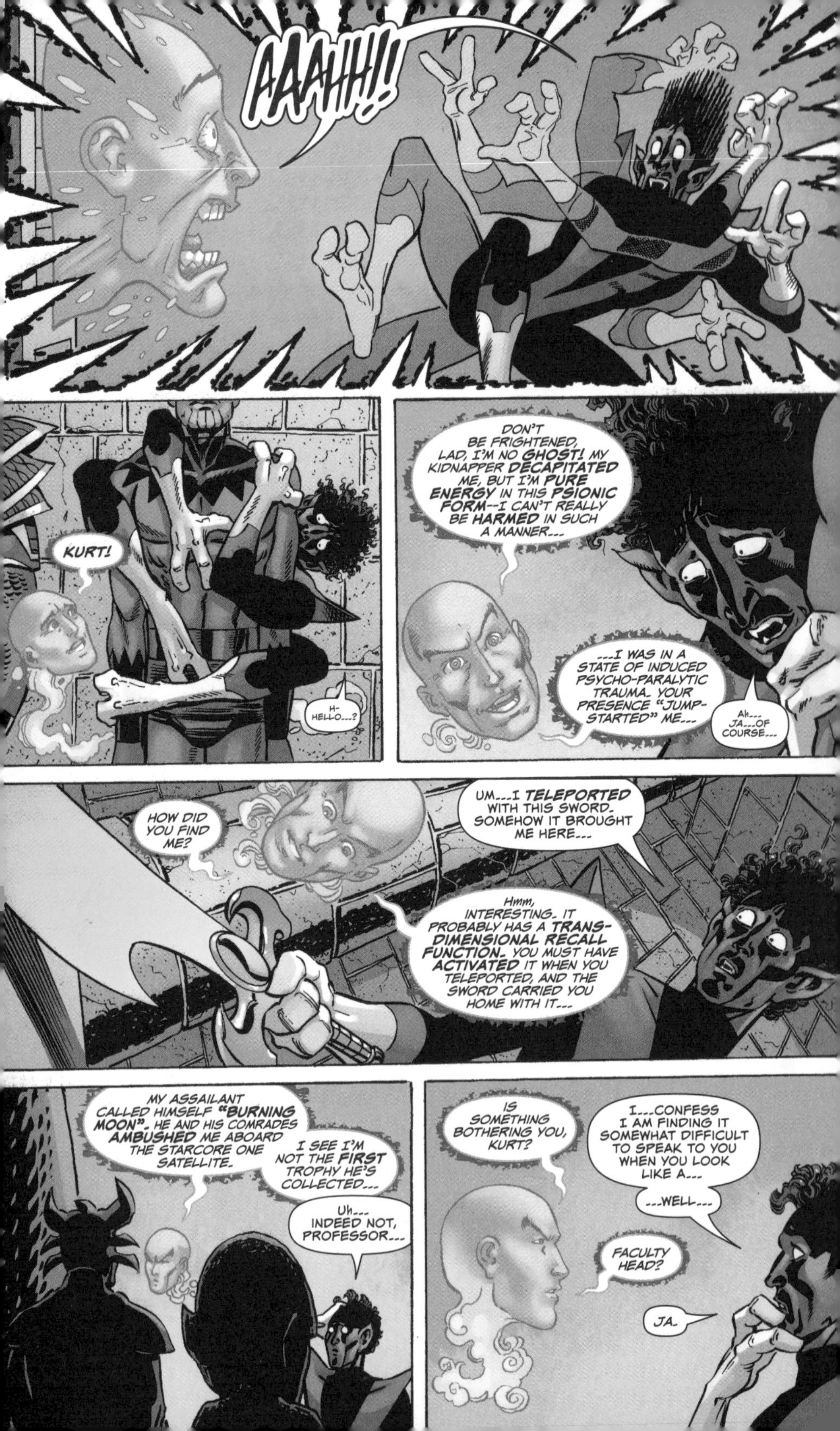
AAAHHH!!
KURT!
H-HELLO...?
DON'T BE FRIGHTENED, LAD, I'M NO GHOST! MY KIDNAPPER DECAPITATED ME, BUT I'M PURE ENERGY IN THIS PSIONIC FORM--I CAN'T REALLY BE HARMED IN SUCH A MANNER...
...I WAS IN A STATE OF INDUCED PSYCHO-PARALYTIC TRAUMA. YOUR PRESENCE "JUMP-STARTED" ME...
Ah... JA...OF COURSE...
HOW DID YOU FIND ME?
UM...I TELEPORTED WITH THIS SWORD. SOMEHOW IT BROUGHT ME HERE...
Hmm, INTERESTING. IT PROBABLY HAS A TRANS-DIMENSIONAL RECALL FUNCTION. YOU MUST HAVE ACTIVATED IT WHEN YOU TELEPORTED, AND THE SWORD CARRIED YOU HOME WITH IT...
MY ASSAILANT CALLED HIMSELF "BURNING MOON". HE AND HIS COMRADES AMBUSHED ME ABOARD THE STARCORE ONE SATELLITE.
I SEE I'M NOT THE FIRST TROPHY HE'S COLLECTED...
Uh... INDEED NOT, PROFESSOR...
IS SOMETHING BOTHERING YOU, KURT?
I...CONFESS I AM FINDING IT SOMEWHAT DIFFICULT TO SPEAK TO YOU WHEN YOU LOOK LIKE A...
...WELL...
FACULTY HEAD?
JA.

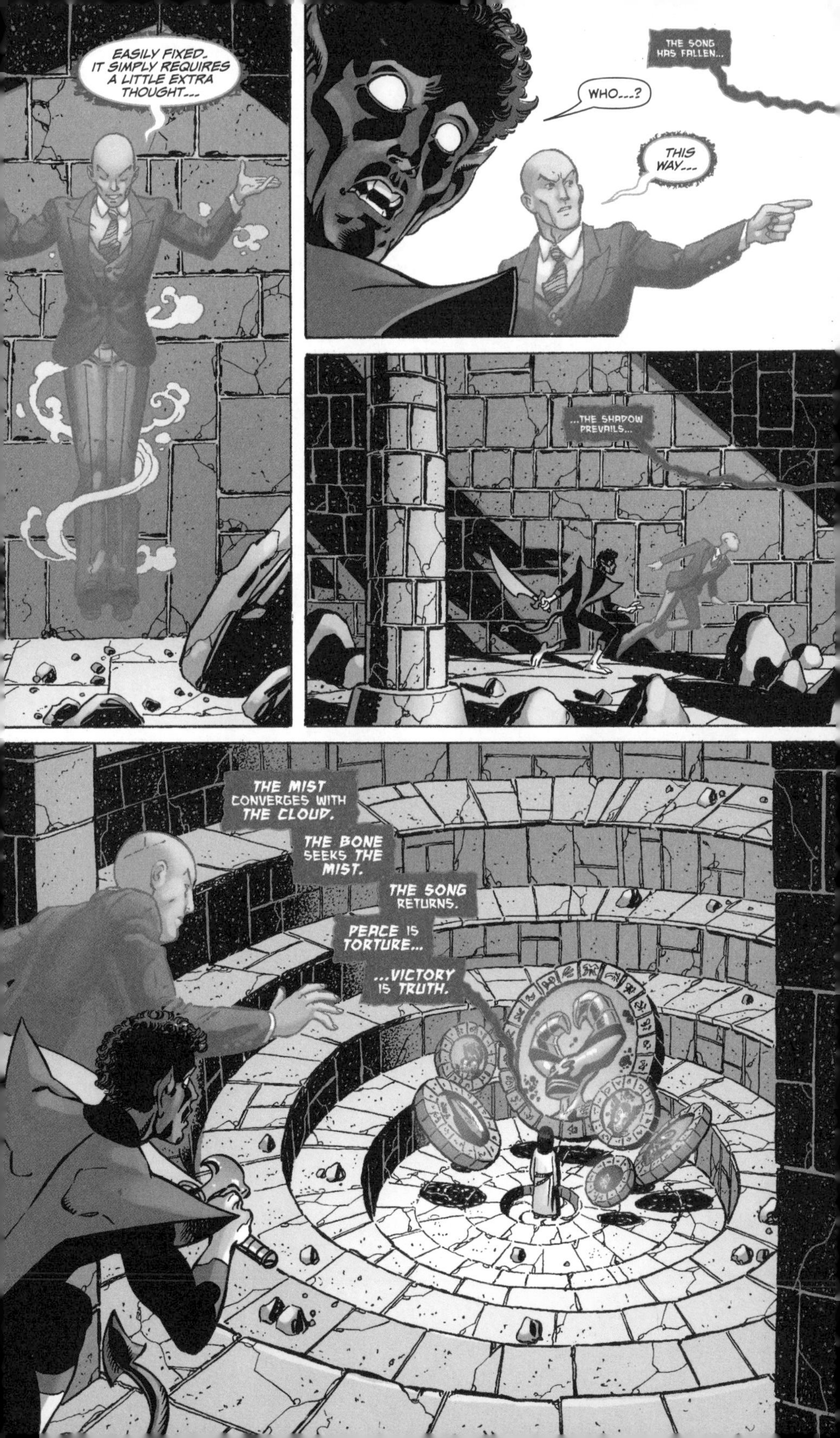
EASILY FIXED. IT SIMPLY REQUIRES A LITTLE EXTRA THOUGHT...
THE SONG HAS FALLEN...
WHO...?
THIS WAY...
...THE SHADOW PREVAILS...
THE MIST CONVERGES WITH THE CLOUD.
THE BONE SEEKS THE MIST.
THE SONG RETURNS.
PEACE IS TORTURE...
...VICTORY IS TRUTH.

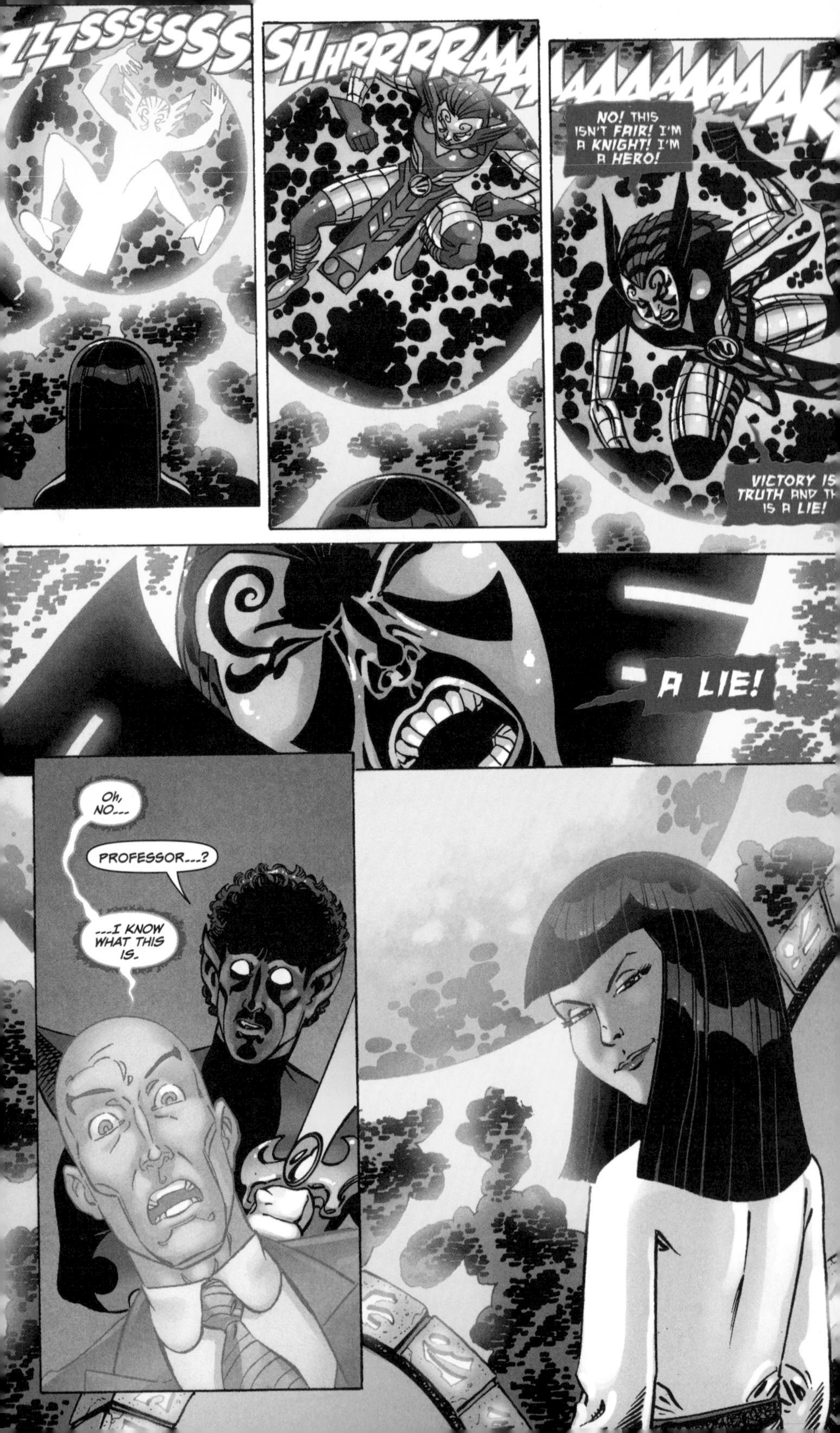

ZZZSSSSSSSS
SHHRRRRAAAAAAAAAAAAAK
NO! THIS ISN'T FAIR! I'M A KNIGHT! I'M A HERO!
VICTORY IS TRUTH AND TH IS A LIE!
A LIE!
Oh, NO---
PROFESSOR---?
---I KNOW WHAT THIS IS.

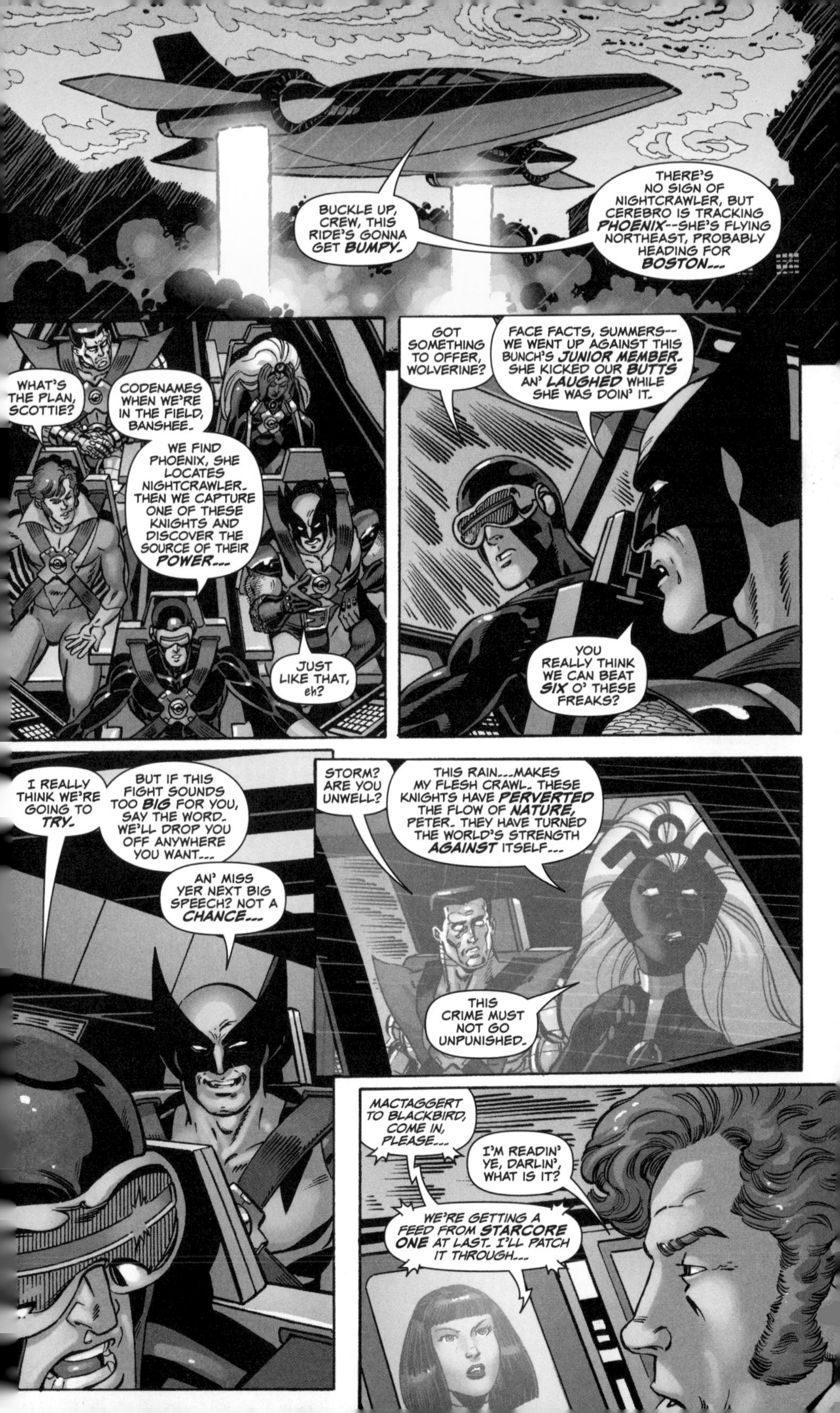

THERE'S NO SIGN OF NIGHTCRAWLER, BUT CEREBRO IS TRACKING PHOENIX--SHE'S FLYING NORTHEAST, PROBABLY HEADING FOR BOSTON...
BUCKLE UP, CREW, THIS RIDE'S GONNA GET BUMPY.
WHAT'S THE PLAN, SCOTTIE?
CODENAMES WHEN WE'RE IN THE FIELD, BANSHEE.
WE FIND PHOENIX, SHE LOCATES NIGHTCRAWLER. THEN WE CAPTURE ONE OF THESE KNIGHTS AND DISCOVER THE SOURCE OF THEIR POWER...
JUST LIKE THAT, eh?
GOT SOMETHING TO OFFER, WOLVERINE?
FACE FACTS, SUMMERS-- WE WENT UP AGAINST THIS BUNCH'S JUNIOR MEMBER. SHE KICKED OUR BUTTS AN' LAUGHED WHILE SHE WAS DOIN' IT.
YOU REALLY THINK WE CAN BEAT SIX O' THESE FREAKS?
I REALLY THINK WE'RE GOING TO TRY.
BUT IF THIS FIGHT SOUNDS TOO BIG FOR YOU, SAY THE WORD. WE'LL DROP YOU OFF ANYWHERE YOU WANT...
AN' MISS YER NEXT BIG SPEECH? NOT A CHANCE...
STORM? ARE YOU UNWELL?
THIS RAIN...MAKES MY FLESH CRAWL. THESE KNIGHTS HAVE PERVERTED THE FLOW OF NATURE, PETER. THEY HAVE TURNED THE WORLD'S STRENGTH AGAINST ITSELF...
THIS CRIME MUST NOT GO UNPUNISHED.
MACTAGGERT TO BLACKBIRD, COME IN, PLEASE...
I'M READIN' YE, DARLIN', WHAT IS IT?
WE'RE GETTING A FEED FROM STARCORE ONE AT LAST. I'LL PATCH IT THROUGH...

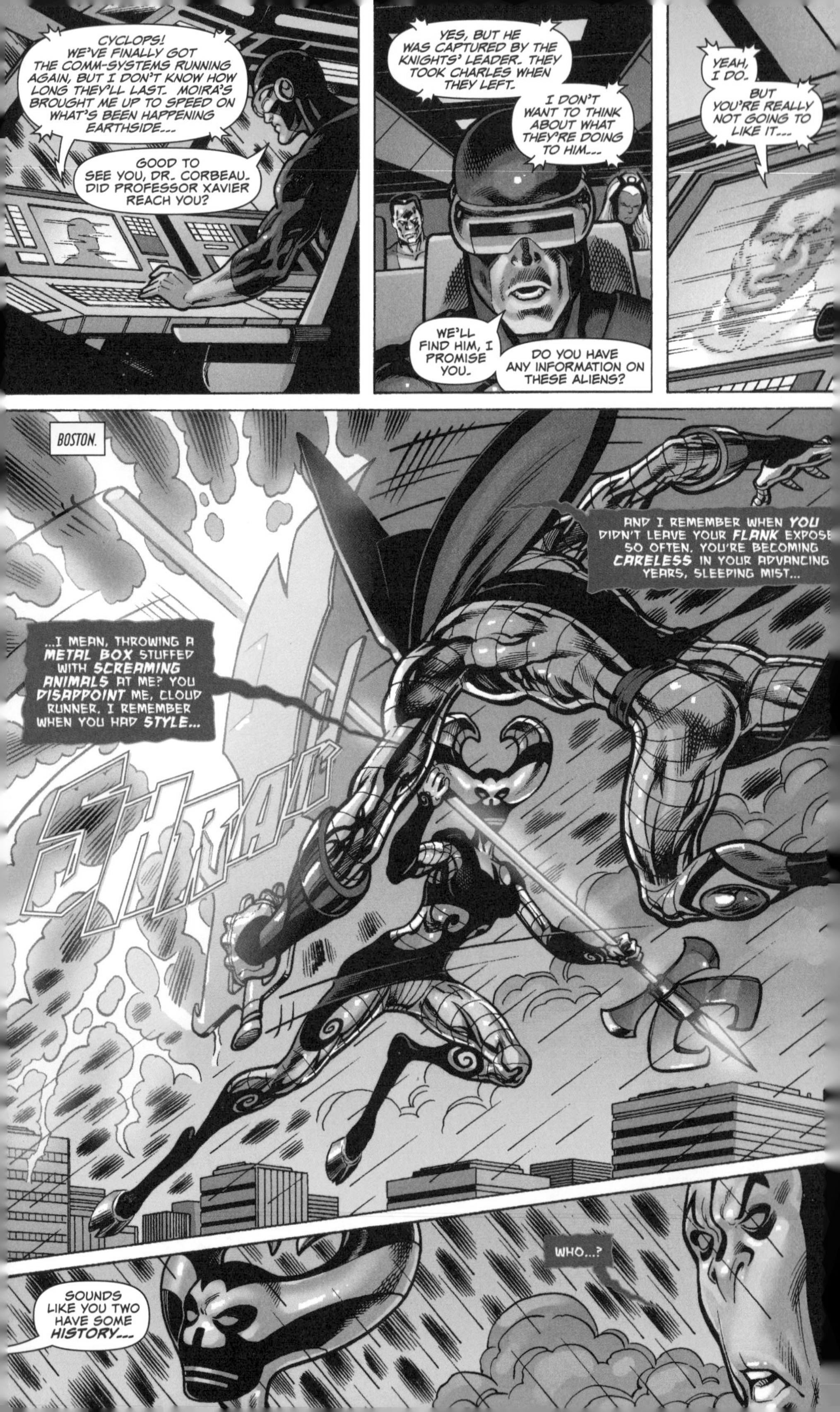
CYCLOPS! WE'VE FINALLY GOT THE COMM-SYSTEMS RUNNING AGAIN, BUT I DON'T KNOW HOW LONG THEY'LL LAST. MOIRA'S BROUGHT ME UP TO SPEED ON WHAT'S BEEN HAPPENING EARTHSIDE...
GOOD TO SEE YOU, DR. CORBEAU. DID PROFESSOR XAVIER REACH YOU?
YES, BUT HE WAS CAPTURED BY THE KNIGHTS' LEADER. THEY TOOK CHARLES WHEN THEY LEFT.
I DON'T WANT TO THINK ABOUT WHAT THEY'RE DOING TO HIM...
WE'LL FIND HIM, I PROMISE YOU.
DO YOU HAVE ANY INFORMATION ON THESE ALIENS?
YEAH, I DO.
BUT YOU'RE REALLY NOT GOING TO LIKE IT...
BOSTON.
...I MEAN, THROWING A METAL BOX STUFFED WITH SCREAMING ANIMALS AT ME? YOU DISAPPOINT ME, CLOUD RUNNER. I REMEMBER WHEN YOU HAD STYLE...
AND I REMEMBER WHEN YOU DIDN'T LEAVE YOUR FLANK EXPOSE SO OFTEN. YOU'RE BECOMING CARELESS IN YOUR ADVANCING YEARS, SLEEPING MIST...
SHRAK
SOUNDS LIKE YOU TWO HAVE SOME HISTORY...
WHO...?

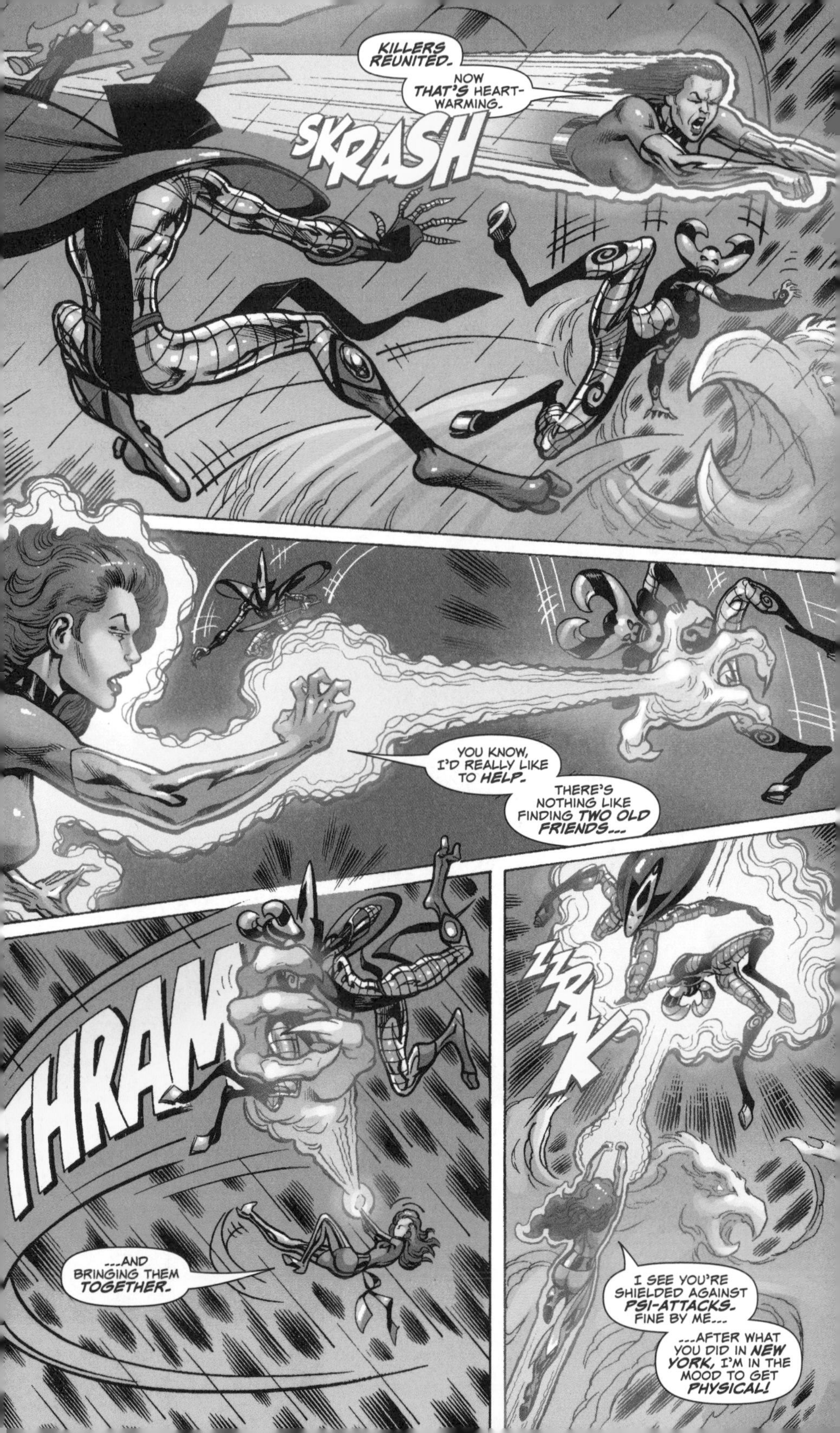
KILLERS REUNITED.
NOW THAT'S HEART-WARMING.
SKRASH
YOU KNOW, I'D REALLY LIKE TO HELP.
THERE'S NOTHING LIKE FINDING TWO OLD FRIENDS...
THRAM
...AND BRINGING THEM TOGETHER.
ZZRAK
I SEE YOU'RE SHIELDED AGAINST PSI-ATTACKS. FINE BY ME...
...AFTER WHAT YOU DID IN NEW YORK, I'M IN THE MOOD TO GET PHYSICAL!

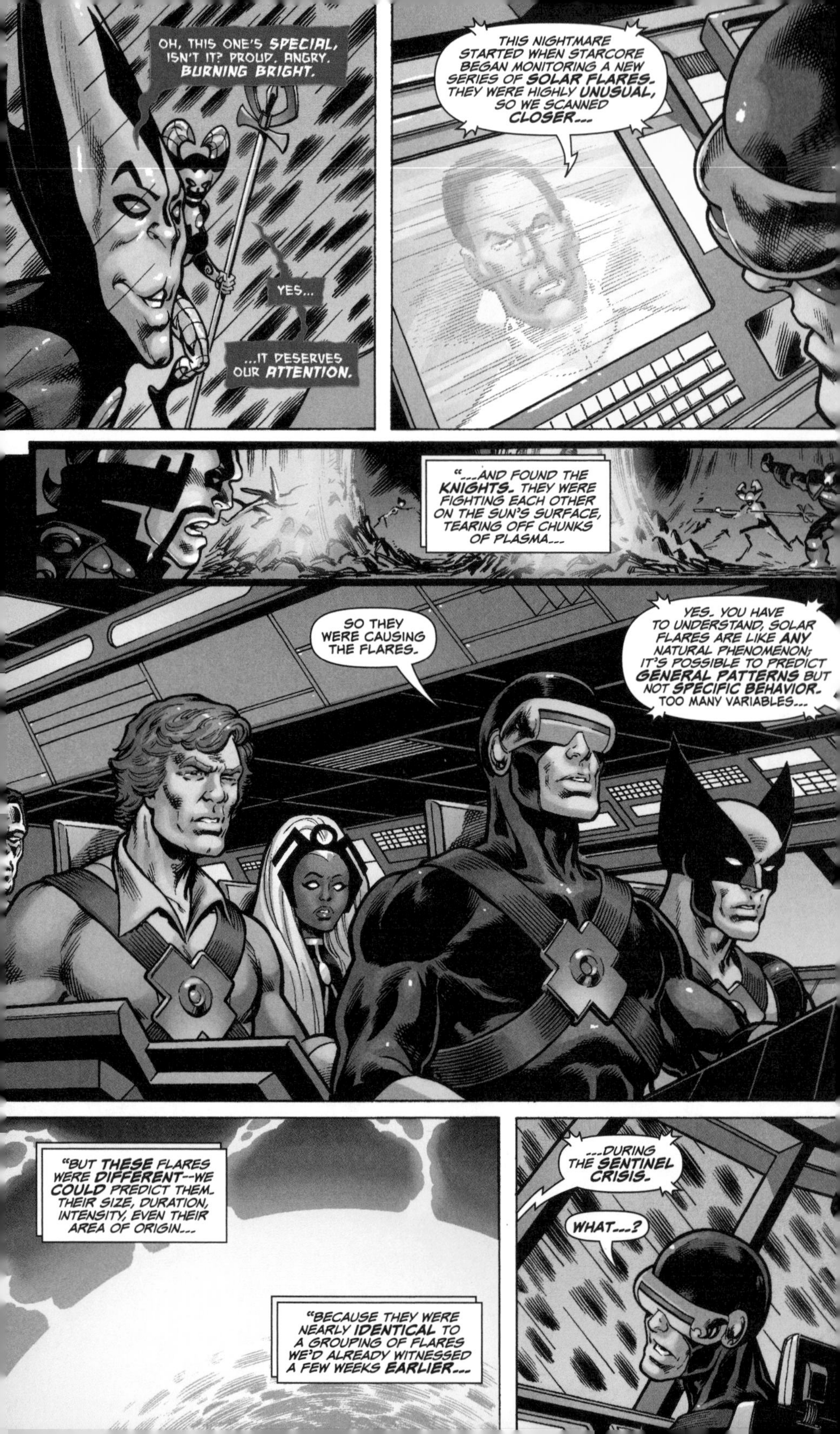
OH, THIS ONE'S SPECIAL, ISN'T IT? PROUD. ANGRY. BURNING BRIGHT.
YES...
...IT DESERVES OUR ATTENTION.
THIS NIGHTMARE STARTED WHEN STARCORE BEGAN MONITORING A NEW SERIES OF SOLAR FLARES. THEY WERE HIGHLY UNUSUAL, SO WE SCANNED CLOSER...
"...AND FOUND THE KNIGHTS. THEY WERE FIGHTING EACH OTHER ON THE SUN'S SURFACE, TEARING OFF CHUNKS OF PLASMA...
SO THEY WERE CAUSING THE FLARES.
YES. YOU HAVE TO UNDERSTAND, SOLAR FLARES ARE LIKE ANY NATURAL PHENOMENON; IT'S POSSIBLE TO PREDICT GENERAL PATTERNS BUT NOT SPECIFIC BEHAVIOR. TOO MANY VARIABLES...
"BUT THESE FLARES WERE DIFFERENT--WE COULD PREDICT THEM. THEIR SIZE, DURATION, INTENSITY, EVEN THEIR AREA OF ORIGIN...
"BECAUSE THEY WERE NEARLY IDENTICAL TO A GROUPING OF FLARES WE'D ALREADY WITNESSED A FEW WEEKS EARLIER...
...DURING THE SENTINEL CRISIS.
WHAT...?

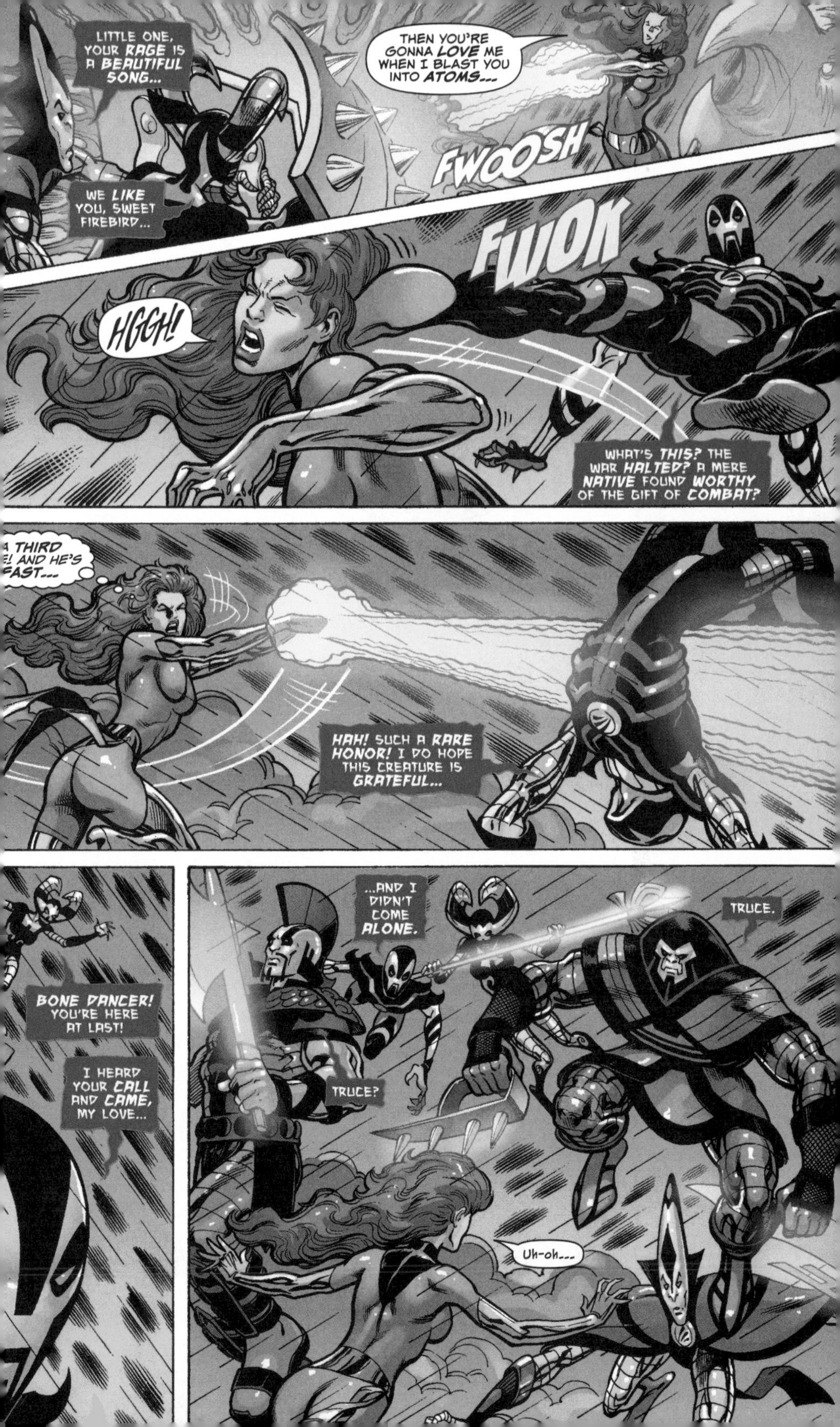
LITTLE ONE, YOUR RAGE IS A BEAUTIFUL SONG...
THEN YOU'RE GONNA LOVE ME WHEN I BLAST YOU INTO ATOMS---
FWOOSH
WE LIKE YOU, SWEET FIREBIRD...
FWOK
HGGH!
WHAT'S THIS? THE WAR HALTED? A MERE NATIVE FOUND WORTHY OF THE GIFT OF COMBAT?
FAST---
HAH! SUCH A RARE HONOR! I DO HOPE THIS CREATURE IS GRATEFUL...
BONE DANCER! YOU'RE HERE AT LAST!
I HEARD YOUR CALL AND CAME, MY LOVE...
...AND I DIDN'T COME ALONE.
TRUCE.
TRUCE?
Uh-oh---

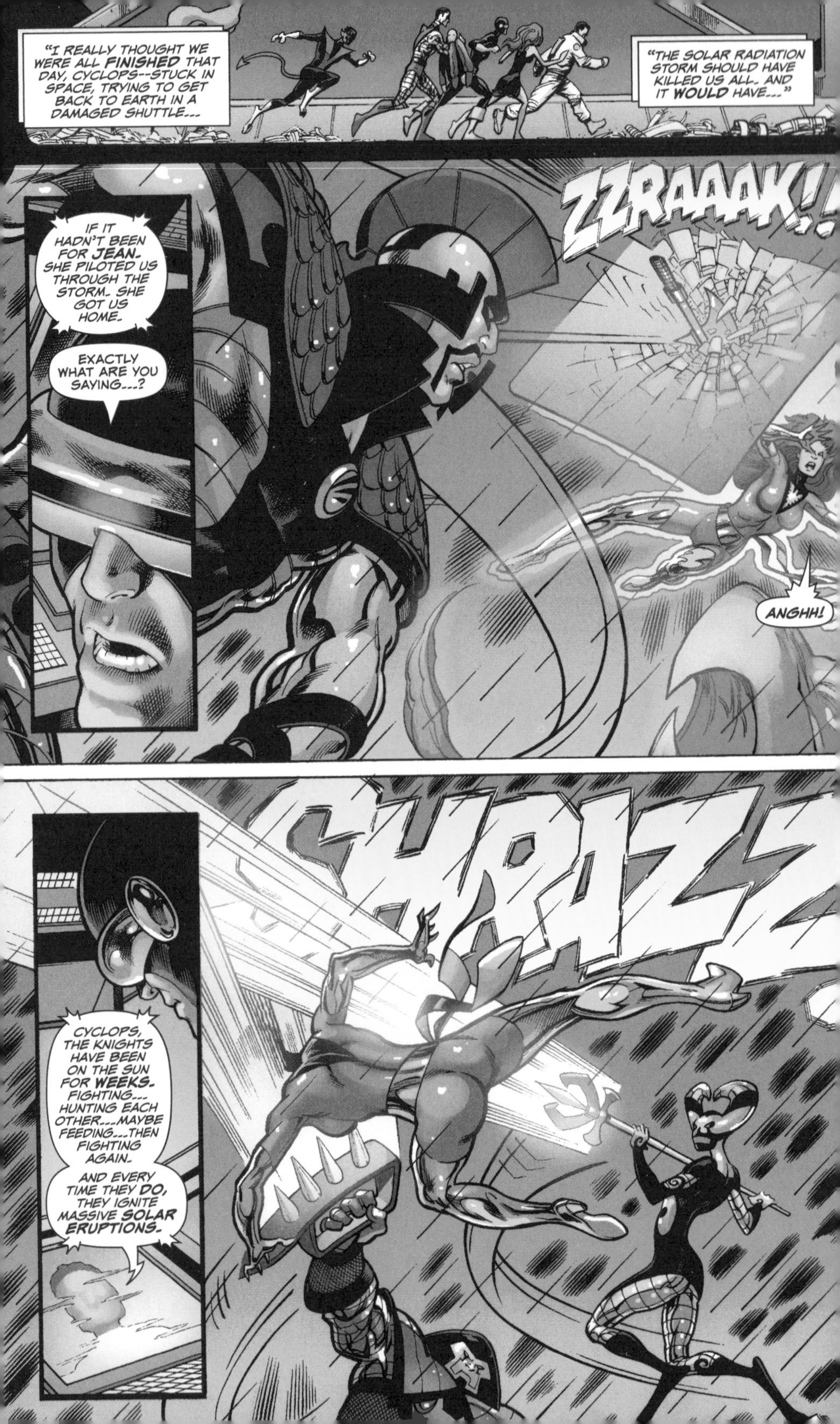
"I REALLY THOUGHT WE WERE ALL FINISHED THAT DAY, CYCLOPS--STUCK IN SPACE, TRYING TO GET BACK TO EARTH IN A DAMAGED SHUTTLE...
"THE SOLAR RADIATION STORM SHOULD HAVE KILLED US ALL. AND IT WOULD HAVE..."
ZZRAAAK!!
IF IT HADN'T BEEN FOR JEAN. SHE PILOTED US THROUGH THE STORM. SHE GOT US HOME.
EXACTLY WHAT ARE YOU SAYING...?
ANGHH!
CYCLOPS, THE KNIGHTS HAVE BEEN ON THE SUN FOR WEEKS. FIGHTING... HUNTING EACH OTHER... MAYBE FEEDING... THEN FIGHTING AGAIN.
AND EVERY TIME THEY DO, THEY IGNITE MASSIVE SOLAR ERUPTIONS.

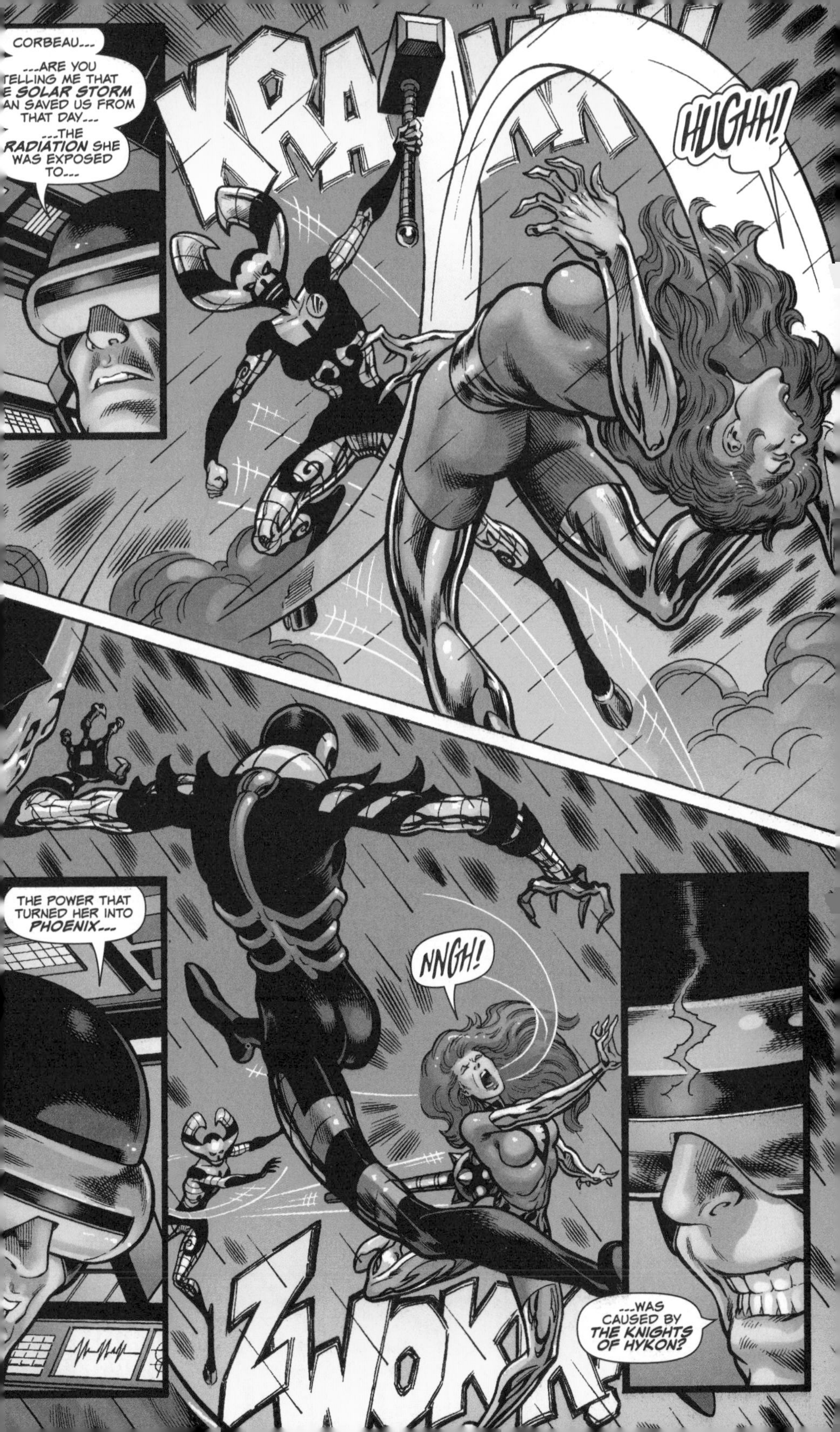
CORBEAU---
---ARE YOU TELLING ME THAT E SOLAR STORM AN SAVED US FROM THAT DAY---
---THE RADIATION SHE WAS EXPOSED TO---
HUGHH!
THE POWER THAT TURNED HER INTO PHOENIX---
NNGH!
---WAS CAUSED BY THE KNIGHTS OF HYKON?

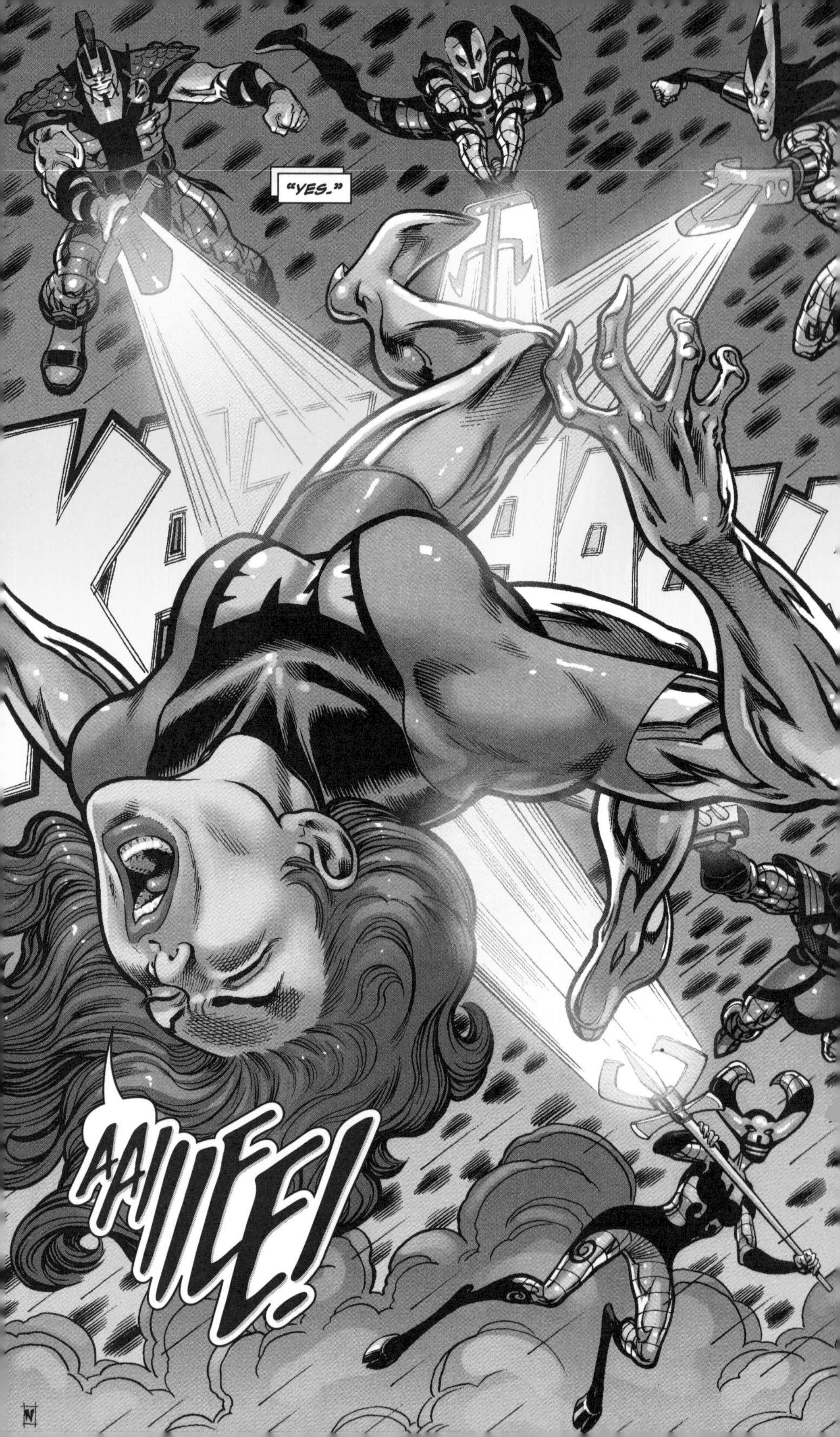
"YES."
AAIIEE!

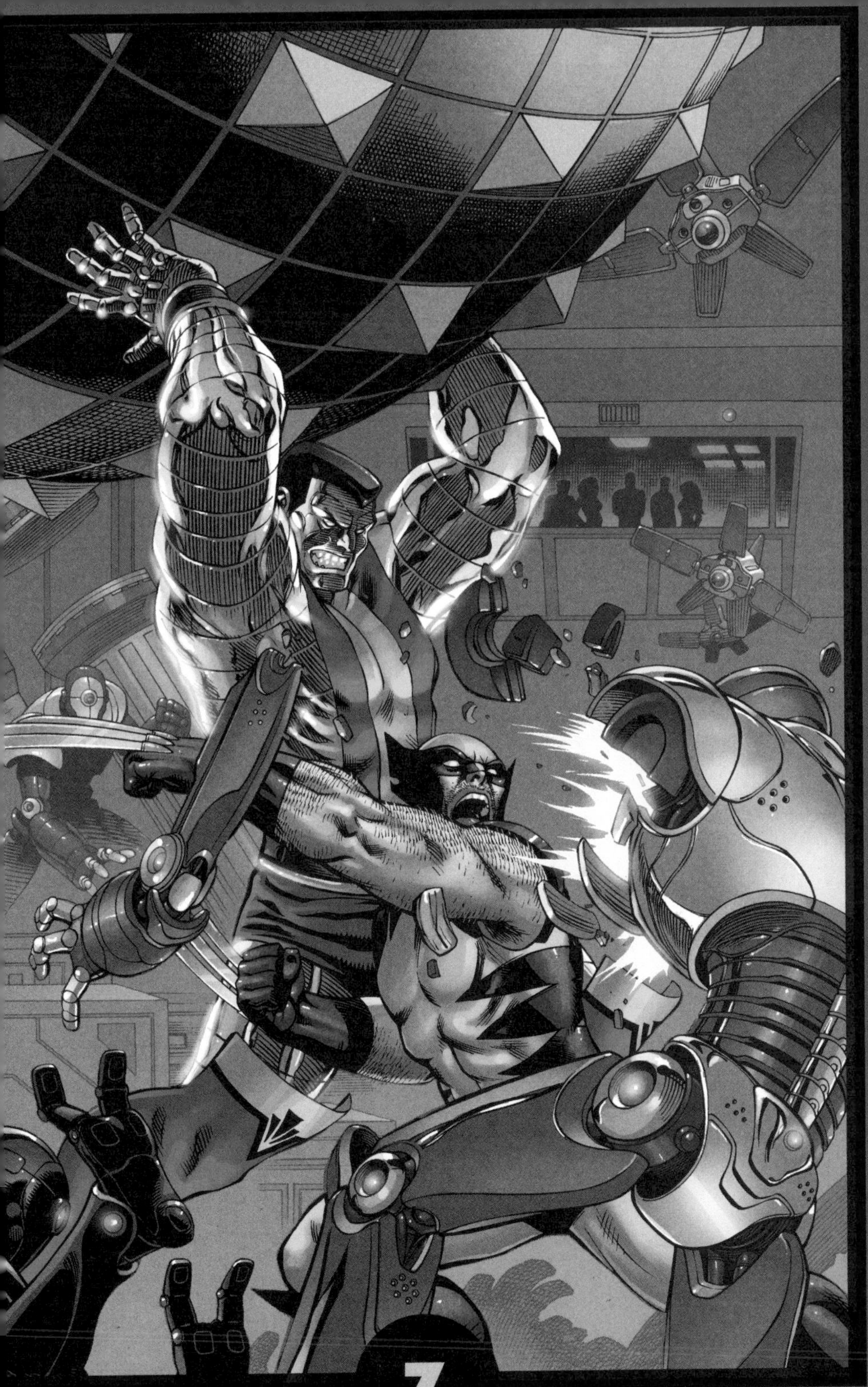

7

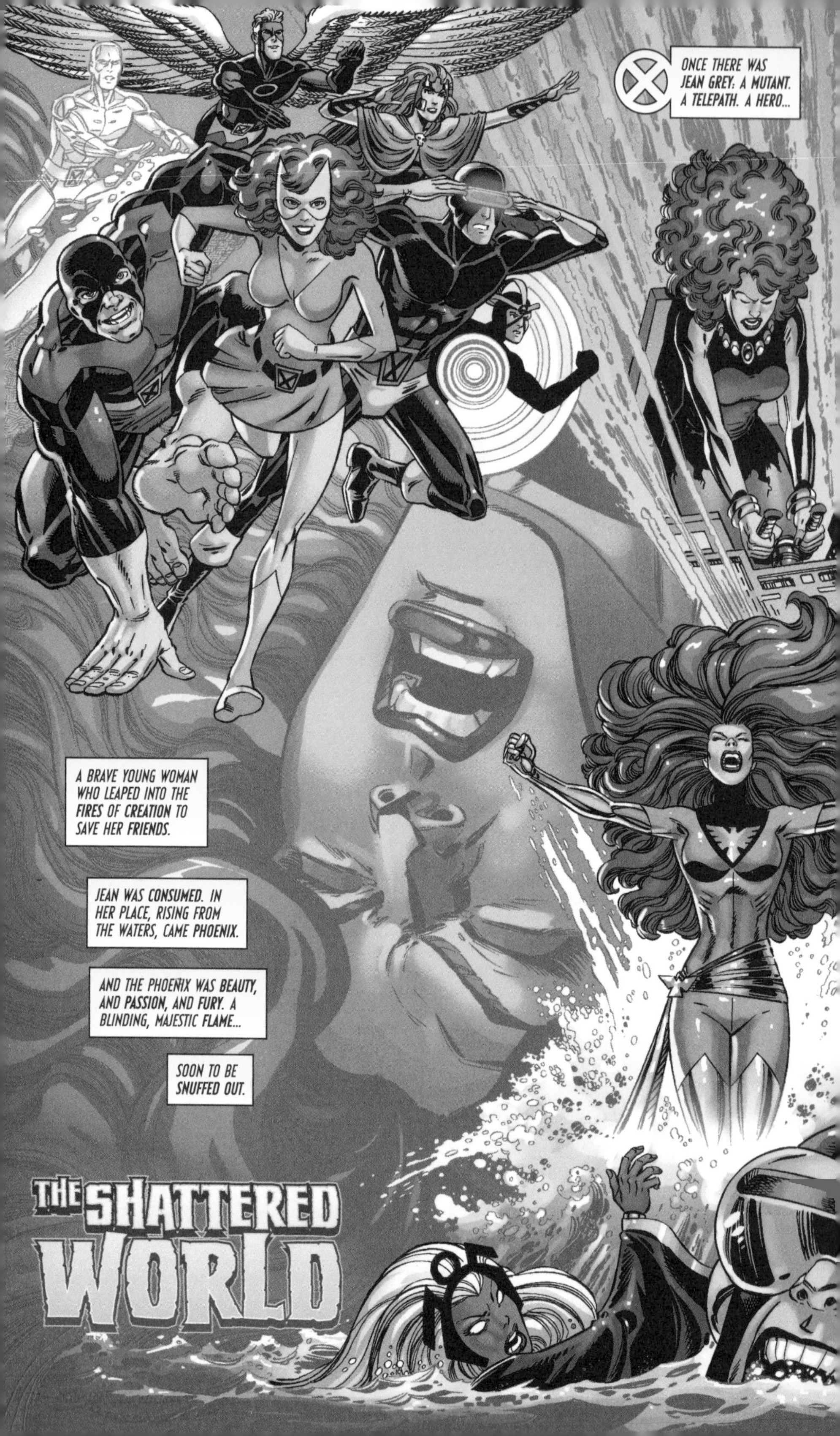
ONCE THERE WAS JEAN GREY: A MUTANT. A TELEPATH. A HERO...
A BRAVE YOUNG WOMAN WHO LEAPED INTO THE FIRES OF CREATION TO SAVE HER FRIENDS.
JEAN WAS CONSUMED. IN HER PLACE, RISING FROM THE WATERS, CAME PHOENIX.
AND THE PHOENIX WAS BEAUTY, AND PASSION, AND FURY. A BLINDING, MAJESTIC FLAME...
SOON TO BE SNUFFED OUT.
THE SHATTERED WORLD

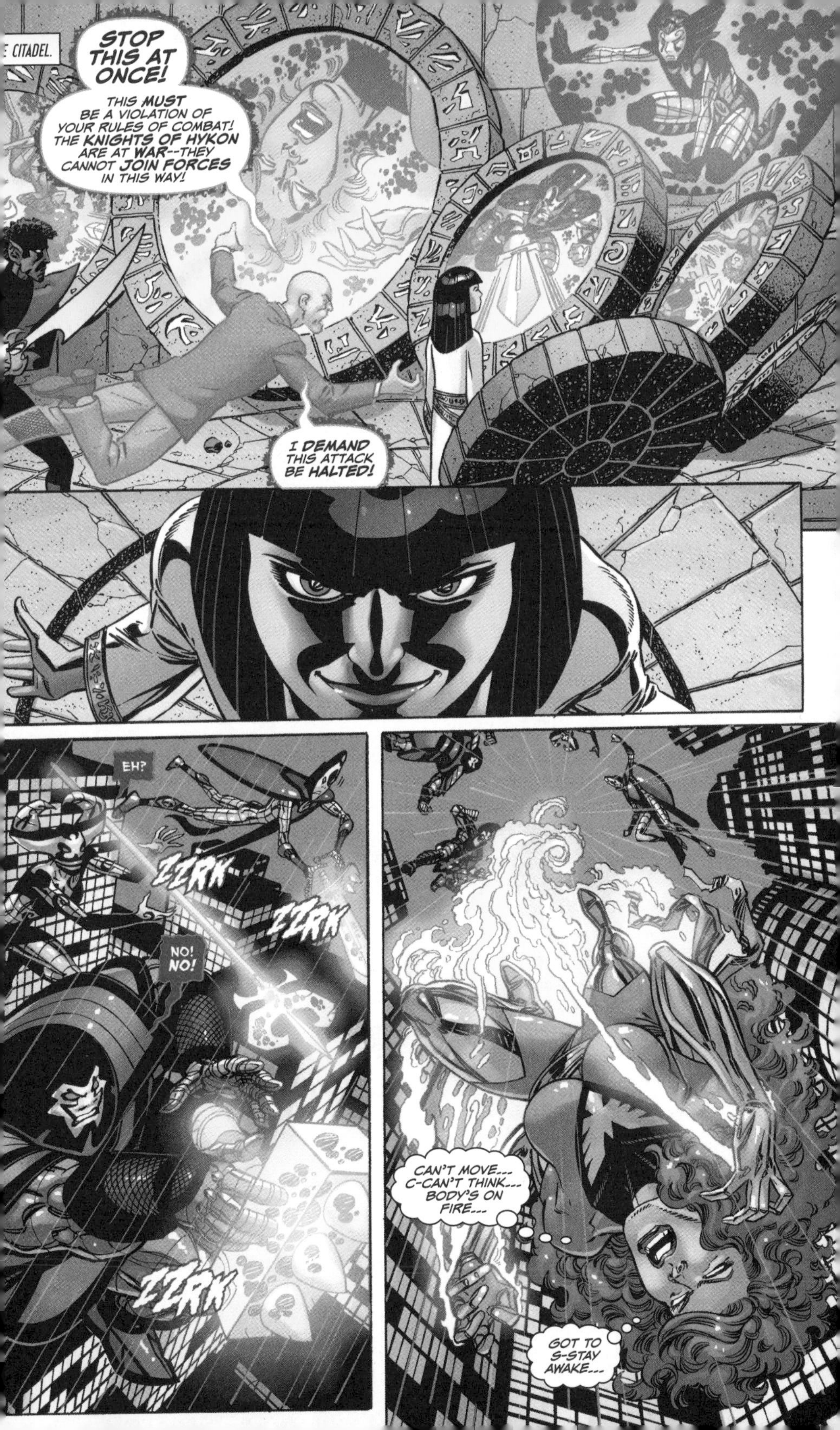
E CITADEL.
STOP THIS AT ONCE!
THIS MUST BE A VIOLATION OF YOUR RULES OF COMBAT! THE KNIGHTS OF HYKON ARE AT WAR--THEY CANNOT JOIN FORCES IN THIS WAY!
I DEMAND THIS ATTACK BE HALTED!
EH?
ZZRK
ZZRK
NO! NO!
ZZRK
CAN'T MOVE... C-CAN'T THINK... BODY'S ON FIRE...
GOT TO S-STAY AWAKE...

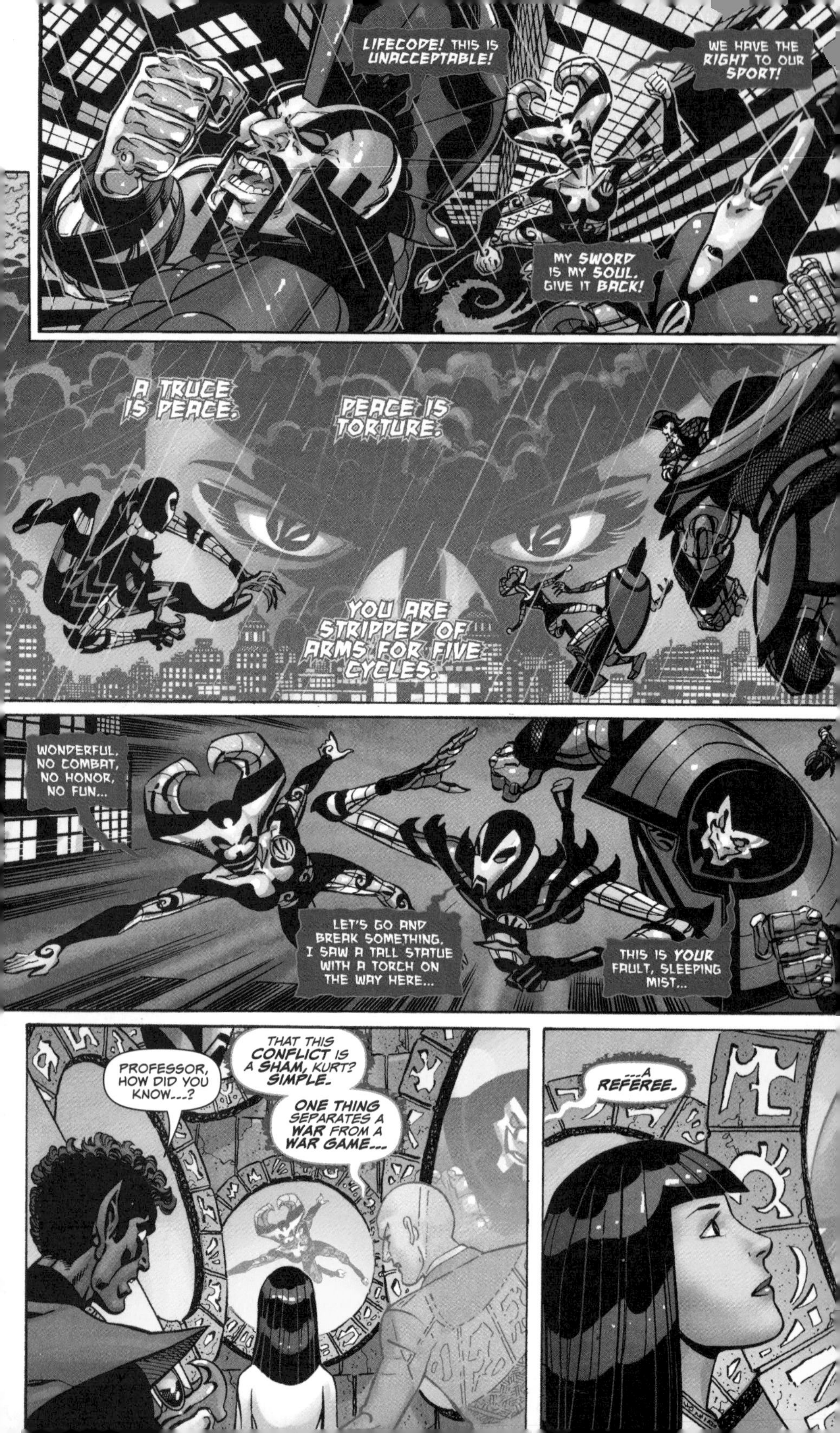
LIFECODE! THIS IS UNACCEPTABLE!
WE HAVE THE RIGHT TO OUR SPORT!
MY SWORD IS MY SOUL. GIVE IT BACK!
A TRUCE IS PEACE.
PEACE IS TORTURE.
YOU ARE STRIPPED OF ARMS FOR FIVE CYCLES.
WONDERFUL. NO COMBAT, NO HONOR, NO FUN...
LET'S GO AND BREAK SOMETHING. I SAW A TALL STATUE WITH A TORCH ON THE WAY HERE...
THIS IS YOUR FAULT, SLEEPING MIST...
PROFESSOR, HOW DID YOU KNOW...?
THAT THIS CONFLICT IS A SHAM, KURT? SIMPLE.
ONE THING SEPARATES A WAR FROM A WAR GAME...
...A REFEREE.

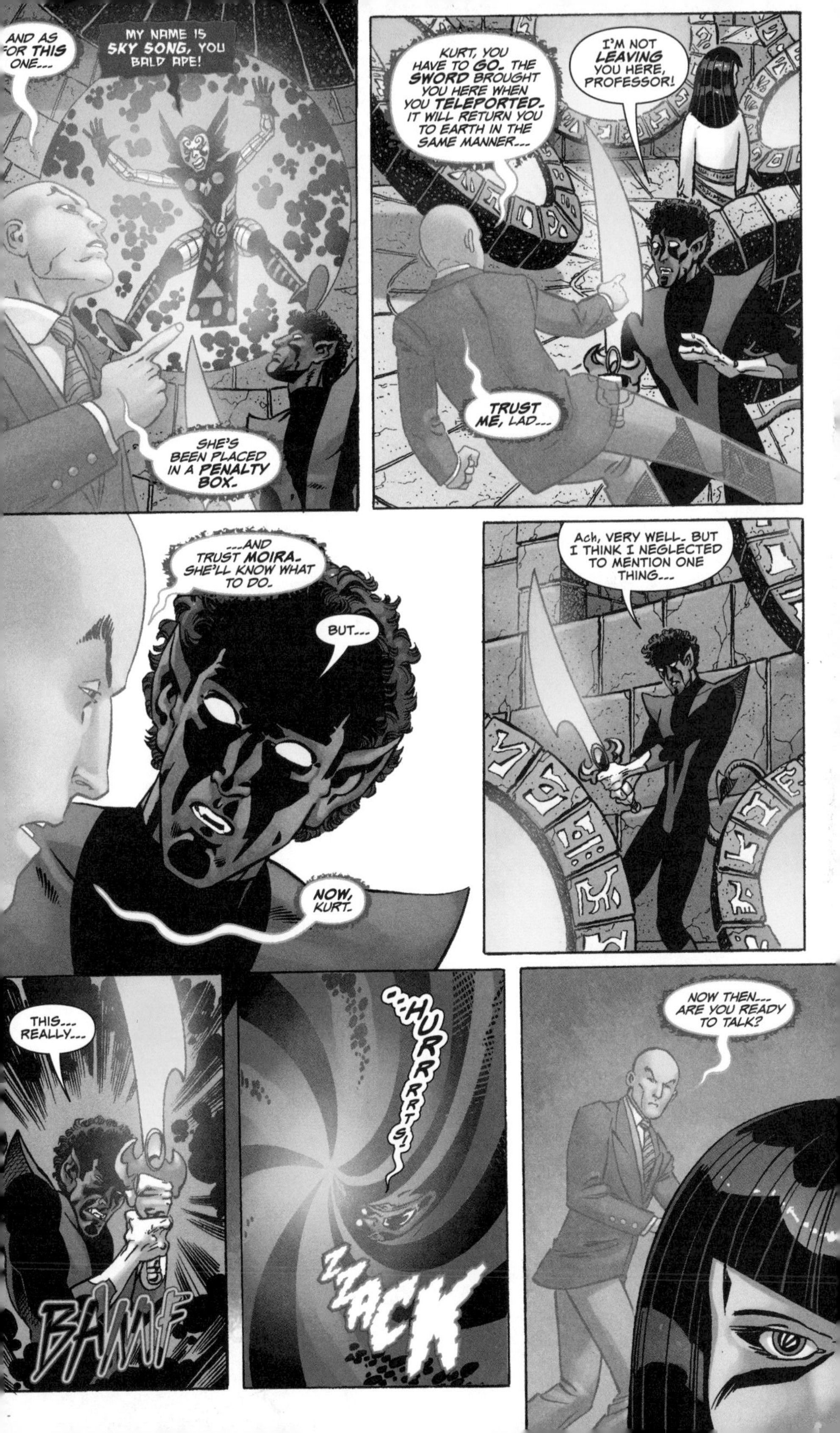
AND AS FOR THIS ONE---
MY NAME IS SKY SONG, YOU BALD APE!
SHE'S BEEN PLACED IN A PENALTY BOX.
KURT, YOU HAVE TO GO. THE SWORD BROUGHT YOU HERE WHEN YOU TELEPORTED. IT WILL RETURN YOU TO EARTH IN THE SAME MANNER---
I'M NOT LEAVING YOU HERE, PROFESSOR!
TRUST ME, LAD---
---AND TRUST MOIRA. SHE'LL KNOW WHAT TO DO.
BUT---
NOW, KURT.
Ach, VERY WELL. BUT I THINK I NEGLECTED TO MENTION ONE THING---
THIS--- REALLY---
BAMF
--HURRRRTS!
ZZACK
NOW THEN--- ARE YOU READY TO TALK?

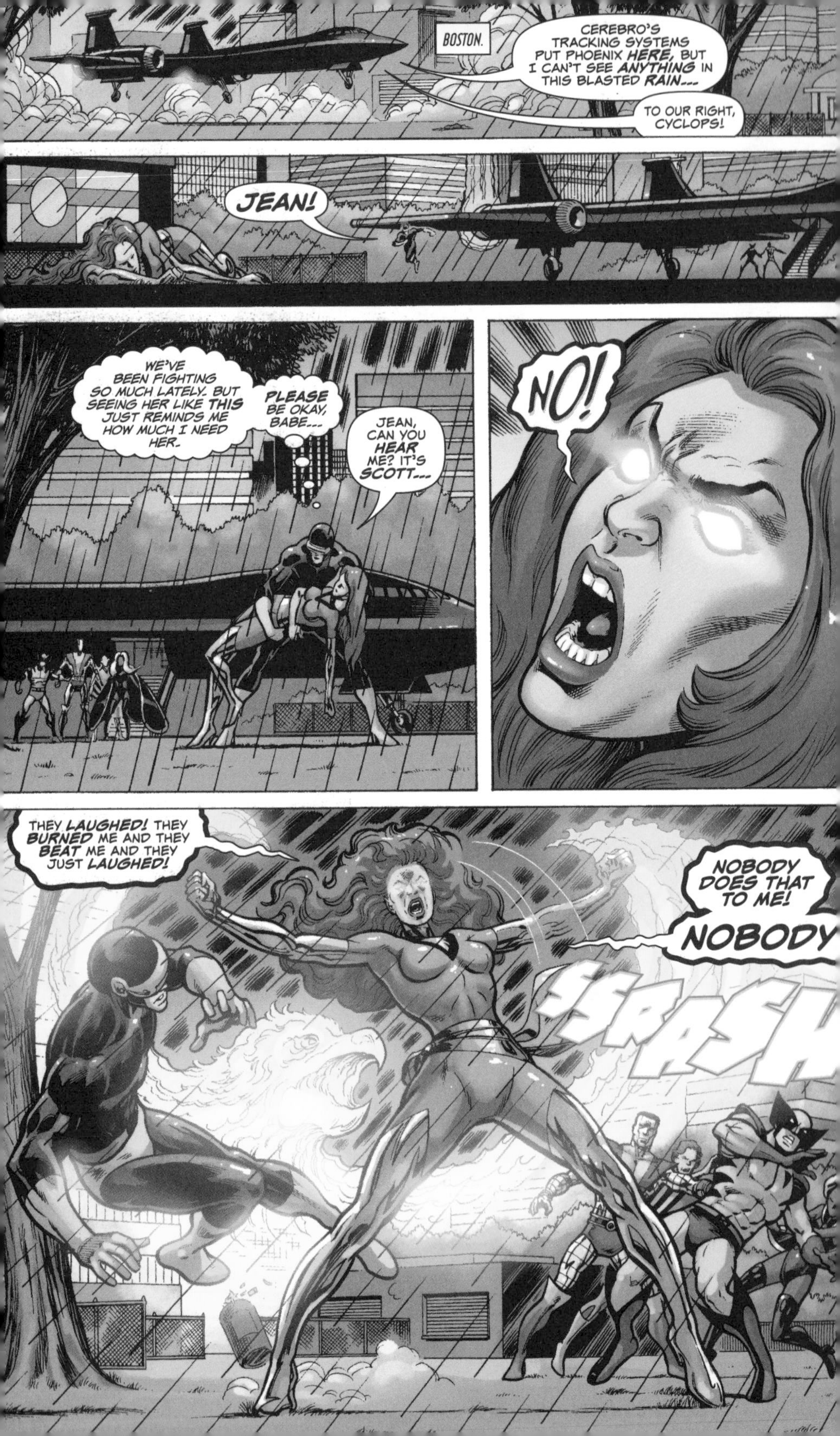
BOSTON.
CEREBRO'S TRACKING SYSTEMS PUT PHOENIX HERE, BUT I CAN'T SEE ANYTHING IN THIS BLASTED RAIN---
TO OUR RIGHT, CYCLOPS!
JEAN!
WE'VE BEEN FIGHTING SO MUCH LATELY. BUT SEEING HER LIKE THIS JUST REMINDS ME HOW MUCH I NEED HER.
PLEASE BE OKAY, BABE---
JEAN, CAN YOU HEAR ME? IT'S SCOTT---
NO!
THEY LAUGHED! THEY BURNED ME AND THEY BEAT ME AND THEY JUST LAUGHED!
NOBODY DOES THAT TO ME!
NOBODY
SSRASH

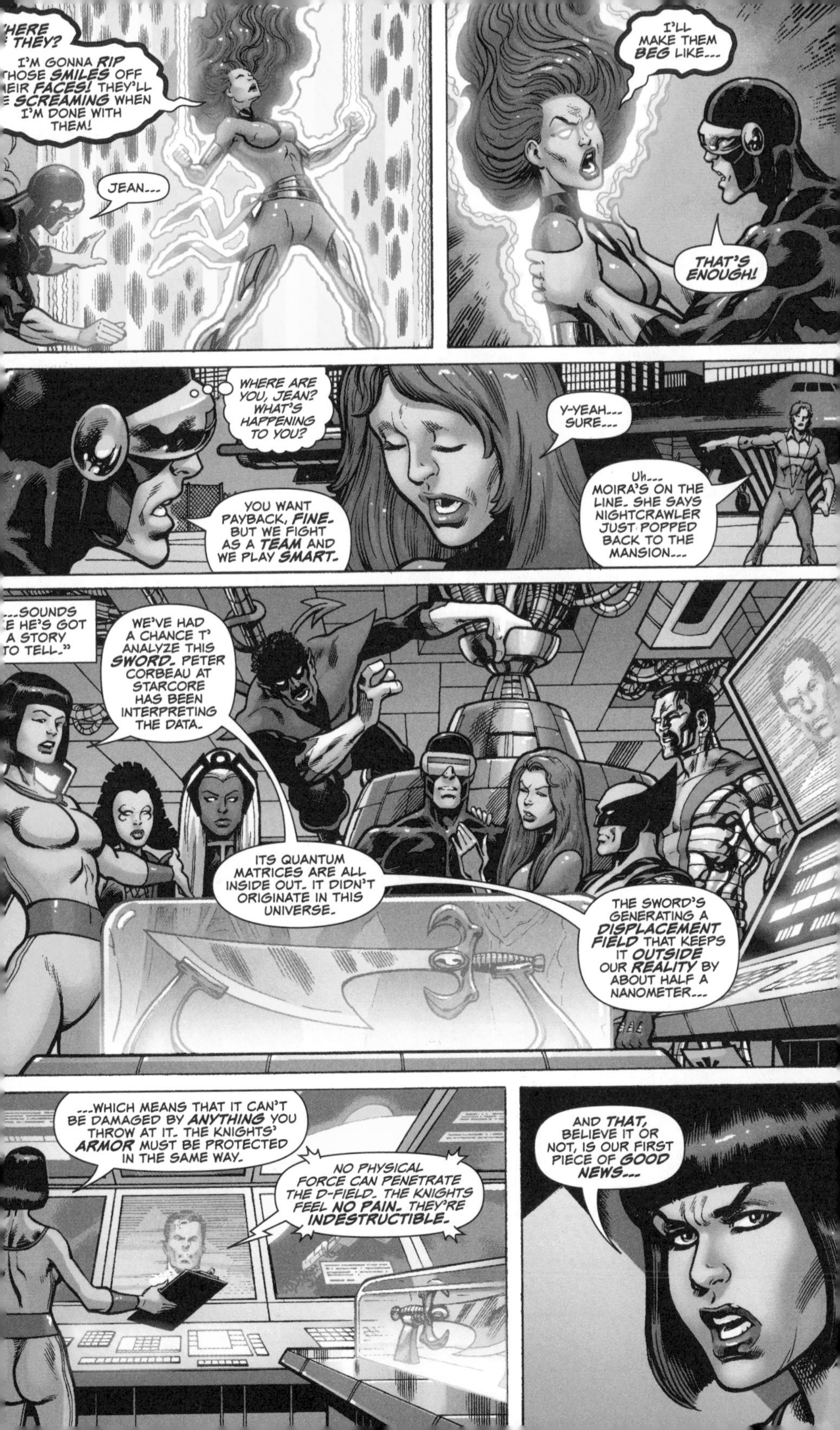

...HERE ...THEY? I'M GONNA RIP THOSE SMILES OFF ...EIR FACES! THEY'LL ...E SCREAMING WHEN I'M DONE WITH THEM!
JEAN...
I'LL MAKE THEM BEG LIKE...
THAT'S ENOUGH!
WHERE ARE YOU, JEAN? WHAT'S HAPPENING TO YOU?
YOU WANT PAYBACK, FINE. BUT WE FIGHT AS A TEAM AND WE PLAY SMART.
Y-YEAH... SURE...
UH... MOIRA'S ON THE LINE. SHE SAYS NIGHTCRAWLER JUST POPPED BACK TO THE MANSION...
"...SOUNDS ...E HE'S GOT A STORY TO TELL."
WE'VE HAD A CHANCE T' ANALYZE THIS SWORD. PETER CORBEAU AT STARCORE HAS BEEN INTERPRETING THE DATA.
ITS QUANTUM MATRICES ARE ALL INSIDE OUT. IT DIDN'T ORIGINATE IN THIS UNIVERSE.
THE SWORD'S GENERATING A DISPLACEMENT FIELD THAT KEEPS IT OUTSIDE OUR REALITY BY ABOUT HALF A NANOMETER...
...WHICH MEANS THAT IT CAN'T BE DAMAGED BY ANYTHING YOU THROW AT IT. THE KNIGHTS' ARMOR MUST BE PROTECTED IN THE SAME WAY.
NO PHYSICAL FORCE CAN PENETRATE THE D-FIELD. THE KNIGHTS FEEL NO PAIN. THEY'RE INDESTRUCTIBLE.
AND THAT, BELIEVE IT OR NOT, IS OUR FIRST PIECE OF GOOD NEWS...

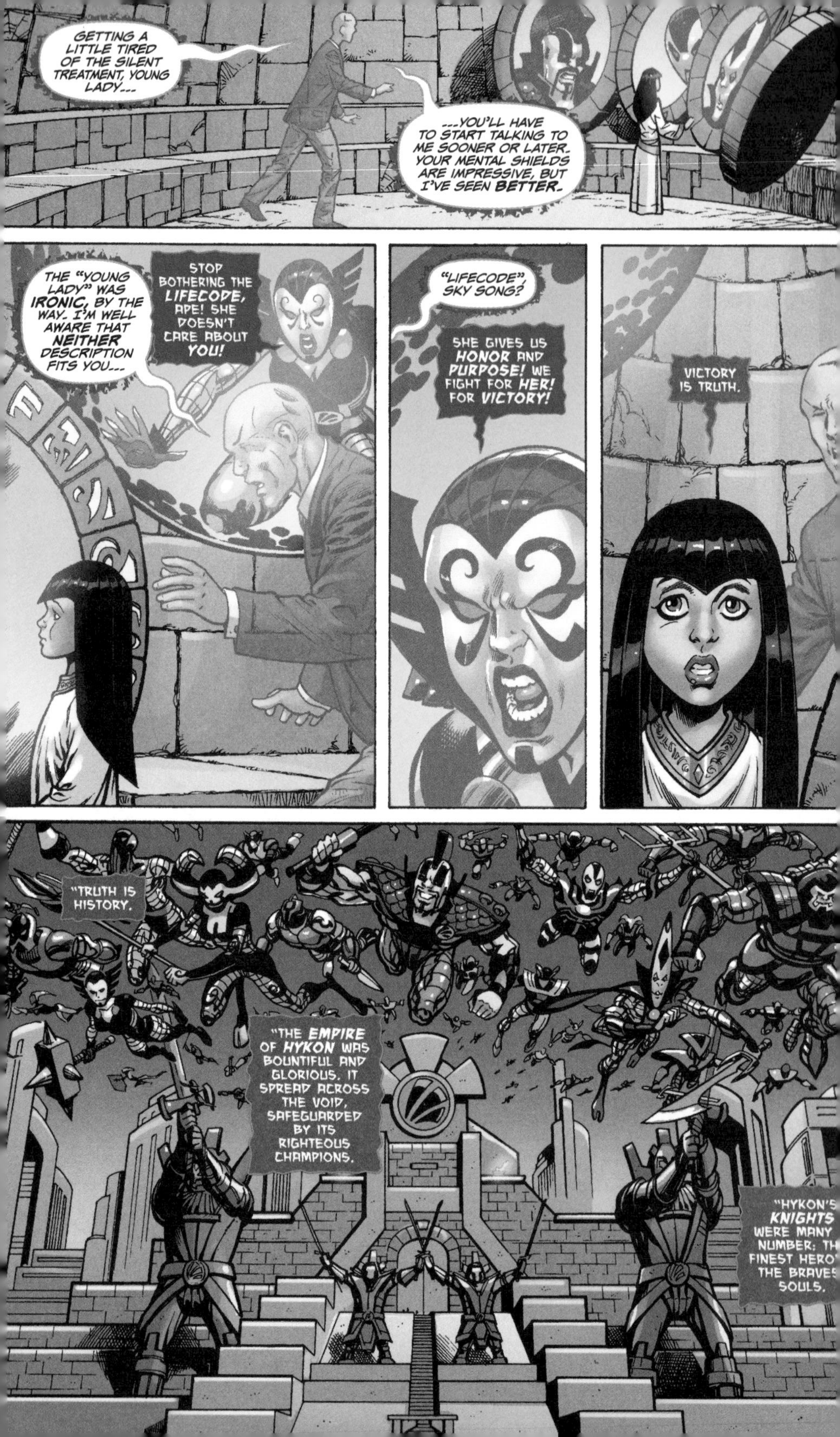
GETTING A LITTLE TIRED OF THE SILENT TREATMENT, YOUNG LADY...
...YOU'LL HAVE TO START TALKING TO ME SOONER OR LATER. YOUR MENTAL SHIELDS ARE IMPRESSIVE, BUT I'VE SEEN BETTER.
THE "YOUNG LADY" WAS IRONIC, BY THE WAY. I'M WELL AWARE THAT NEITHER DESCRIPTION FITS YOU...
STOP BOTHERING THE LIFECODE, APE! SHE DOESN'T CARE ABOUT YOU!
"LIFECODE", SKY SONG?
SHE GIVES US HONOR AND PURPOSE! WE FIGHT FOR HER! FOR VICTORY!
VICTORY IS TRUTH.
"TRUTH IS HISTORY.
"THE EMPIRE OF HYKON WAS BOUNTIFUL AND GLORIOUS. IT SPREAD ACROSS THE VOID, SAFEGUARDED BY ITS RIGHTEOUS CHAMPIONS.
"HYKON'S KNIGHTS WERE MANY

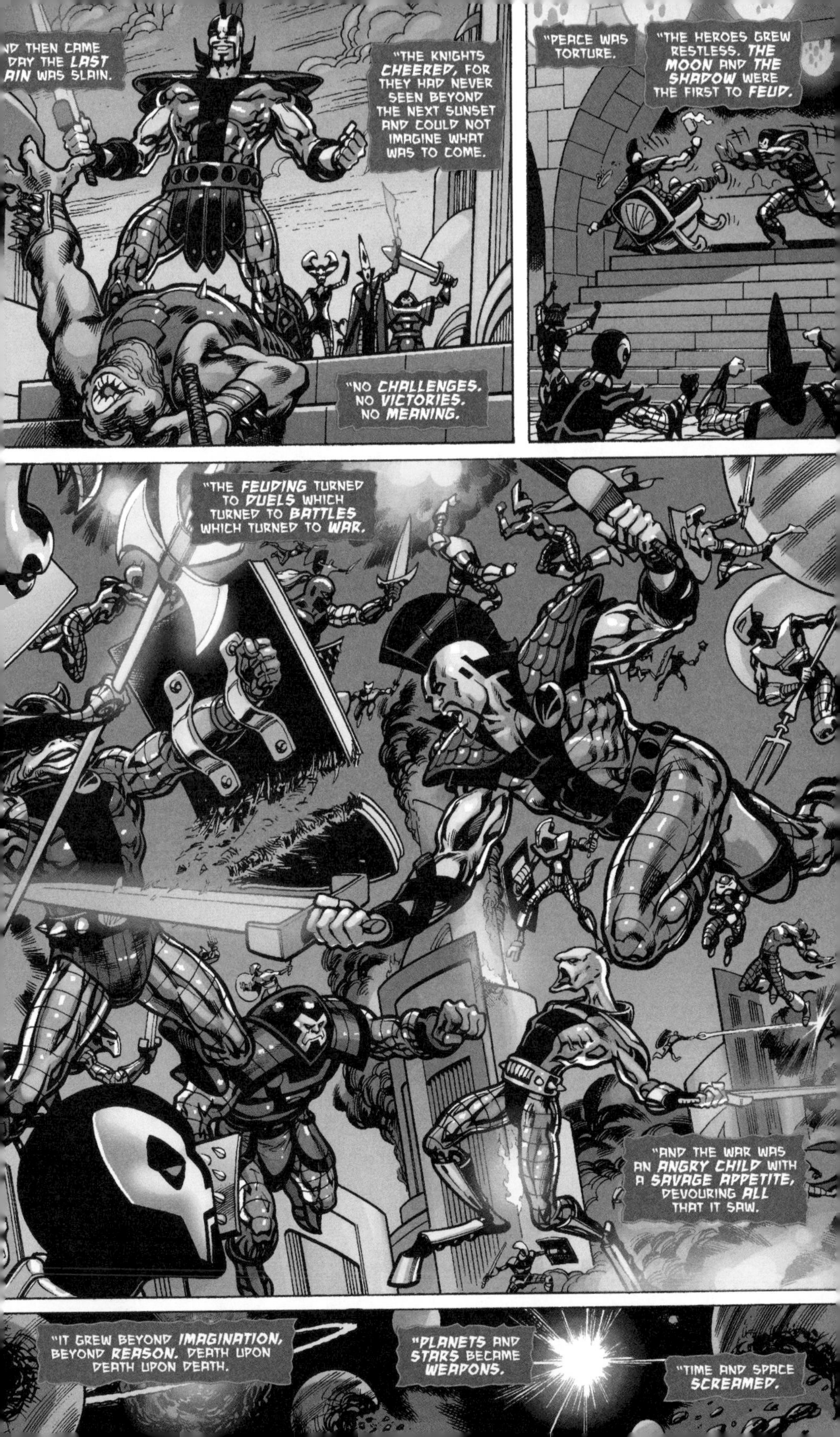
ND THEN CAME DAY THE LAST AIN WAS SLAIN.
"THE KNIGHTS CHEERED, FOR THEY HAD NEVER SEEN BEYOND THE NEXT SUNSET AND COULD NOT IMAGINE WHAT WAS TO COME.
"NO CHALLENGES. NO VICTORIES. NO MEANING.
"PEACE WAS TORTURE.
"THE HEROES GREW RESTLESS. THE MOON AND THE SHADOW WERE THE FIRST TO FEUD.
"THE FEUDING TURNED TO DUELS WHICH TURNED TO BATTLES WHICH TURNED TO WAR.
"AND THE WAR WAS AN ANGRY CHILD WITH A SAVAGE APPETITE, DEVOURING ALL THAT IT SAW.
"IT GREW BEYOND IMAGINATION, BEYOND REASON. DEATH UPON DEATH UPON DEATH.
"PLANETS AND STARS BECAME WEAPONS.
"TIME AND SPACE SCREAMED.

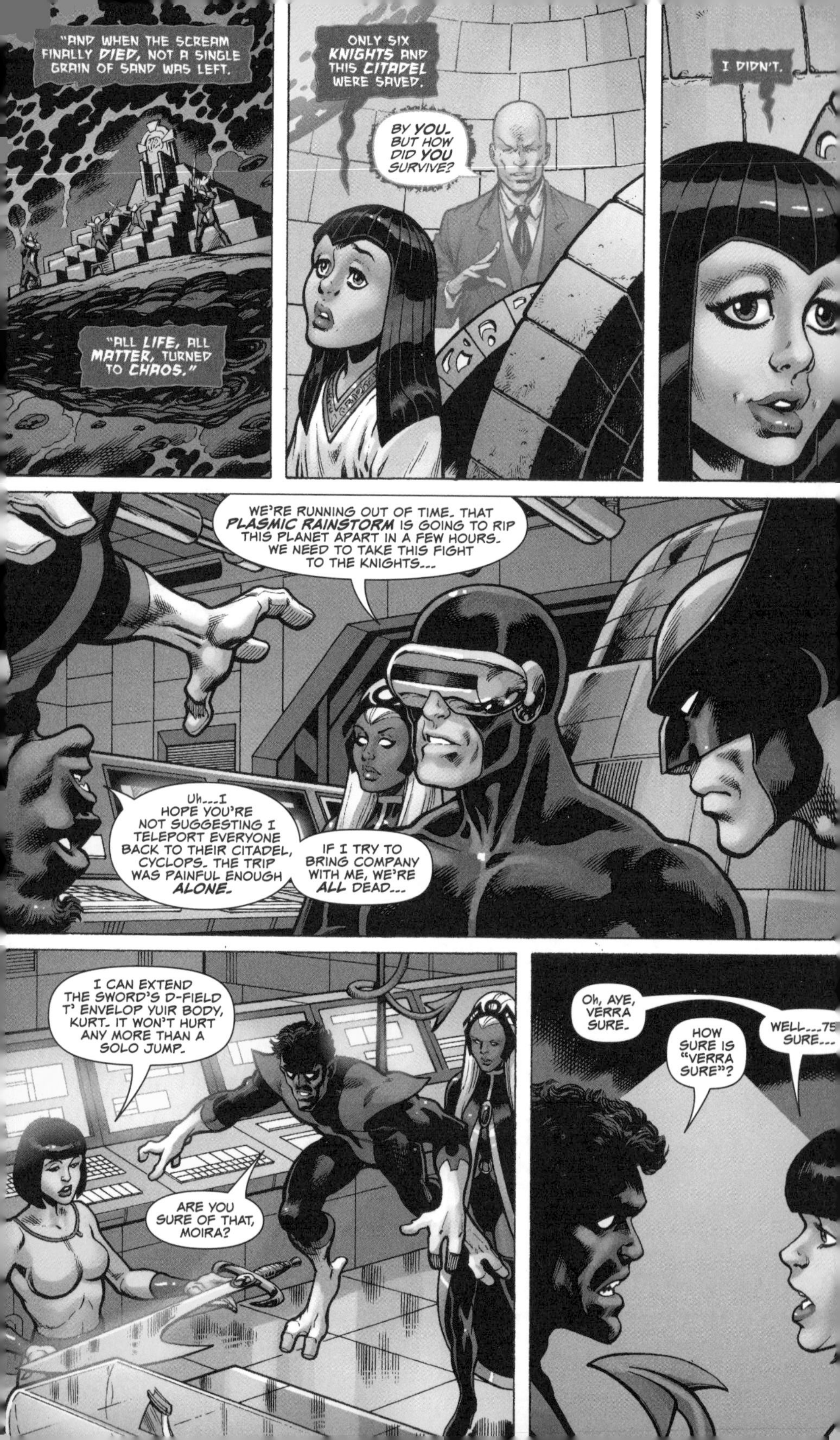
"AND WHEN THE SCREAM FINALLY DIED, NOT A SINGLE GRAIN OF SAND WAS LEFT.
"ALL LIFE, ALL MATTER, TURNED TO CHAOS."
ONLY SIX KNIGHTS AND THIS CITADEL WERE SAVED.
BY YOU. BUT HOW DID YOU SURVIVE?
I DIDN'T.
WE'RE RUNNING OUT OF TIME. THAT PLASMIC RAINSTORM IS GOING TO RIP THIS PLANET APART IN A FEW HOURS. WE NEED TO TAKE THIS FIGHT TO THE KNIGHTS...
Uh...I HOPE YOU'RE NOT SUGGESTING I TELEPORT EVERYONE BACK TO THEIR CITADEL, CYCLOPS. THE TRIP WAS PAINFUL ENOUGH ALONE.
IF I TRY TO BRING COMPANY WITH ME, WE'RE ALL DEAD...
I CAN EXTEND THE SWORD'S D-FIELD T' ENVELOP YUIR BODY, KURT. IT WON'T HURT ANY MORE THAN A SOLO JUMP.
ARE YOU SURE OF THAT, MOIRA?
Oh, AYE, VERRA SURE.
HOW SURE IS "VERRA SURE"?
WELL...75 SURE...

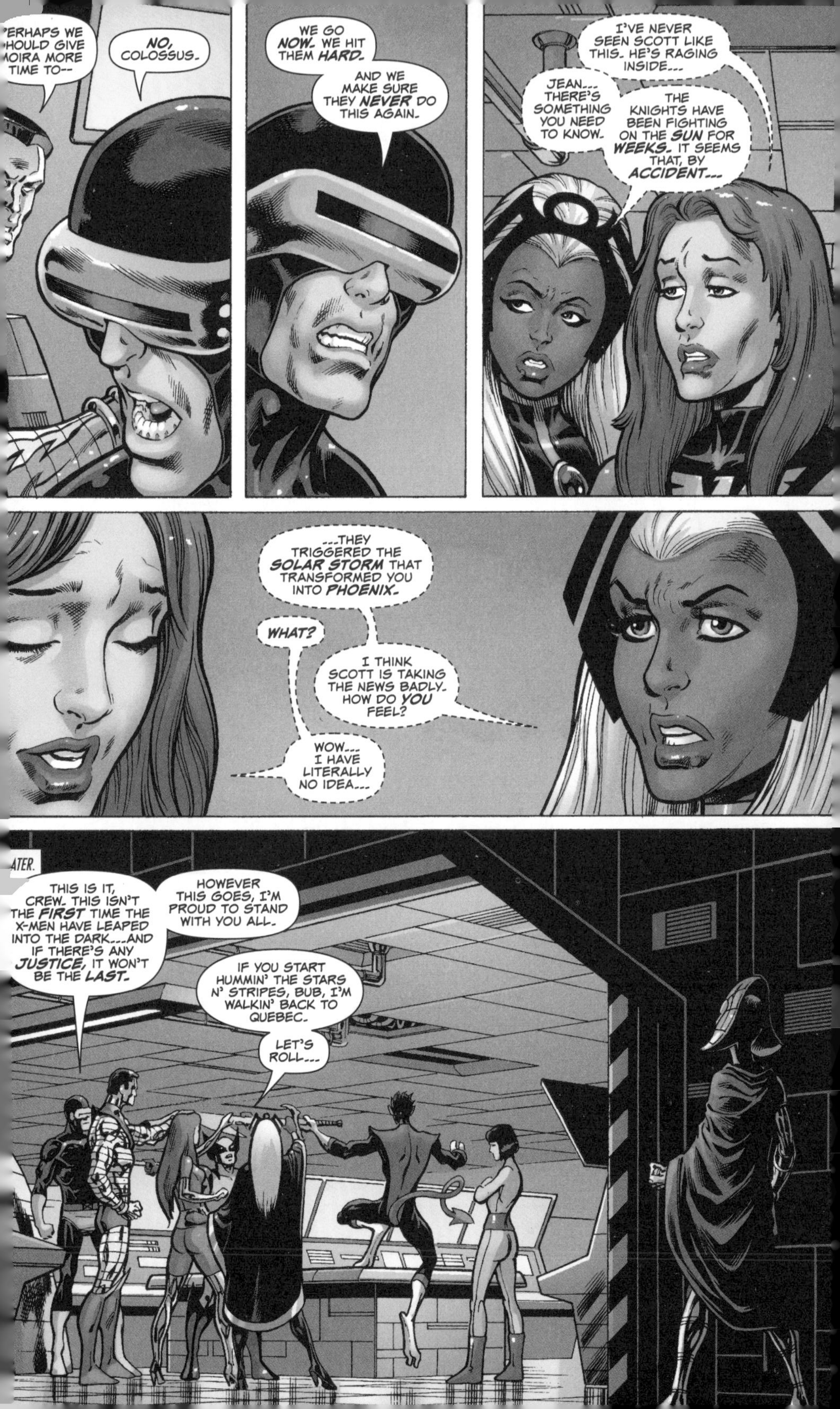
PERHAPS WE SHOULD GIVE MOIRA MORE TIME TO--
NO, COLOSSUS.
WE GO NOW. WE HIT THEM HARD.
AND WE MAKE SURE THEY NEVER DO THIS AGAIN.
I'VE NEVER SEEN SCOTT LIKE THIS. HE'S RAGING INSIDE...
JEAN... THERE'S SOMETHING YOU NEED TO KNOW.
THE KNIGHTS HAVE BEEN FIGHTING ON THE SUN FOR WEEKS. IT SEEMS THAT, BY ACCIDENT...
...THEY TRIGGERED THE SOLAR STORM THAT TRANSFORMED YOU INTO PHOENIX.
WHAT?
I THINK SCOTT IS TAKING THE NEWS BADLY. HOW DO YOU FEEL?
WOW... I HAVE LITERALLY NO IDEA...
ATER.
THIS IS IT, CREW. THIS ISN'T THE FIRST TIME THE X-MEN HAVE LEAPED INTO THE DARK...AND IF THERE'S ANY JUSTICE, IT WON'T BE THE LAST.
HOWEVER THIS GOES, I'M PROUD TO STAND WITH YOU ALL.
IF YOU START HUMMIN' THE STARS N' STRIPES, BUB, I'M WALKIN' BACK TO QUEBEC.
LET'S ROLL...

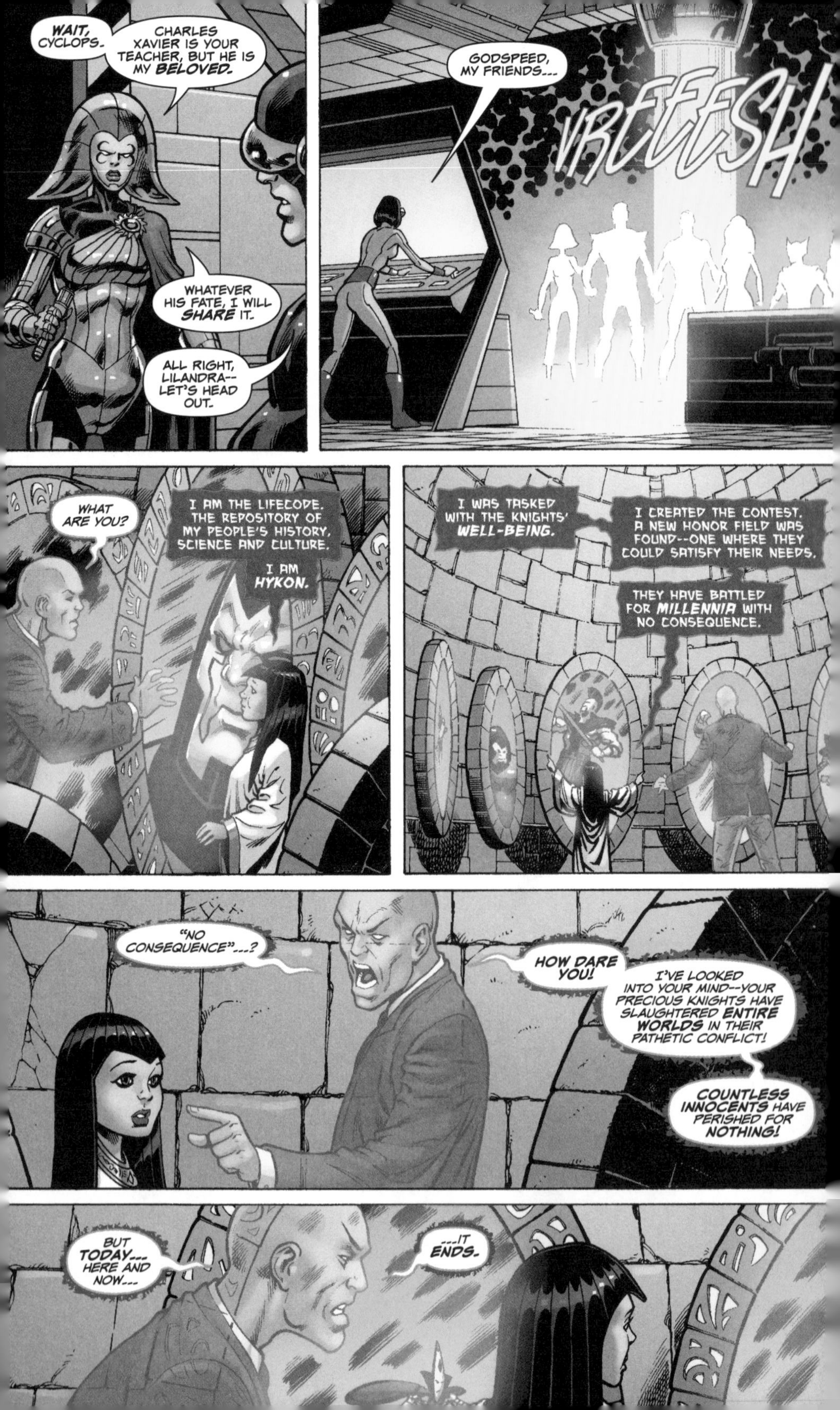
WAIT, CYCLOPS.
CHARLES XAVIER IS YOUR TEACHER, BUT HE IS MY BELOVED.
WHATEVER HIS FATE, I WILL SHARE IT.
ALL RIGHT, LILANDRA-- LET'S HEAD OUT.
GODSPEED, MY FRIENDS...
VREEEESH
WHAT ARE YOU?
I AM THE LIFECODE. THE REPOSITORY OF MY PEOPLE'S HISTORY, SCIENCE AND CULTURE.
I AM HYKON.
I WAS TASKED WITH THE KNIGHTS' WELL-BEING.
I CREATED THE CONTEST. A NEW HONOR FIELD WAS FOUND--ONE WHERE THEY COULD SATISFY THEIR NEEDS.
THEY HAVE BATTLED FOR MILLENNIA WITH NO CONSEQUENCE.
"NO CONSEQUENCE"...?
HOW DARE YOU!
I'VE LOOKED INTO YOUR MIND--YOUR PRECIOUS KNIGHTS HAVE SLAUGHTERED ENTIRE WORLDS IN THEIR PATHETIC CONFLICT!
COUNTLESS INNOCENTS HAVE PERISHED FOR NOTHING!
BUT TODAY... HERE AND NOW...
...IT ENDS.

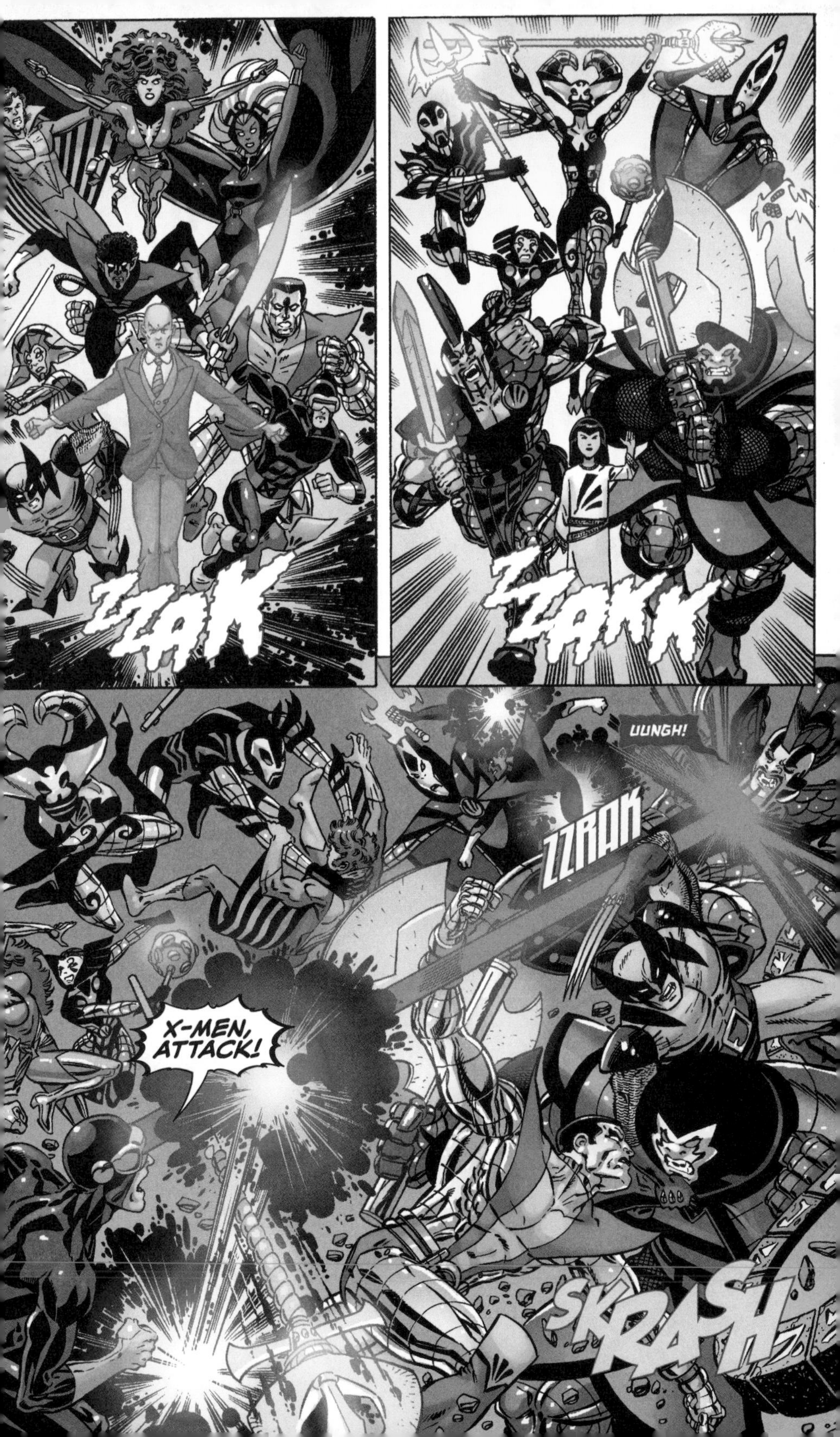
ZZAK
ZZAKK
UUNGH!
ZZRAK
X-MEN, ATTACK!
SKRASH

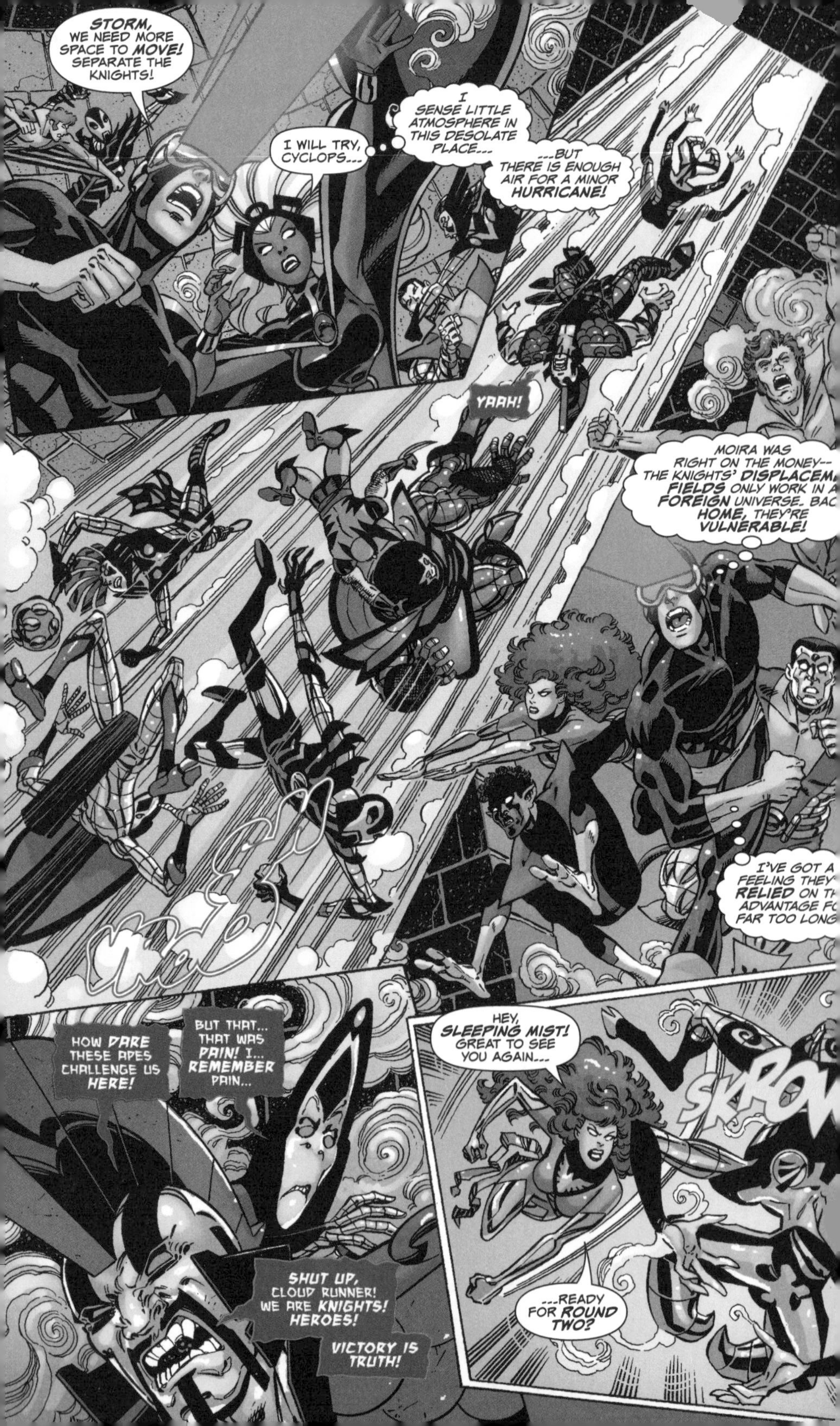
STORM, WE NEED MORE SPACE TO MOVE! SEPARATE THE KNIGHTS!
I WILL TRY, CYCLOPS...
I SENSE LITTLE ATMOSPHERE IN THIS DESOLATE PLACE...
...BUT THERE IS ENOUGH AIR FOR A MINOR HURRICANE!
YAAH!
MOIRA WAS RIGHT ON THE MONEY-- THE KNIGHTS' DISPLACEM FIELDS ONLY WORK IN A FOREIGN UNIVERSE. BAC HOME, THEY'RE VULNERABLE!
I'VE GOT A FEELING THEY RELIED ON TH ADVANTAGE FO FAR TOO LONG
HOW DARE THESE APES CHALLENGE US HERE!
BUT THAT... THAT WAS PAIN! I... REMEMBER PAIN...
SHUT UP, CLOUD RUNNER! WE ARE KNIGHTS! HEROES!
VICTORY IS TRUTH!
HEY, SLEEPING MIST! GREAT TO SEE YOU AGAIN...
...READY FOR ROUND TWO?
SKROW

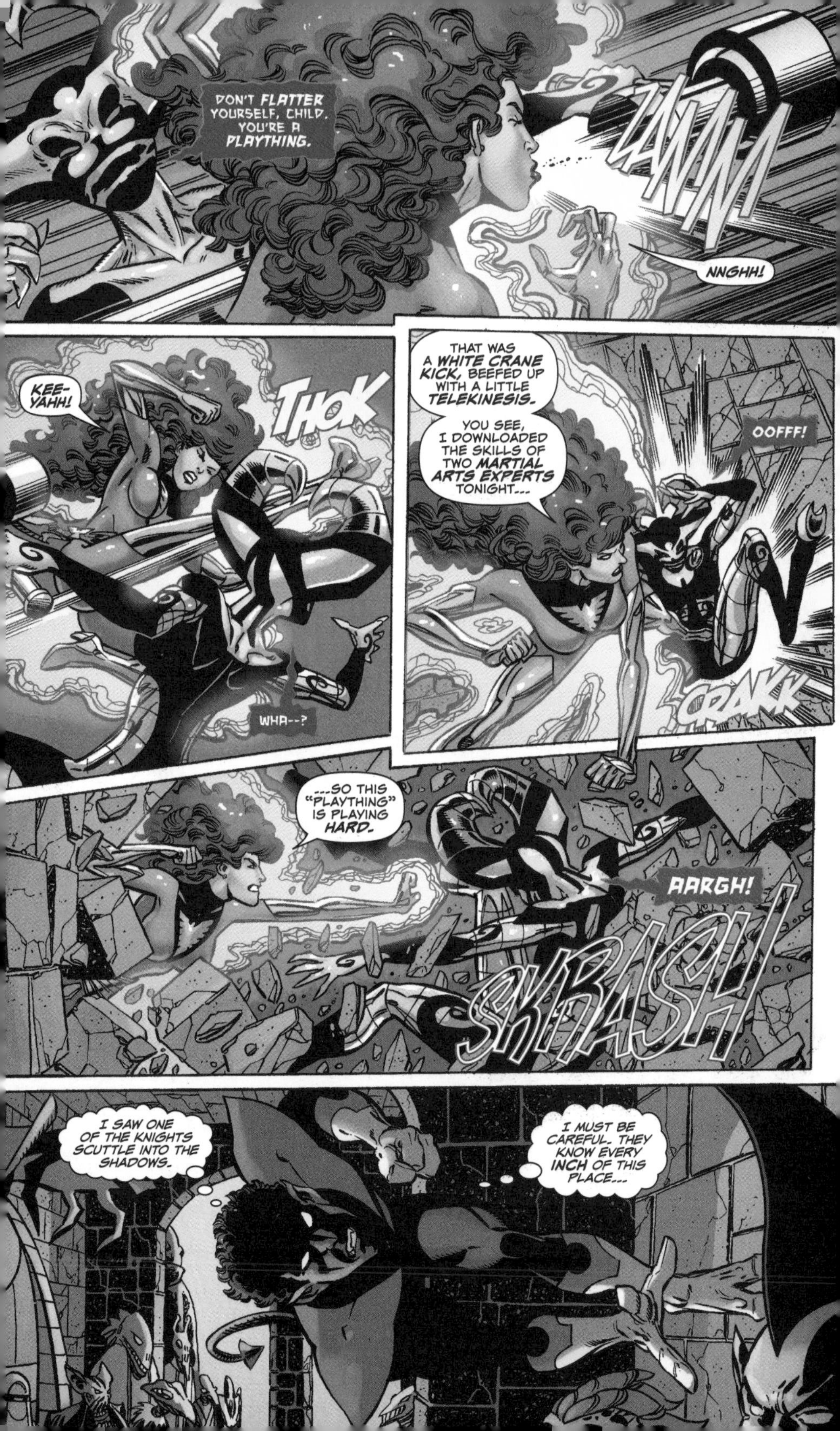
DON'T FLATTER YOURSELF, CHILD. YOU'RE A PLAYTHING.
NNGHH!
KEE-YAHH!
THOK
WHA--?
THAT WAS A WHITE CRANE KICK, BEEFED UP WITH A LITTLE TELEKINESIS.
YOU SEE, I DOWNLOADED THE SKILLS OF TWO MARTIAL ARTS EXPERTS TONIGHT...
OOFFF!
CRAKK
...SO THIS "PLAYTHING" IS PLAYING HARD.
AARGH!
SKRASH
I SAW ONE OF THE KNIGHTS SCUTTLE INTO THE SHADOWS.
I MUST BE CAREFUL. THEY KNOW EVERY INCH OF THIS PLACE...

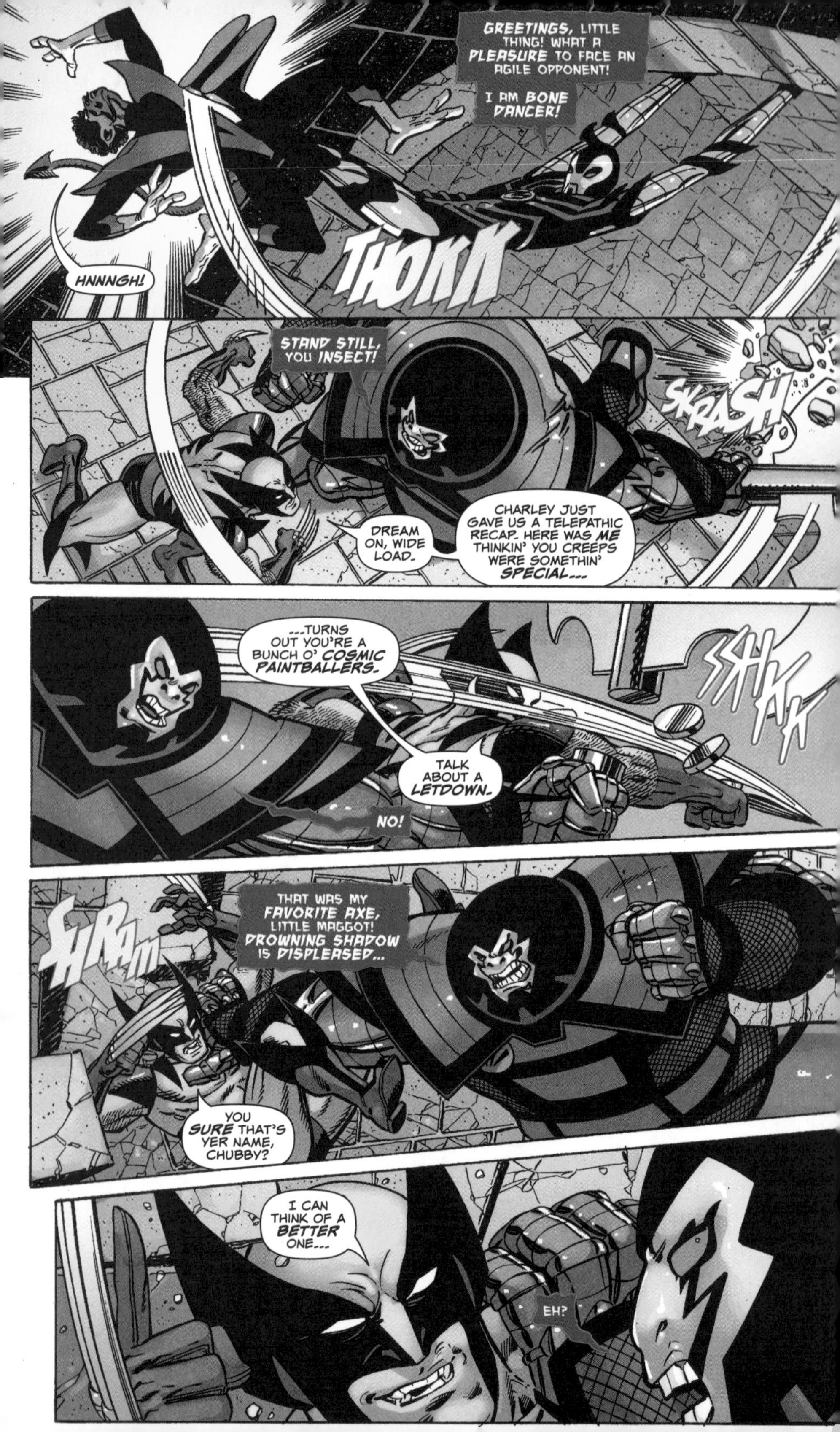
GREETINGS, LITTLE THING! WHAT A PLEASURE TO FACE AN AGILE OPPONENT!
I AM BONE DANCER!
HNNNGH!
THOKK
STAND STILL, YOU INSECT!
SKRASH
DREAM ON, WIDE LOAD.
CHARLEY JUST GAVE US A TELEPATHIC RECAP. HERE WAS ME THINKIN' YOU CREEPS WERE SOMETHIN' SPECIAL...
...TURNS OUT YOU'RE A BUNCH O' COSMIC PAINTBALLERS.
SSHKKK
TALK ABOUT A LETDOWN.
NO!
SHRAM
THAT WAS MY FAVORITE AXE, LITTLE MAGGOT! DROWNING SHADOW IS DISPLEASED...
YOU SURE THAT'S YER NAME, CHUBBY?
I CAN THINK OF A BETTER ONE...
EH?

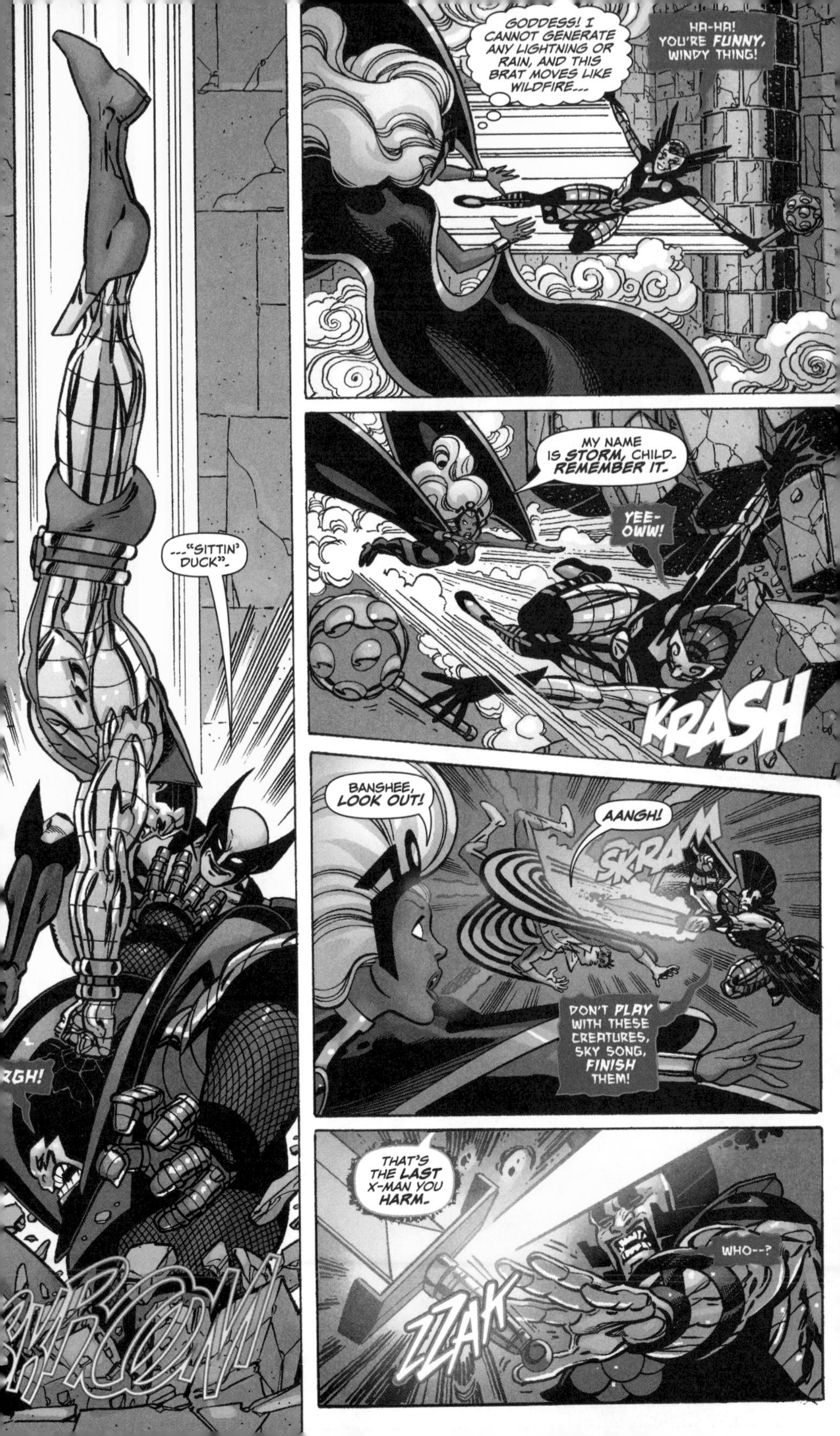

...."SITTIN' DUCK".
RGH!
VROOM
GODDESS! I CANNOT GENERATE ANY LIGHTNING OR RAIN, AND THIS BRAT MOVES LIKE WILDFIRE...
HA-HA! YOU'RE FUNNY, WINDY THING!
MY NAME IS STORM, CHILD. REMEMBER IT.
YEE-OWW!
KRASH
BANSHEE, LOOK OUT!
AANGH!
SKRAM
DON'T PLAY WITH THESE CREATURES, SKY SONG, FINISH THEM!
THAT'S THE LAST X-MAN YOU HARM.
WHO--?
ZZAK

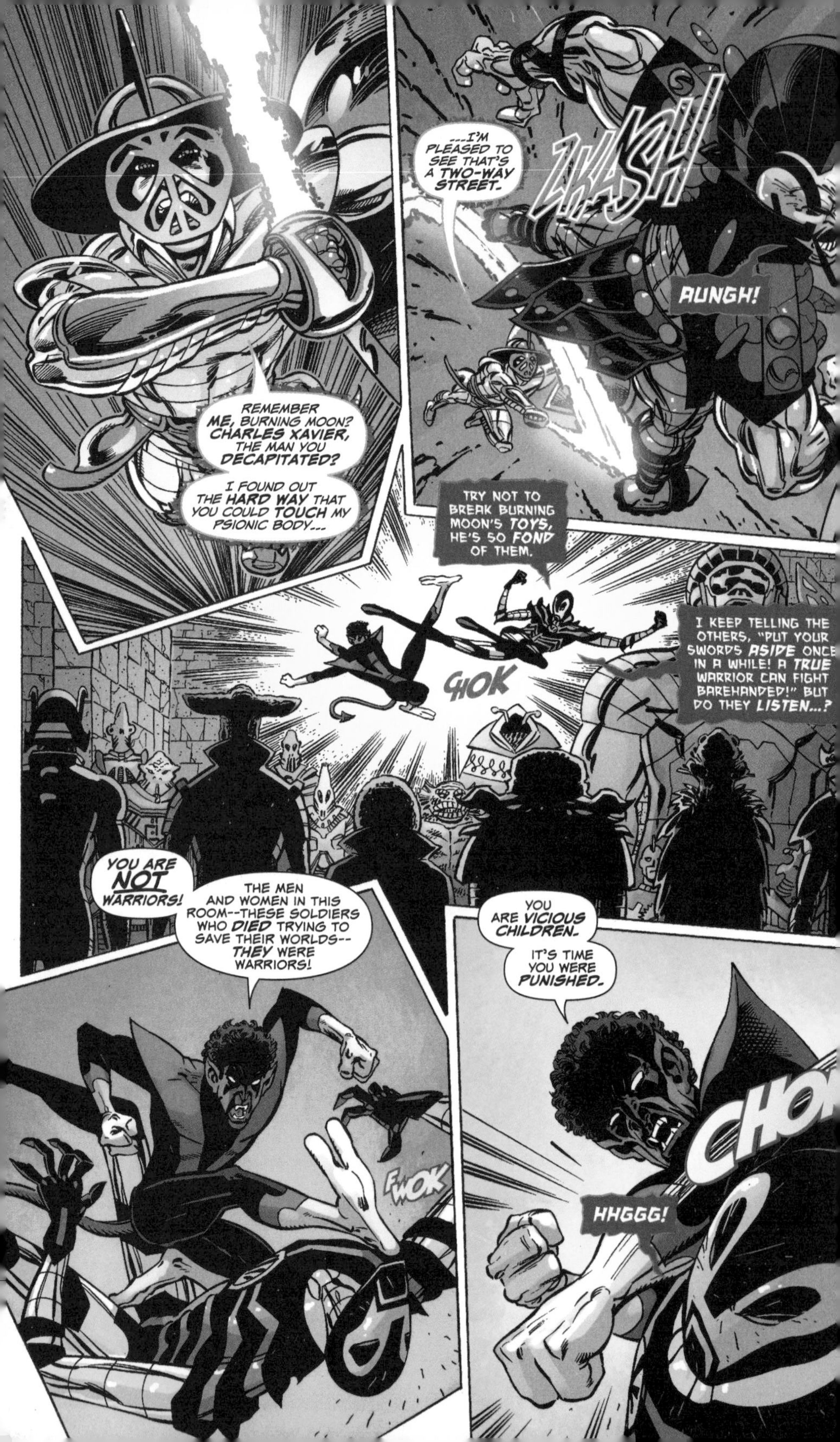
REMEMBER ME, BURNING MOON? CHARLES XAVIER, THE MAN YOU DECAPITATED?
I FOUND OUT THE HARD WAY THAT YOU COULD TOUCH MY PSIONIC BODY---
---I'M PLEASED TO SEE THAT'S A TWO-WAY STREET.
ZKASH
AUNGH!
TRY NOT TO BREAK BURNING MOON'S TOYS, HE'S SO FOND OF THEM.
I KEEP TELLING THE OTHERS, "PUT YOUR SWORDS ASIDE ONCE IN A WHILE! A TRUE WARRIOR CAN FIGHT BAREHANDED!" BUT DO THEY LISTEN...?
GHOK
YOU ARE NOT WARRIORS!
THE MEN AND WOMEN IN THIS ROOM--THESE SOLDIERS WHO DIED TRYING TO SAVE THEIR WORLDS--THEY WERE WARRIORS!
FWOK
YOU ARE VICIOUS CHILDREN.
IT'S TIME YOU WERE PUNISHED.
HHGGG!

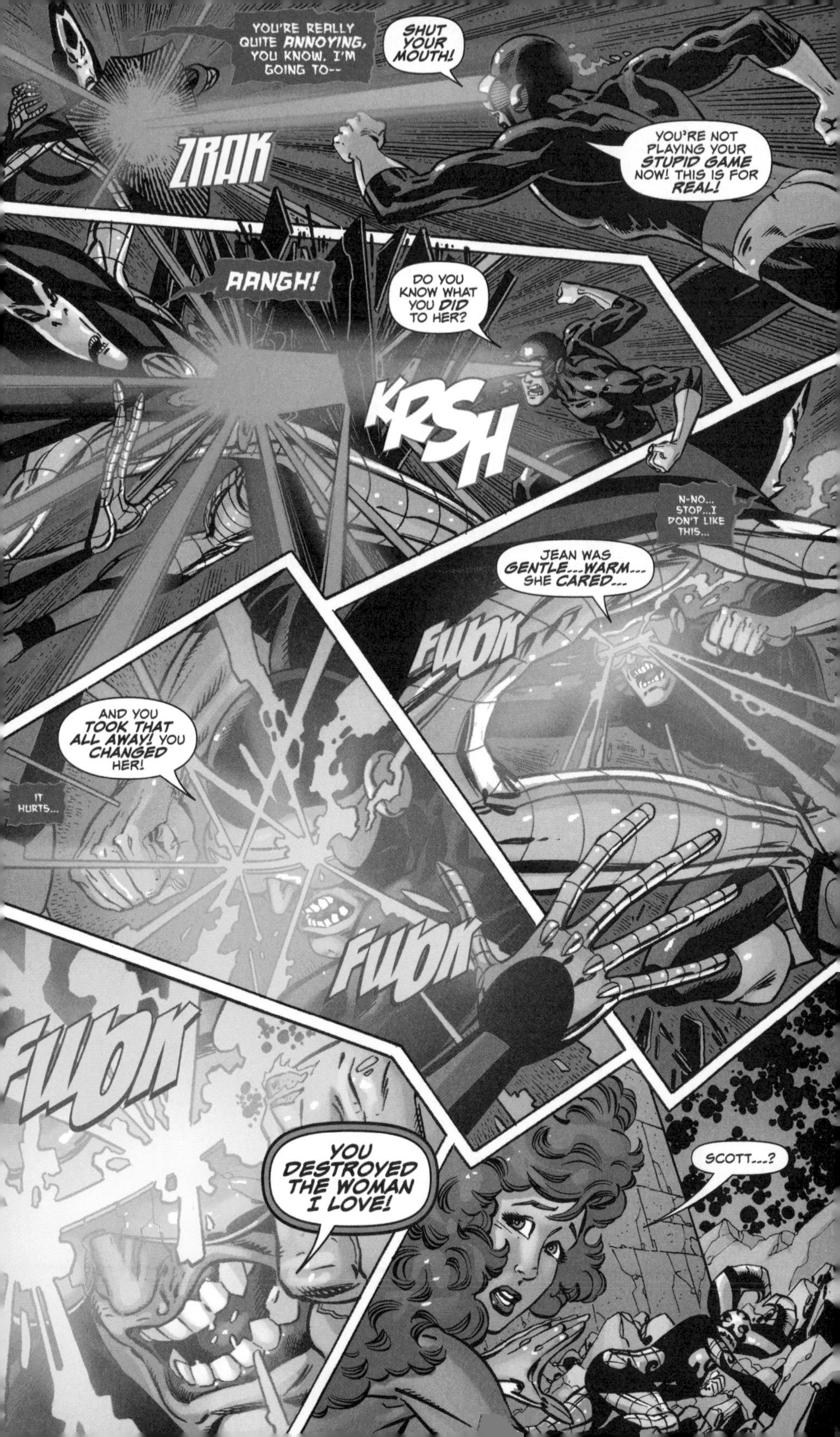
YOU'RE REALLY QUITE ANNOYING, YOU KNOW. I'M GOING TO--
SHUT YOUR MOUTH!
ZRAK
YOU'RE NOT PLAYING YOUR STUPID GAME NOW! THIS IS FOR REAL!
AANGH!
DO YOU KNOW WHAT YOU DID TO HER?
KRSH
N-NO... STOP...I DON'T LIKE THIS...
JEAN WAS GENTLE...WARM... SHE CARED...
FWOM
AND YOU TOOK THAT ALL AWAY! YOU CHANGED HER!
IT HURTS...
FWOM
FWOM
YOU DESTROYED THE WOMAN I LOVE!
SCOTT...?

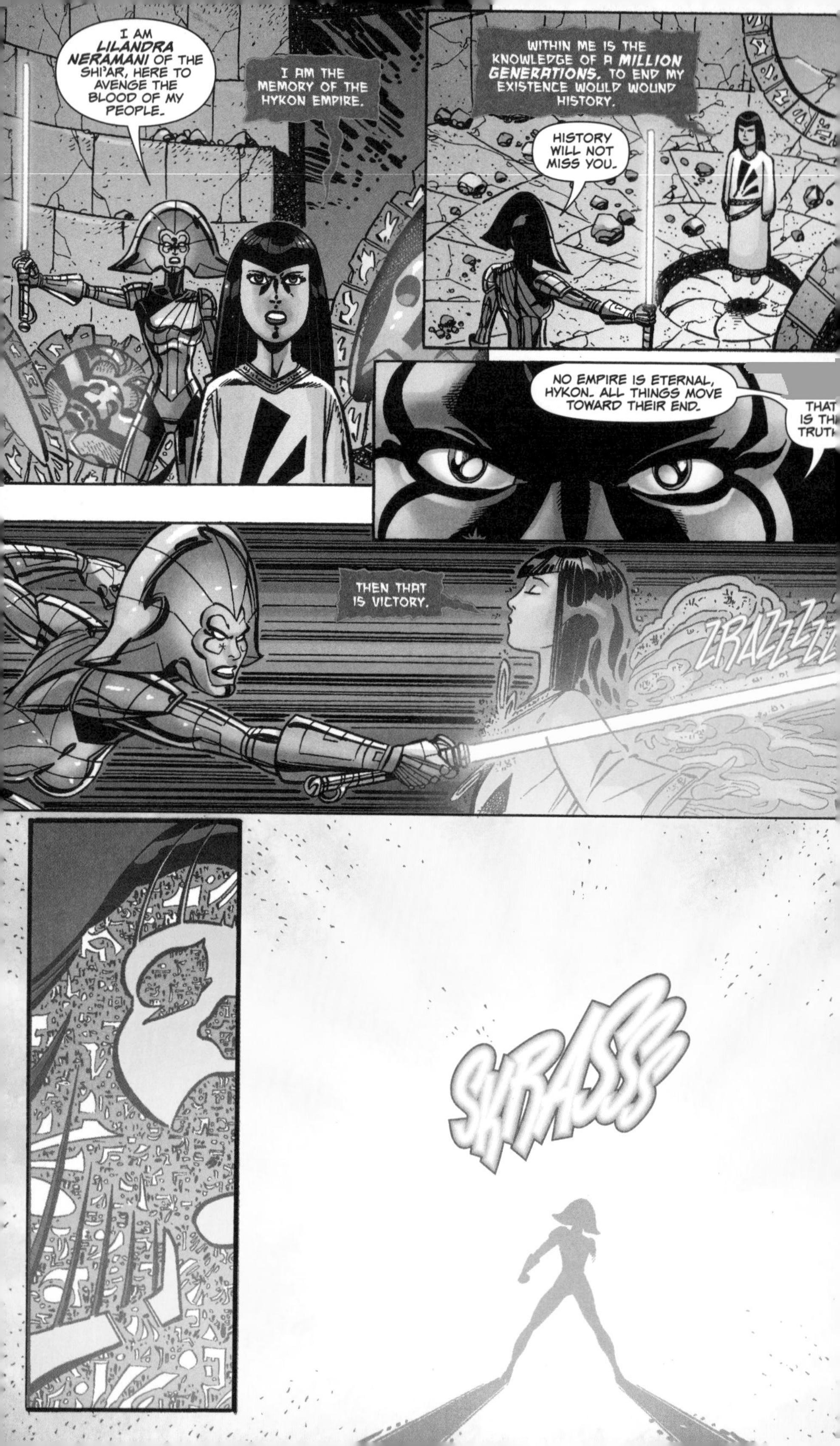
I AM LILANDRA NERAMANI OF THE SHI'AR, HERE TO AVENGE THE BLOOD OF MY PEOPLE.
I AM THE MEMORY OF THE HYKON EMPIRE.
WITHIN ME IS THE KNOWLEDGE OF A MILLION GENERATIONS. TO END MY EXISTENCE WOULD WOUND HISTORY.
HISTORY WILL NOT MISS YOU.
NO EMPIRE IS ETERNAL, HYKON. ALL THINGS MOVE TOWARD THEIR END.
THEN THAT IS VICTORY.
ZRAZZZZ
SKRASSS

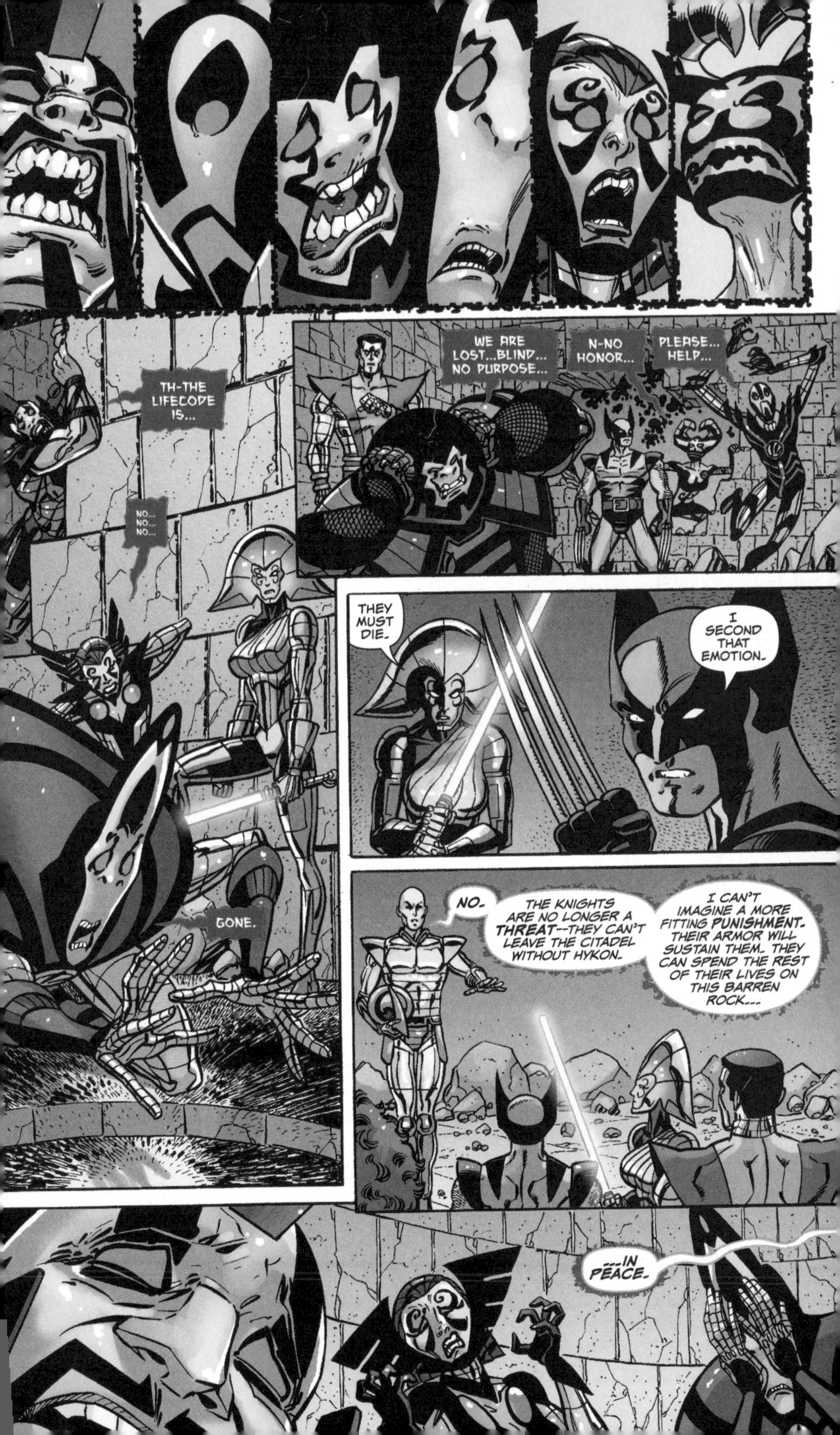
TH-THE LIFECODE IS...
NO... NO... NO...
GONE.
WE ARE LOST...BLIND... NO PURPOSE...
N-NO HONOR...
PLEASE... HELP...
THEY MUST DIE.
I SECOND THAT EMOTION.
NO.
THE KNIGHTS ARE NO LONGER A THREAT--THEY CAN'T LEAVE THE CITADEL WITHOUT HYKON.
I CAN'T IMAGINE A MORE FITTING PUNISHMENT. THEIR ARMOR WILL SUSTAIN THEM. THEY CAN SPEND THE REST OF THEIR LIVES ON THIS BARREN ROCK...
...IN PEACE.

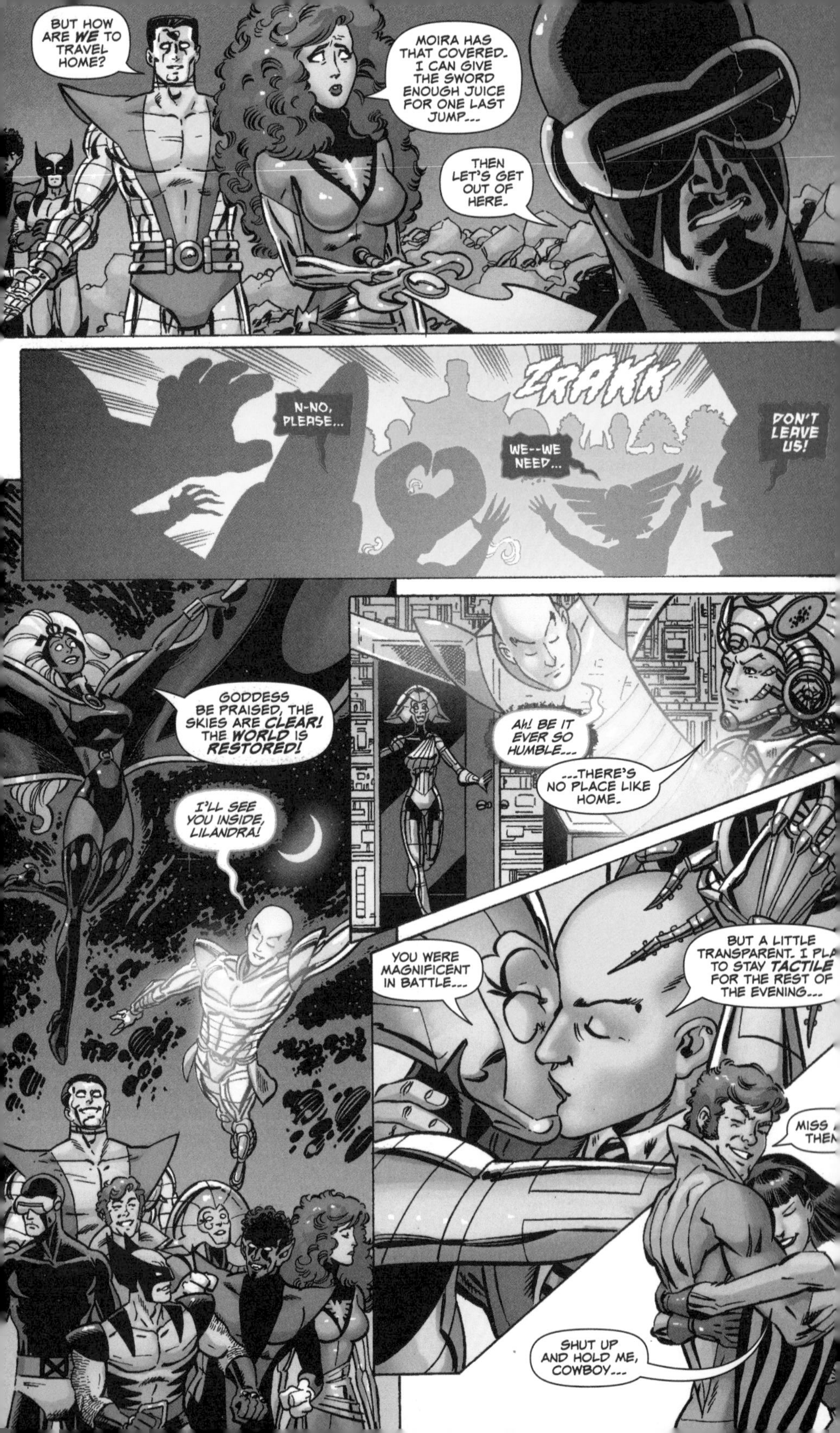
BUT HOW ARE WE TO TRAVEL HOME?
MOIRA HAS THAT COVERED. I CAN GIVE THE SWORD ENOUGH JUICE FOR ONE LAST JUMP...
THEN LET'S GET OUT OF HERE.
ZRAKK
N-NO, PLEASE...
WE--WE NEED...
DON'T LEAVE US!
GODDESS BE PRAISED, THE SKIES ARE CLEAR! THE WORLD IS RESTORED!
I'LL SEE YOU INSIDE, LILANDRA!
AH! BE IT EVER SO HUMBLE...
...THERE'S NO PLACE LIKE HOME.
YOU WERE MAGNIFICENT IN BATTLE...
BUT A LITTLE TRANSPARENT. I PLA TO STAY TACTILE FOR THE REST OF THE EVENING...
MISS THEM
SHUT UP AND HOLD ME, COWBOY...

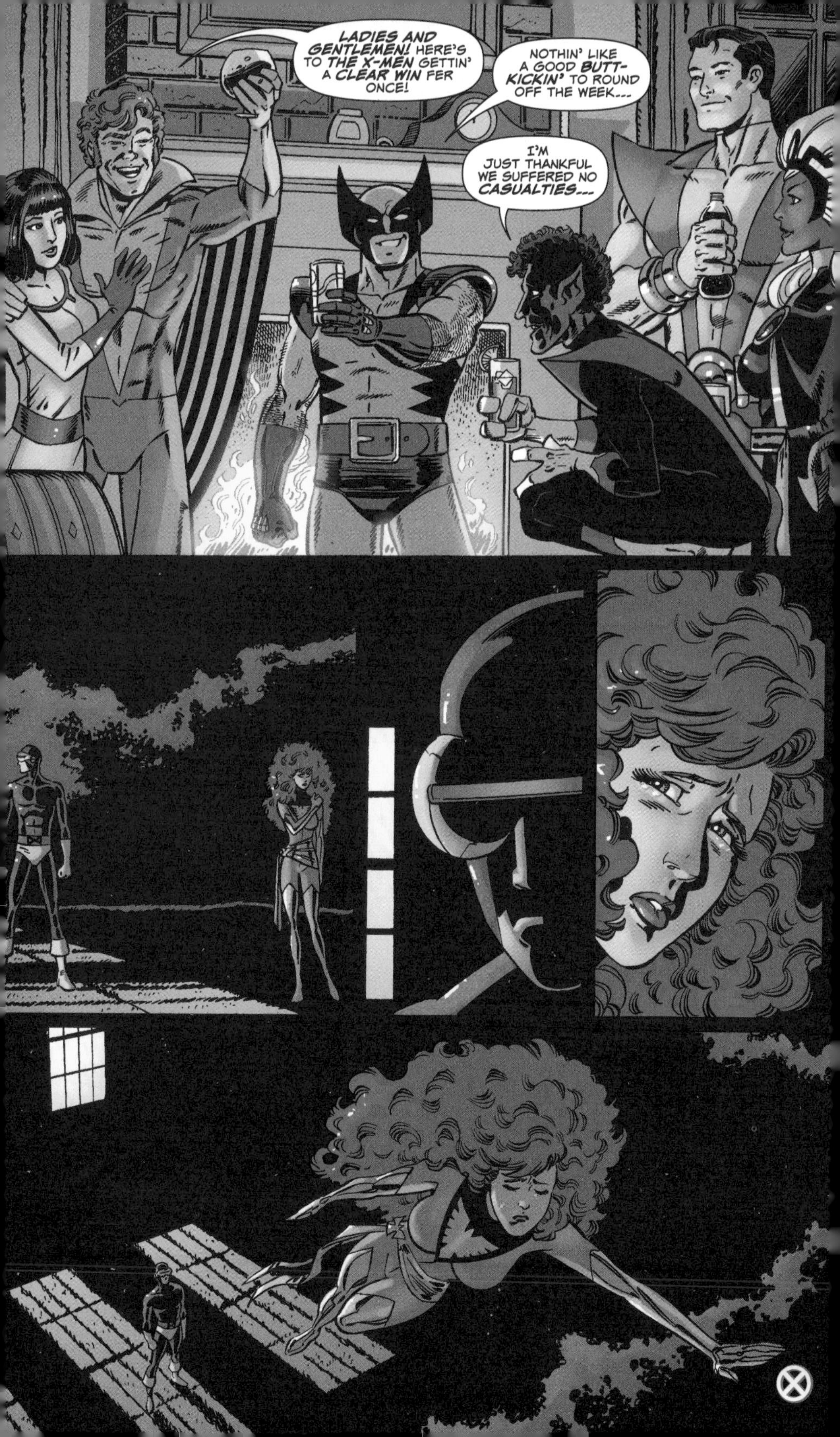
LADIES AND GENTLEMEN! HERE'S TO THE X-MEN GETTIN' A CLEAR WIN FER ONCE!
NOTHIN' LIKE A GOOD BUTT-KICKIN' TO ROUND OFF THE WEEK...
I'M JUST THANKFUL WE SUFFERED NO CASUALTIES...

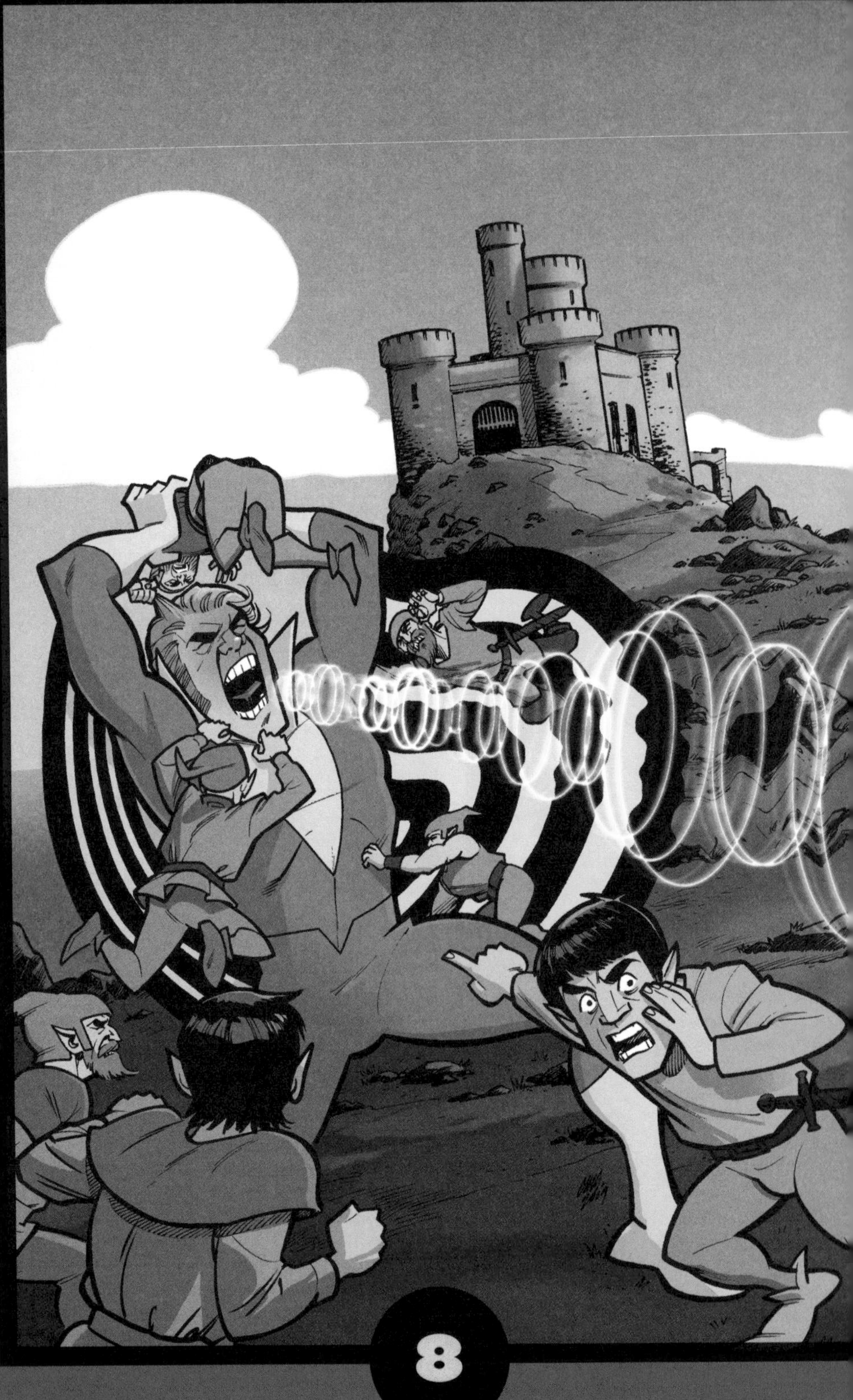

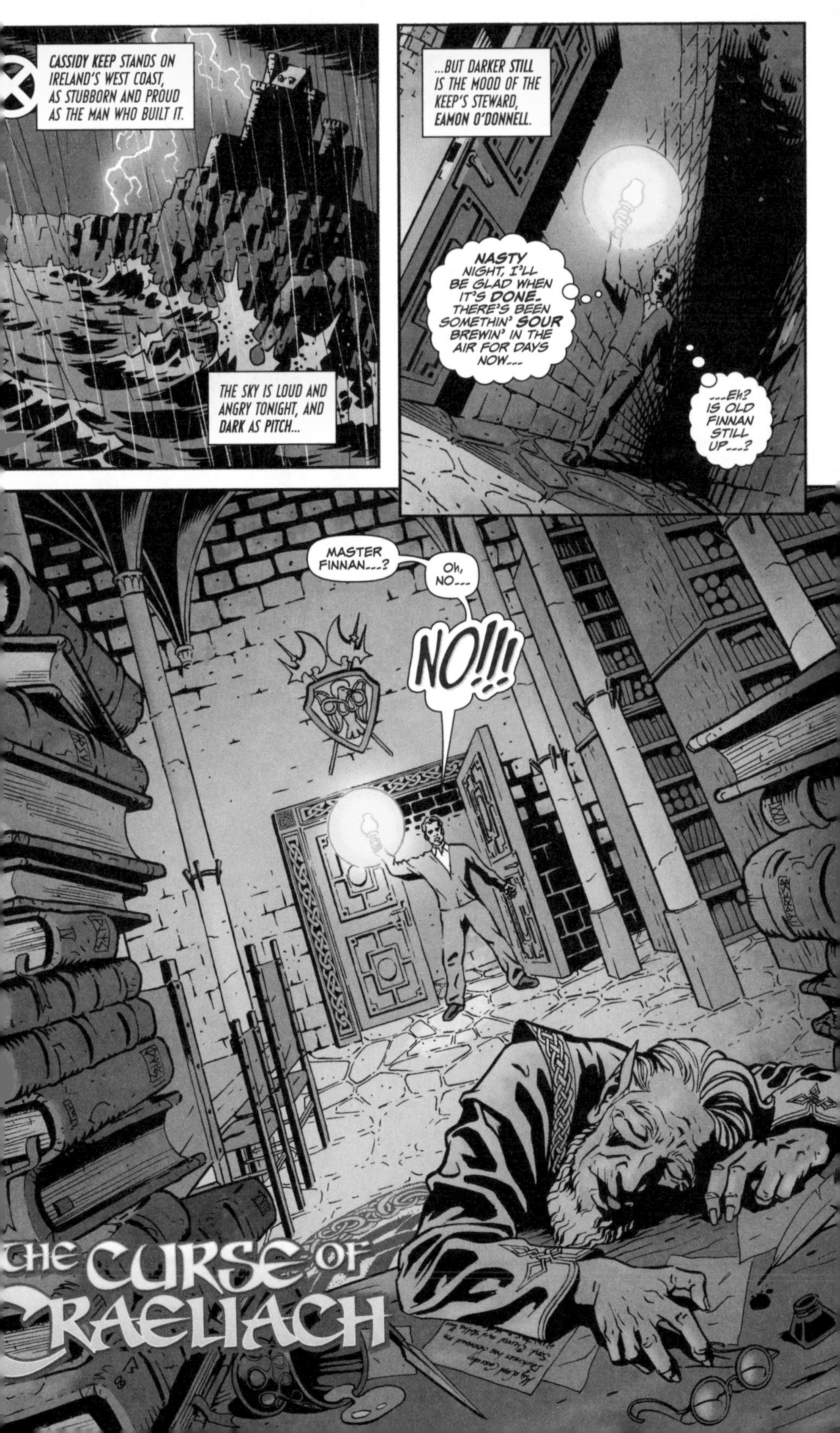
CASSIDY KEEP STANDS ON IRELAND'S WEST COAST, AS STUBBORN AND PROUD AS THE MAN WHO BUILT IT.
THE SKY IS LOUD AND ANGRY TONIGHT, AND DARK AS PITCH...
...BUT DARKER STILL IS THE MOOD OF THE KEEP'S STEWARD, EAMON O'DONNELL.
NASTY NIGHT, I'LL BE GLAD WHEN IT'S DONE. THERE'S BEEN SOMETHIN' SOUR BREWIN' IN THE AIR FOR DAYS NOW...
...EH? IS OLD FINNAN STILL UP...?
MASTER FINNAN...?
Oh, NO...
NO!!!
THE CURSE OF CRAELIACH

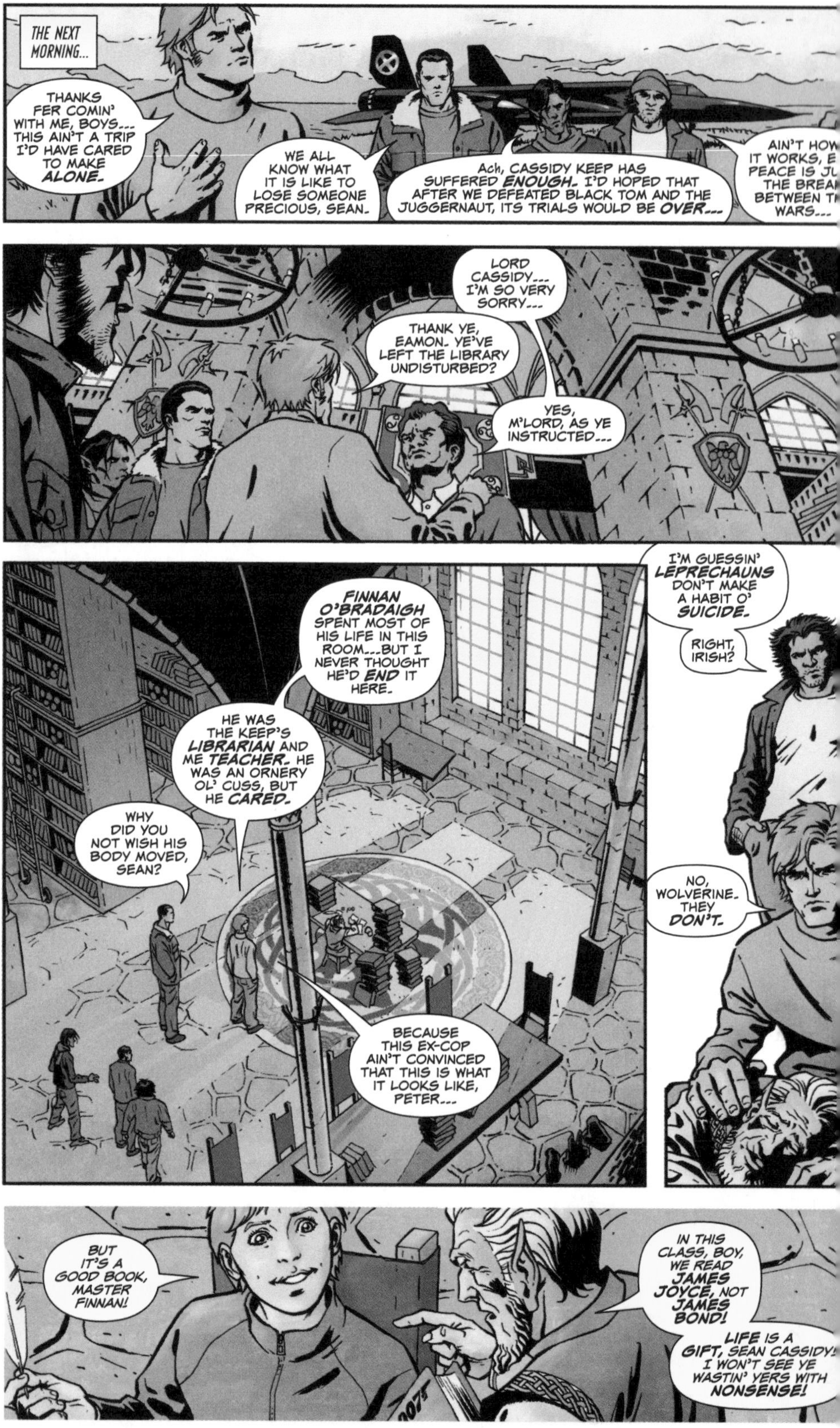
THE NEXT MORNING...
THANKS FER COMIN' WITH ME, BOYS... THIS AIN'T A TRIP I'D HAVE CARED TO MAKE ALONE.
WE ALL KNOW WHAT IT IS LIKE TO LOSE SOMEONE PRECIOUS, SEAN.
Ach, CASSIDY KEEP HAS SUFFERED ENOUGH. I'D HOPED THAT AFTER WE DEFEATED BLACK TOM AND THE JUGGERNAUT, ITS TRIALS WOULD BE OVER...
AIN'T HOW IT WORKS, E PEACE IS JU THE BREA BETWEEN T WARS...
LORD CASSIDY... I'M SO VERY SORRY...
THANK YE, EAMON. YE'VE LEFT THE LIBRARY UNDISTURBED?
YES, M'LORD, AS YE INSTRUCTED...
FINNAN O'BRADAIGH SPENT MOST OF HIS LIFE IN THIS ROOM...BUT I NEVER THOUGHT HE'D END IT HERE.
HE WAS THE KEEP'S LIBRARIAN AND ME TEACHER. HE WAS AN ORNERY OL' CUSS, BUT HE CARED.
WHY DID YOU NOT WISH HIS BODY MOVED, SEAN?
BECAUSE THIS EX-COP AIN'T CONVINCED THAT THIS IS WHAT IT LOOKS LIKE, PETER...
I'M GUESSIN' LEPRECHAUNS DON'T MAKE A HABIT O' SUICIDE.
RIGHT, IRISH?
NO, WOLVERINE. THEY DON'T.
BUT IT'S A GOOD BOOK, MASTER FINNAN!
IN THIS CLASS, BOY, WE READ JAMES JOYCE, NOT JAMES BOND!
LIFE IS A GIFT, SEAN CASSIDY! I WON'T SEE YE WASTIN' YERS WITH NONSENSE!
007

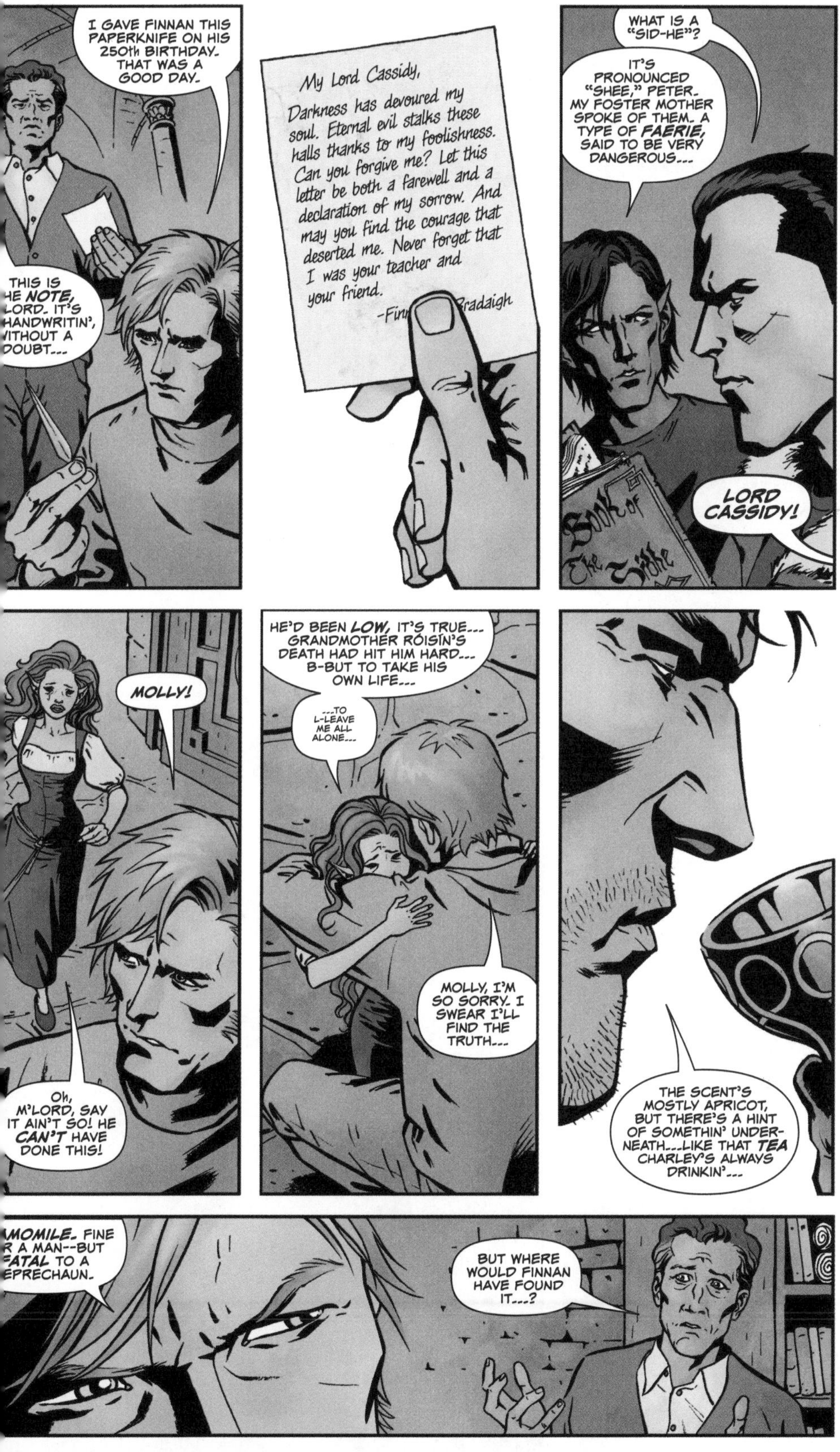
I GAVE FINNAN THIS PAPERKNIFE ON HIS 250th BIRTHDAY. THAT WAS A GOOD DAY.
THIS IS HE NOTE, LORD. IT'S HANDWRITIN', WITHOUT A DOUBT...
My Lord Cassidy,
Darkness has devoured my soul. Eternal evil stalks these halls thanks to my foolishness. Can you forgive me? Let this letter be both a farewell and a declaration of my sorrow. And may you find the courage that deserted me. Never forget that I was your teacher and your friend.
-Fin Bradaigh
WHAT IS A "SID-HE"?
IT'S PRONOUNCED "SHEE," PETER. MY FOSTER MOTHER SPOKE OF THEM. A TYPE OF FAERIE, SAID TO BE VERY DANGEROUS...
LORD CASSIDY!
MOLLY!
Oh, M'LORD, SAY IT AIN'T SO! HE CAN'T HAVE DONE THIS!
HE'D BEEN LOW, IT'S TRUE... GRANDMOTHER RÓISÍN'S DEATH HAD HIT HIM HARD... B-BUT TO TAKE HIS OWN LIFE...
...TO L-LEAVE ME ALL ALONE...
MOLLY, I'M SO SORRY. I SWEAR I'LL FIND THE TRUTH...
THE SCENT'S MOSTLY APRICOT, BUT THERE'S A HINT OF SOMETHIN' UNDER-NEATH...LIKE THAT TEA CHARLEY'S ALWAYS DRINKIN'...
AMOMILE. FINE R A MAN--BUT FATAL TO A EPRECHAUN.
BUT WHERE WOULD FINNAN HAVE FOUND IT...?

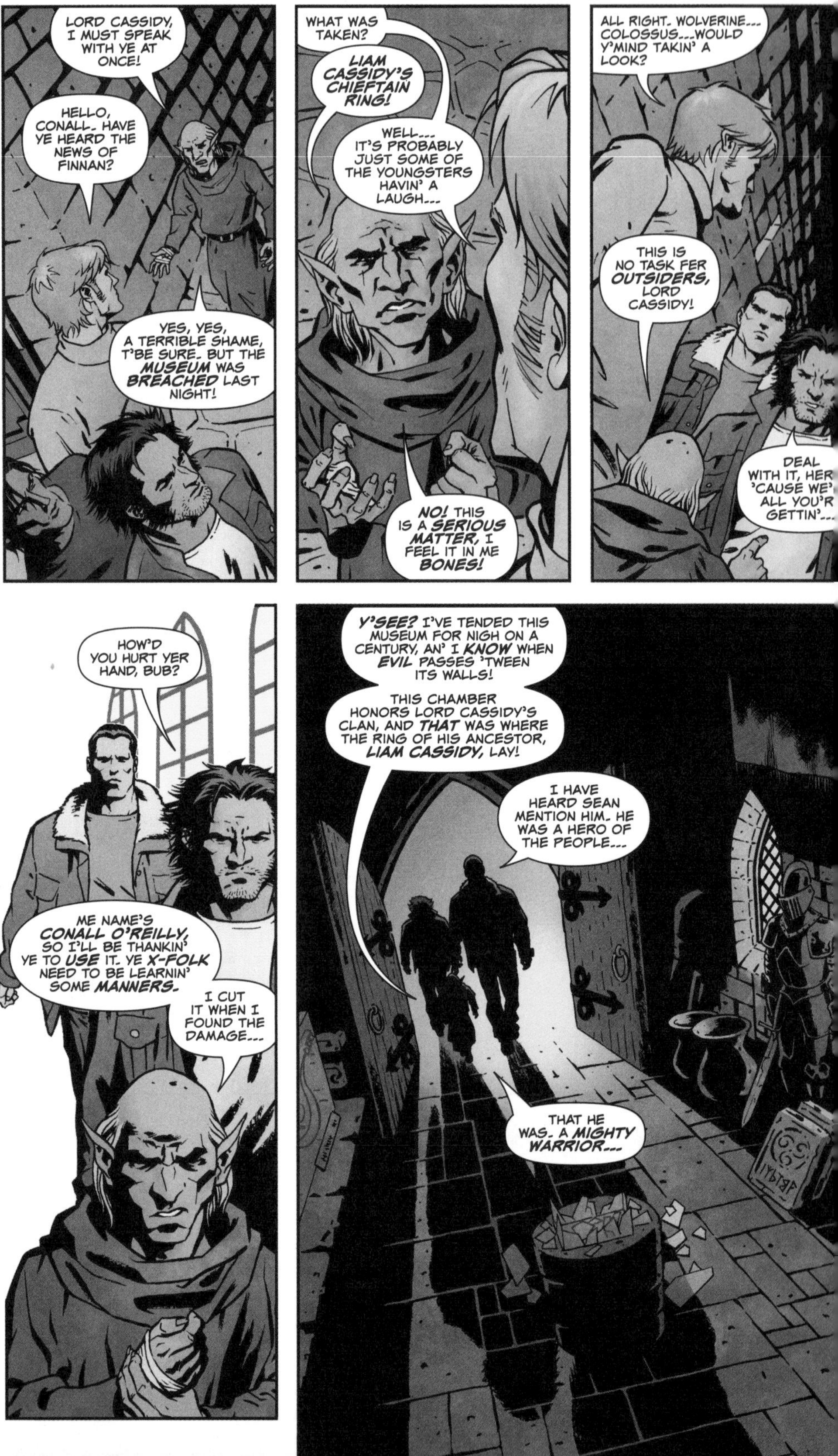
LORD CASSIDY, I MUST SPEAK WITH YE AT ONCE!
HELLO, CONALL. HAVE YE HEARD THE NEWS OF FINNAN?
YES, YES, A TERRIBLE SHAME, T'BE SURE. BUT THE MUSEUM WAS BREACHED LAST NIGHT!
WHAT WAS TAKEN?
LIAM CASSIDY'S CHIEFTAIN RING!
WELL... IT'S PROBABLY JUST SOME OF THE YOUNGSTERS HAVIN' A LAUGH...
NO! THIS IS A SERIOUS MATTER, I FEEL IT IN ME BONES!
ALL RIGHT. WOLVERINE... COLOSSUS...WOULD Y'MIND TAKIN' A LOOK?
THIS IS NO TASK FER OUTSIDERS, LORD CASSIDY!
DEAL WITH IT, HER 'CAUSE WE' ALL YOU'R GETTIN'...
HOW'D YOU HURT YER HAND, BUB?
ME NAME'S CONALL O'REILLY, SO I'LL BE THANKIN' YE TO USE IT. YE X-FOLK NEED TO BE LEARNIN' SOME MANNERS.
I CUT IT WHEN I FOUND THE DAMAGE...
Y'SEE? I'VE TENDED THIS MUSEUM FOR NIGH ON A CENTURY, AN' I KNOW WHEN EVIL PASSES 'TWEEN ITS WALLS!
THIS CHAMBER HONORS LORD CASSIDY'S CLAN, AND THAT WAS WHERE THE RING OF HIS ANCESTOR, LIAM CASSIDY, LAY!
I HAVE HEARD SEAN MENTION HIM. HE WAS A HERO OF THE PEOPLE...
THAT HE WAS. A MIGHTY WARRIOR...

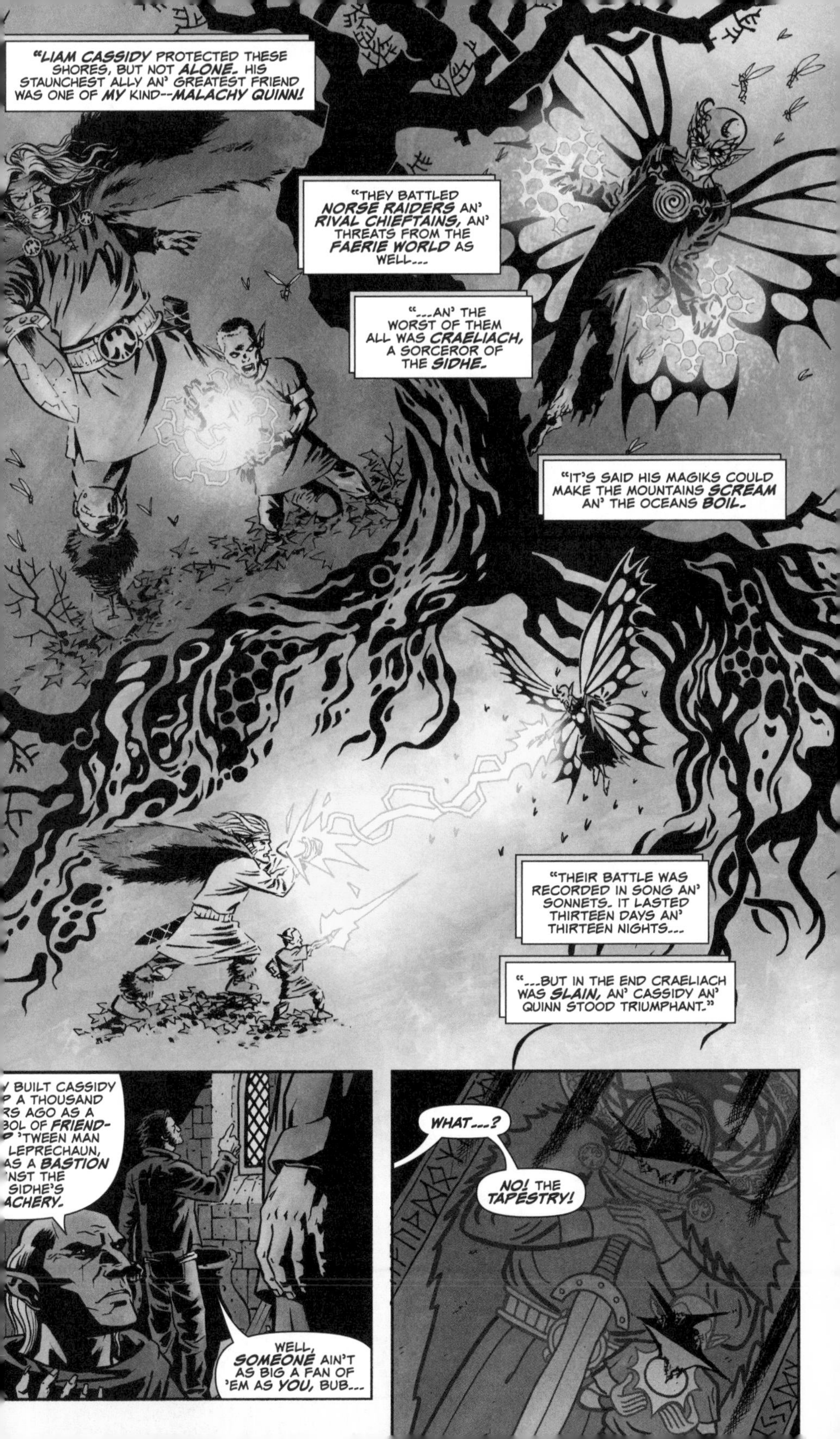

"LIAM CASSIDY PROTECTED THESE SHORES, BUT NOT ALONE. HIS STAUNCHEST ALLY AN' GREATEST FRIEND WAS ONE OF MY KIND--MALACHY QUINN!
"THEY BATTLED NORSE RAIDERS AN' RIVAL CHIEFTAINS, AN' THREATS FROM THE FAERIE WORLD AS WELL...
"...AN' THE WORST OF THEM ALL WAS CRAELIACH, A SORCEROR OF THE SIDHE.
"IT'S SAID HIS MAGIKS COULD MAKE THE MOUNTAINS SCREAM AN' THE OCEANS BOIL.
"THEIR BATTLE WAS RECORDED IN SONG AN' SONNETS. IT LASTED THIRTEEN DAYS AN' THIRTEEN NIGHTS...
"...BUT IN THE END CRAELIACH WAS SLAIN, AN' CASSIDY AN' QUINN STOOD TRIUMPHANT."
Y BUILT CASSIDY P A THOUSAND RS AGO AS A BOL OF FRIEND- P 'TWEEN MAN LEPRECHAUN, AS A BASTION NST THE SIDHE'S ACHERY.
WELL, SOMEONE AIN'T AS BIG A FAN OF 'EM AS YOU, BUB...
WHAT...?
NO! THE TAPESTRY!

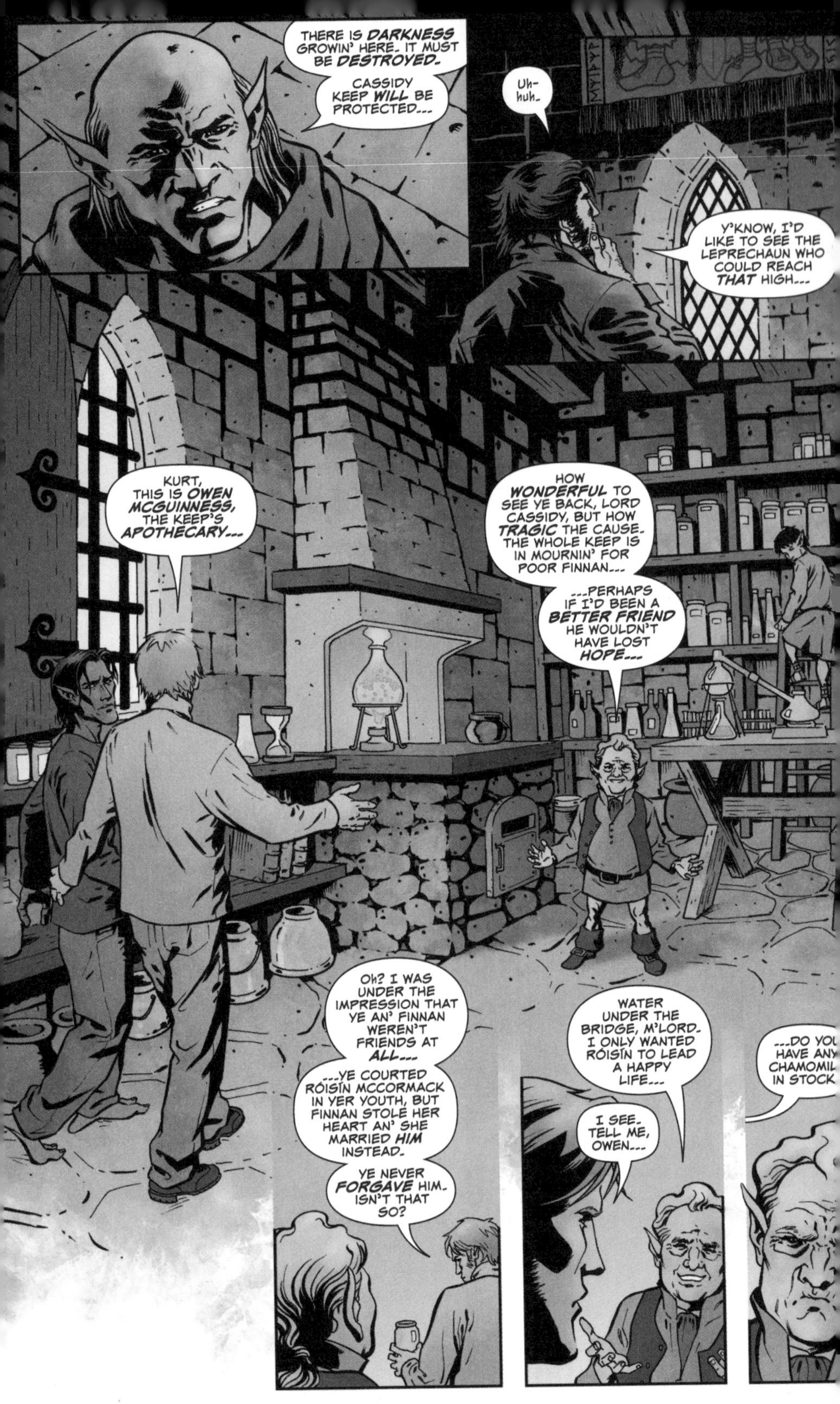
THERE IS DARKNESS GROWIN' HERE. IT MUST BE DESTROYED.
CASSIDY KEEP WILL BE PROTECTED...
Uh-huh.
Y'KNOW, I'D LIKE TO SEE THE LEPRECHAUN WHO COULD REACH THAT HIGH...
KURT, THIS IS OWEN MCGUINNESS, THE KEEP'S APOTHECARY...
HOW WONDERFUL TO SEE YE BACK, LORD CASSIDY, BUT HOW TRAGIC THE CAUSE. THE WHOLE KEEP IS IN MOURNIN' FOR POOR FINNAN...
...PERHAPS IF I'D BEEN A BETTER FRIEND HE WOULDN'T HAVE LOST HOPE...
Oh? I WAS UNDER THE IMPRESSION THAT YE AN' FINNAN WEREN'T FRIENDS AT ALL...
...YE COURTED RÓISÍN MCCORMACK IN YER YOUTH, BUT FINNAN STOLE HER HEART AN' SHE MARRIED HIM INSTEAD.
YE NEVER FORGAVE HIM. ISN'T THAT SO?
WATER UNDER THE BRIDGE, M'LORD. I ONLY WANTED RÓISÍN TO LEAD A HAPPY LIFE...
I SEE. TELL ME, OWEN...
...DO YOU HAVE ANY CHAMOMIL IN STOCK

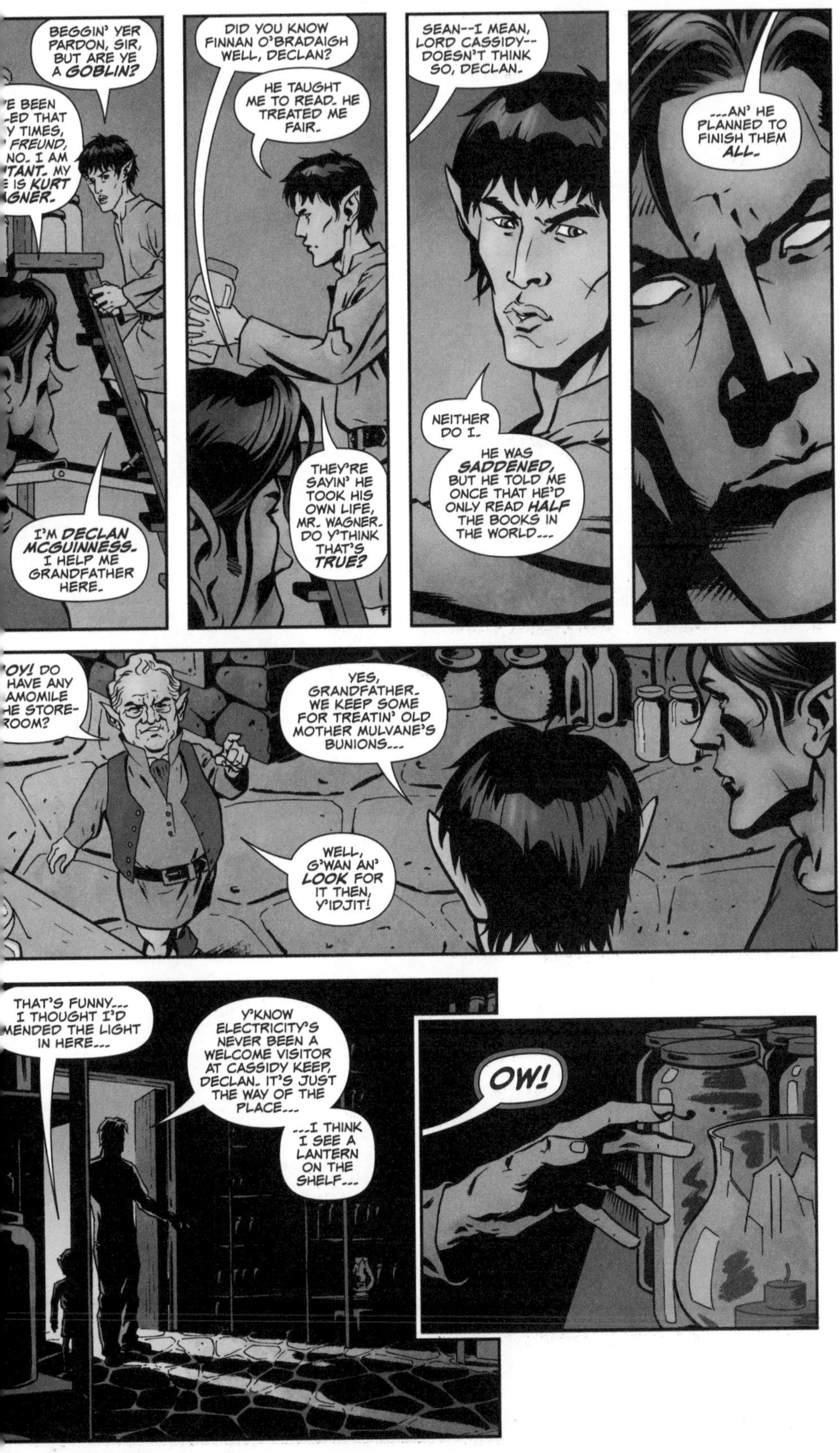
BEGGIN' YER PARDON, SIR, BUT ARE YE A GOBLIN?
'VE BEEN ...ED THAT ...Y TIMES, ... FREUND, NO. I AM ...TANT. MY ...E IS KURT ...GNER.
I'M DECLAN MCGUINNESS. I HELP ME GRANDFATHER HERE.
DID YOU KNOW FINNAN O'BRADAIGH WELL, DECLAN?
HE TAUGHT ME TO READ. HE TREATED ME FAIR.
THEY'RE SAYIN' HE TOOK HIS OWN LIFE, MR. WAGNER. DO Y'THINK THAT'S TRUE?
SEAN--I MEAN, LORD CASSIDY--DOESN'T THINK SO, DECLAN.
NEITHER DO I.
HE WAS SADDENED, BUT HE TOLD ME ONCE THAT HE'D ONLY READ HALF THE BOOKS IN THE WORLD...
...AN' HE PLANNED TO FINISH THEM ALL.
...OY! DO ... HAVE ANY ...AMOMILE ...HE STORE-ROOM?
YES, GRANDFATHER. WE KEEP SOME FOR TREATIN' OLD MOTHER MULVANE'S BUNIONS...
WELL, G'WAN AN' LOOK FOR IT THEN, Y'IDJIT!
THAT'S FUNNY... I THOUGHT I'D MENDED THE LIGHT IN HERE...
Y'KNOW ELECTRICITY'S NEVER BEEN A WELCOME VISITOR AT CASSIDY KEEP, DECLAN. IT'S JUST THE WAY OF THE PLACE...
...I THINK I SEE A LANTERN ON THE SHELF...
OW!

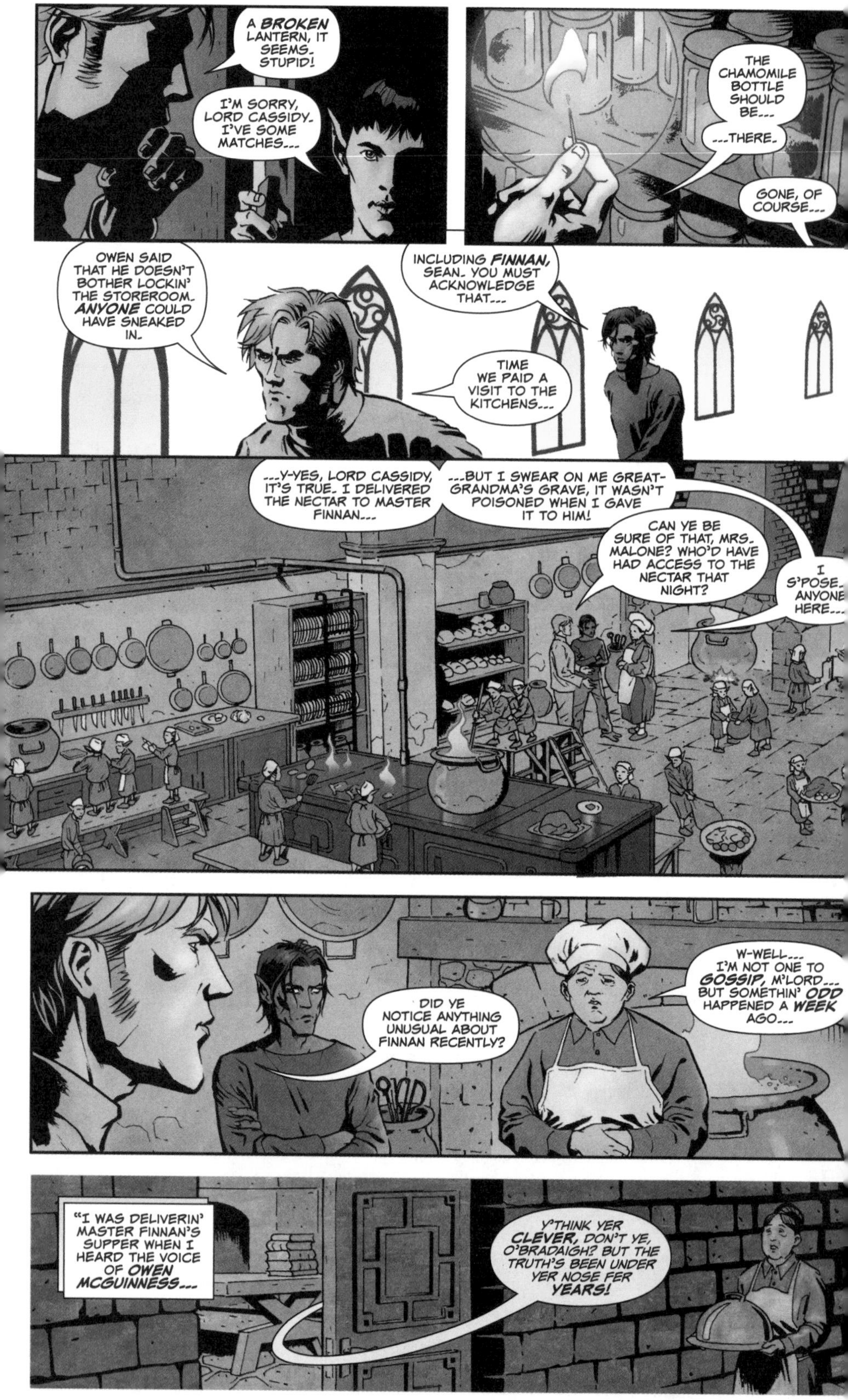
A BROKEN LANTERN, IT SEEMS. STUPID!
I'M SORRY, LORD CASSIDY. I'VE SOME MATCHES...
THE CHAMOMILE BOTTLE SHOULD BE...
...THERE.
GONE, OF COURSE...
OWEN SAID THAT HE DOESN'T BOTHER LOCKIN' THE STOREROOM. ANYONE COULD HAVE SNEAKED IN.
INCLUDING FINNAN, SEAN. YOU MUST ACKNOWLEDGE THAT...
TIME WE PAID A VISIT TO THE KITCHENS...
...Y-YES, LORD CASSIDY, IT'S TRUE. I DELIVERED THE NECTAR TO MASTER FINNAN...
...BUT I SWEAR ON ME GREAT-GRANDMA'S GRAVE, IT WASN'T POISONED WHEN I GAVE IT TO HIM!
CAN YE BE SURE OF THAT, MRS. MALONE? WHO'D HAVE HAD ACCESS TO THE NECTAR THAT NIGHT?
I S'POSE. ANYONE HERE...
DID YE NOTICE ANYTHING UNUSUAL ABOUT FINNAN RECENTLY?
W-WELL... I'M NOT ONE TO GOSSIP, M'LORD... BUT SOMETHIN' ODD HAPPENED A WEEK AGO...
"I WAS DELIVERIN' MASTER FINNAN'S SUPPER WHEN I HEARD THE VOICE OF OWEN MCGUINNESS...
Y'THINK YER CLEVER, DON'T YE, O'BRADAIGH? BUT THE TRUTH'S BEEN UNDER YER NOSE FER YEARS!

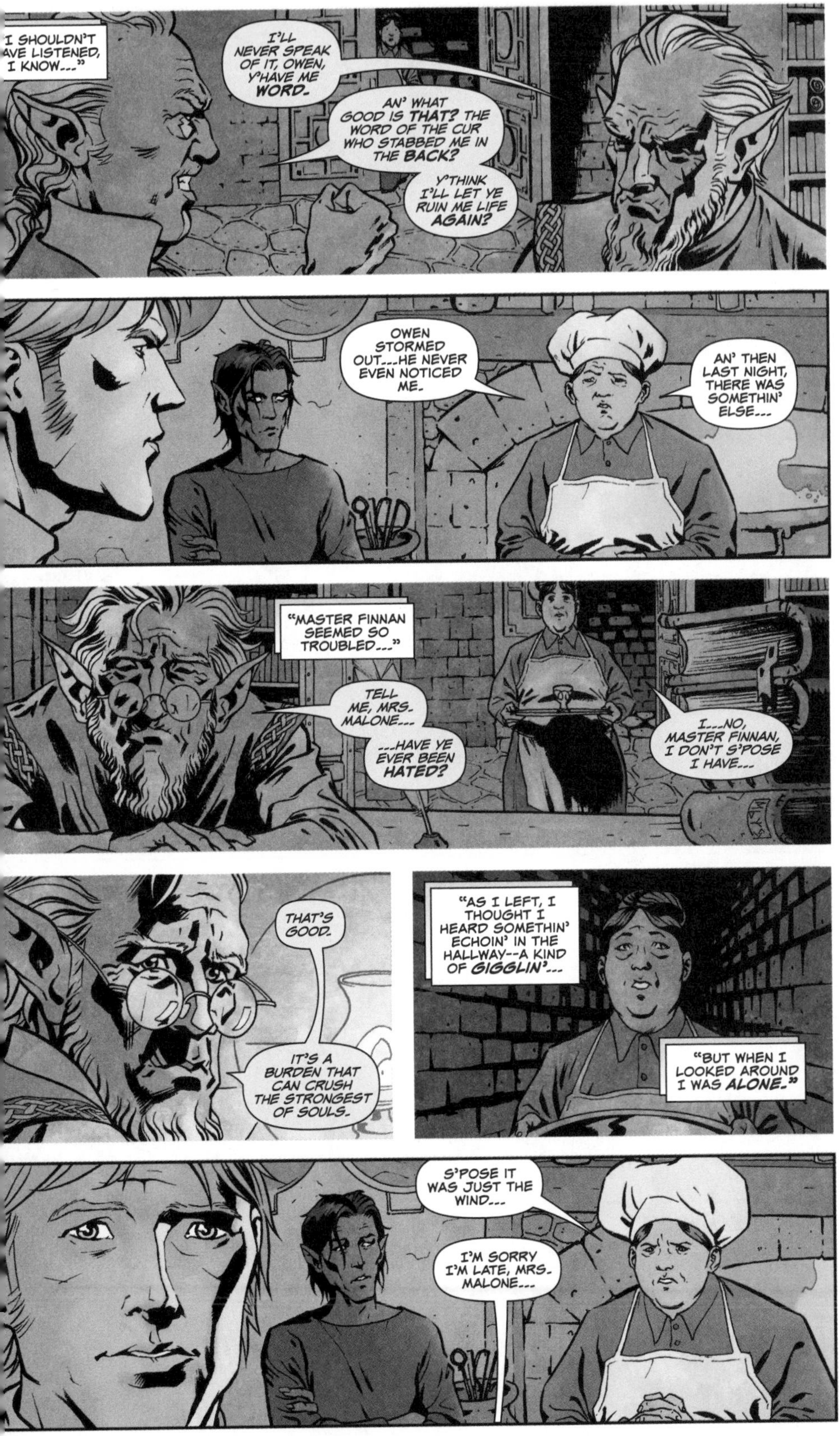

I SHOULDN'T
AVE LISTENED, I KNOW..."
I'LL NEVER SPEAK OF IT, OWEN, Y'HAVE ME WORD.
AN' WHAT GOOD IS THAT? THE WORD OF THE CUR WHO STABBED ME IN THE BACK?
Y'THINK I'LL LET YE RUIN ME LIFE AGAIN?
OWEN STORMED OUT...HE NEVER EVEN NOTICED ME.
AN' THEN LAST NIGHT, THERE WAS SOMETHIN' ELSE...
"MASTER FINNAN SEEMED SO TROUBLED..."
TELL ME, MRS. MALONE...
...HAVE YE EVER BEEN HATED?
I...NO, MASTER FINNAN, I DON'T S'POSE I HAVE...
THAT'S GOOD.
IT'S A BURDEN THAT CAN CRUSH THE STRONGEST OF SOULS.
"AS I LEFT, I THOUGHT I HEARD SOMETHIN' ECHOIN' IN THE HALLWAY--A KIND OF GIGGLIN'...
"BUT WHEN I LOOKED AROUND I WAS ALONE."
S'POSE IT WAS JUST THE WIND...
I'M SORRY I'M LATE, MRS. MALONE...

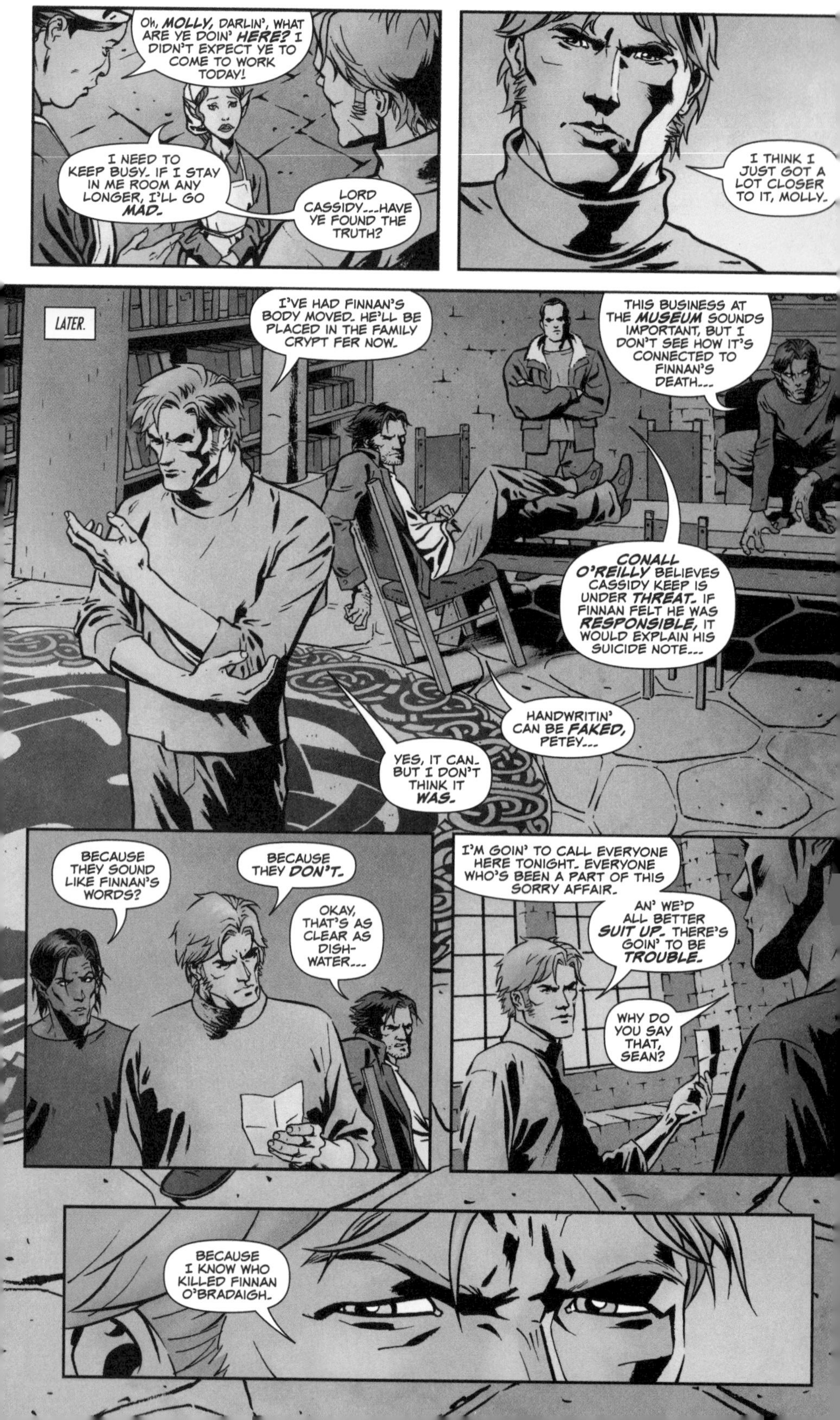
Oh, MOLLY, DARLIN', WHAT ARE YE DOIN' HERE? I DIDN'T EXPECT YE TO COME TO WORK TODAY!
I NEED TO KEEP BUSY. IF I STAY IN ME ROOM ANY LONGER, I'LL GO MAD.
LORD CASSIDY...HAVE YE FOUND THE TRUTH?
I THINK I JUST GOT A LOT CLOSER TO IT, MOLLY.
LATER.
I'VE HAD FINNAN'S BODY MOVED. HE'LL BE PLACED IN THE FAMILY CRYPT FER NOW.
THIS BUSINESS AT THE MUSEUM SOUNDS IMPORTANT, BUT I DON'T SEE HOW IT'S CONNECTED TO FINNAN'S DEATH...
CONALL O'REILLY BELIEVES CASSIDY KEEP IS UNDER THREAT. IF FINNAN FELT HE WAS RESPONSIBLE, IT WOULD EXPLAIN HIS SUICIDE NOTE...
HANDWRITIN' CAN BE FAKED, PETEY...
YES, IT CAN. BUT I DON'T THINK IT WAS.
BECAUSE THEY SOUND LIKE FINNAN'S WORDS?
BECAUSE THEY DON'T.
OKAY, THAT'S AS CLEAR AS DISH-WATER...
I'M GOIN' TO CALL EVERYONE HERE TONIGHT. EVERYONE WHO'S BEEN A PART OF THIS SORRY AFFAIR.
AN' WE'D ALL BETTER SUIT UP. THERE'S GOIN' TO BE TROUBLE.
WHY DO YOU SAY THAT, SEAN?
BECAUSE I KNOW WHO KILLED FINNAN O'BRADAIGH.

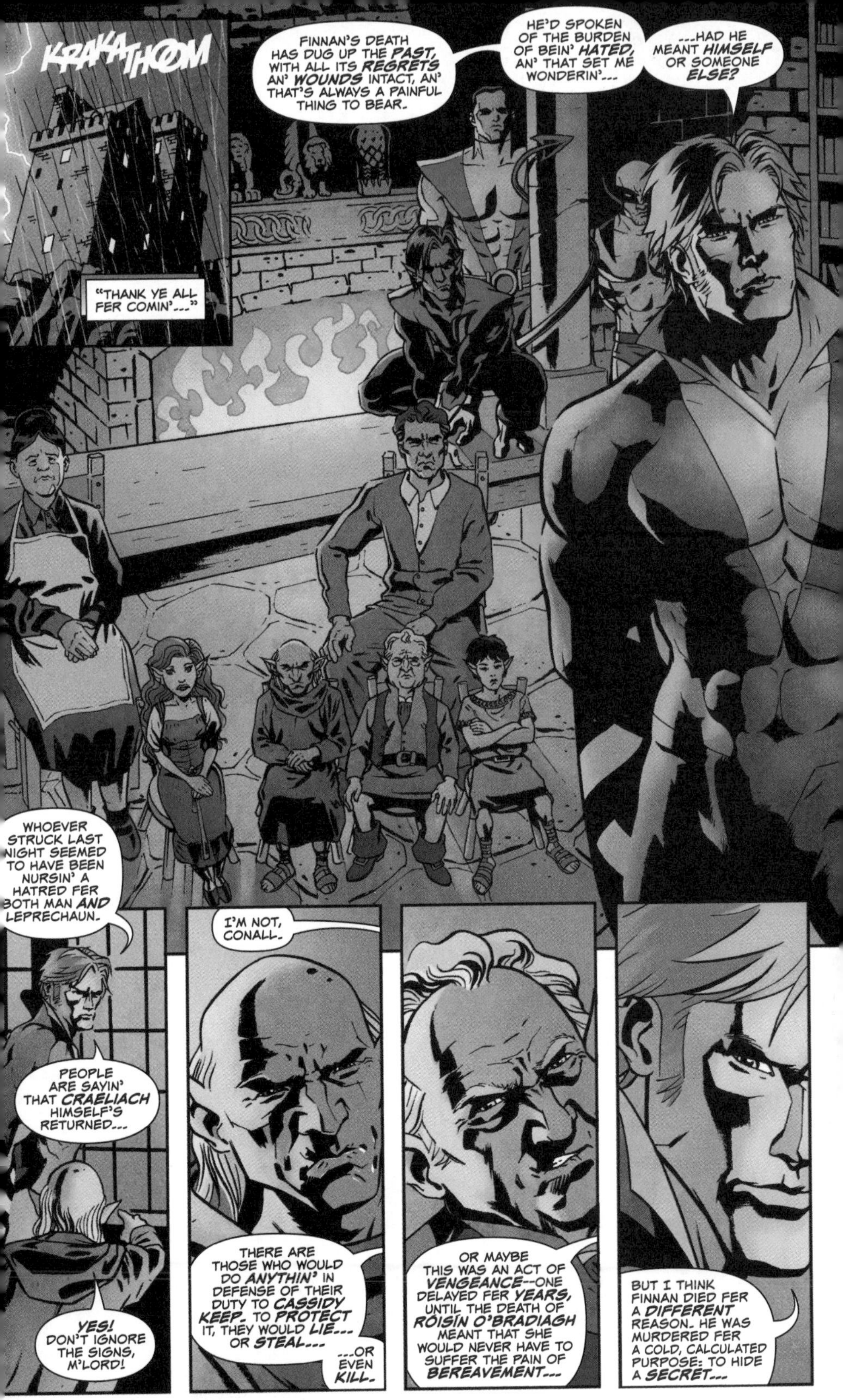

KRAKATHOOM
"THANK YE ALL FER COMIN'..."
FINNAN'S DEATH HAS DUG UP THE PAST, WITH ALL ITS REGRETS AN' WOUNDS INTACT, AN' THAT'S ALWAYS A PAINFUL THING TO BEAR.
HE'D SPOKEN OF THE BURDEN OF BEIN' HATED, AN' THAT SET ME WONDERIN'...
...HAD HE MEANT HIMSELF OR SOMEONE ELSE?
WHOEVER STRUCK LAST NIGHT SEEMED TO HAVE BEEN NURSIN' A HATRED FER BOTH MAN AND LEPRECHAUN.
PEOPLE ARE SAYIN' THAT CRAELIACH HIMSELF'S RETURNED...
YES! DON'T IGNORE THE SIGNS, M'LORD!
I'M NOT, CONALL.
THERE ARE THOSE WHO WOULD DO ANYTHIN' IN DEFENSE OF THEIR DUTY TO CASSIDY KEEP. TO PROTECT IT, THEY WOULD LIE... OR STEAL...
...OR EVEN KILL.
OR MAYBE THIS WAS AN ACT OF VENGEANCE--ONE DELAYED FER YEARS, UNTIL THE DEATH OF ROISIN O'BRADIAGH MEANT THAT SHE WOULD NEVER HAVE TO SUFFER THE PAIN OF BEREAVEMENT...
BUT I THINK FINNAN DIED FER A DIFFERENT REASON. HE WAS MURDERED FER A COLD, CALCULATED PURPOSE: TO HIDE A SECRET...

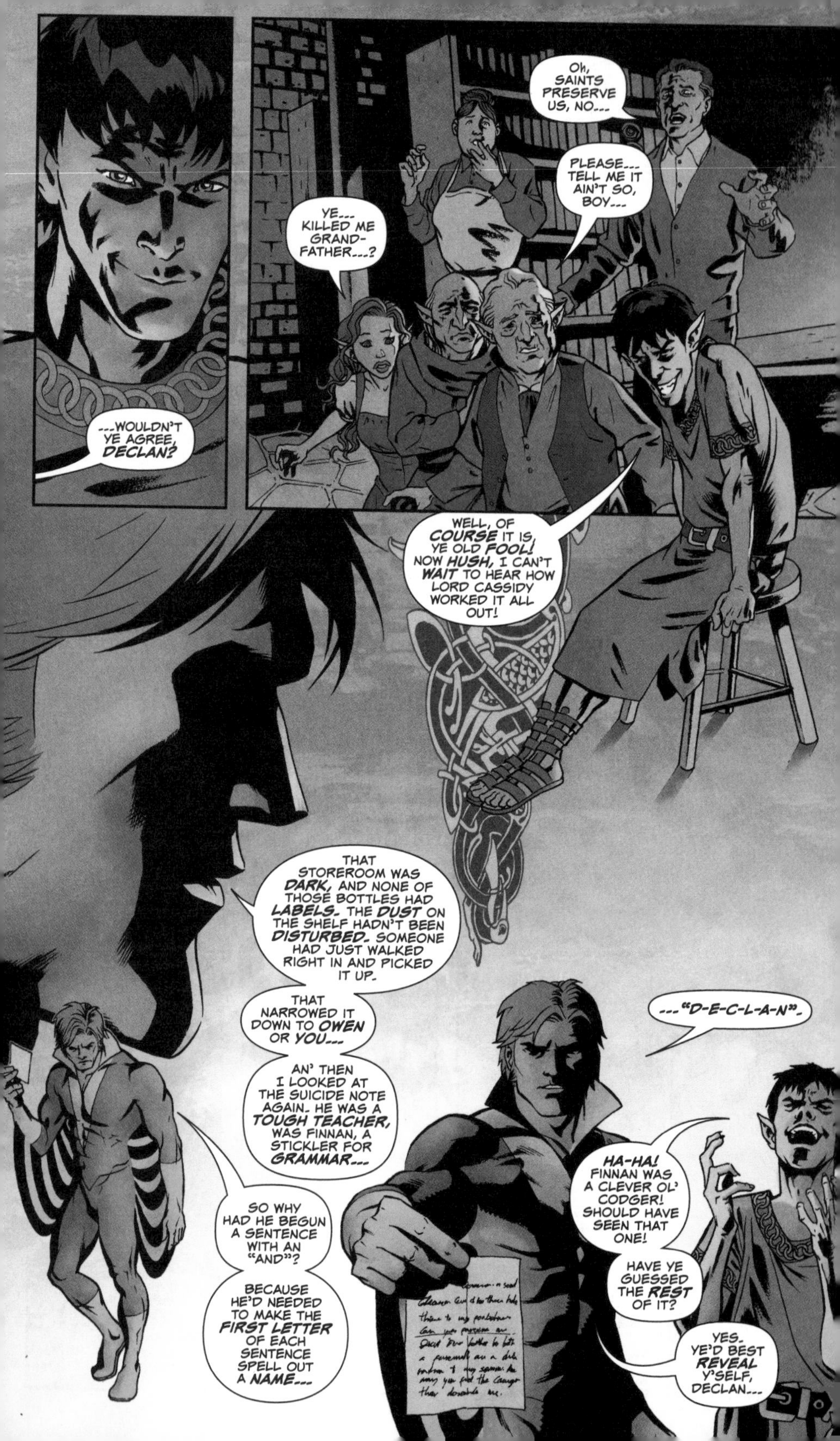

---WOULDN'T YE AGREE, DECLAN?
Oh, SAINTS PRESERVE US, NO---
PLEASE--- TELL ME IT AIN'T SO, BOY---
YE--- KILLED ME GRAND-FATHER---?
WELL, OF COURSE IT IS, YE OLD FOOL! NOW HUSH, I CAN'T WAIT TO HEAR HOW LORD CASSIDY WORKED IT ALL OUT!
THAT STOREROOM WAS DARK, AND NONE OF THOSE BOTTLES HAD LABELS. THE DUST ON THE SHELF HADN'T BEEN DISTURBED. SOMEONE HAD JUST WALKED RIGHT IN AND PICKED IT UP.
THAT NARROWED IT DOWN TO OWEN OR YOU---
AN' THEN I LOOKED AT THE SUICIDE NOTE AGAIN. HE WAS A TOUGH TEACHER, WAS FINNAN, A STICKLER FOR GRAMMAR---
SO WHY HAD HE BEGUN A SENTENCE WITH AN "AND"?
BECAUSE HE'D NEEDED TO MAKE THE FIRST LETTER OF EACH SENTENCE SPELL OUT A NAME---
---"D-E-C-L-A-N".
HA-HA! FINNAN WAS A CLEVER OL' CODGER! SHOULD HAVE SEEN THAT ONE!
HAVE YE GUESSED THE REST OF IT?
YES. YE'D BEST REVEAL Y'SELF, DECLAN---

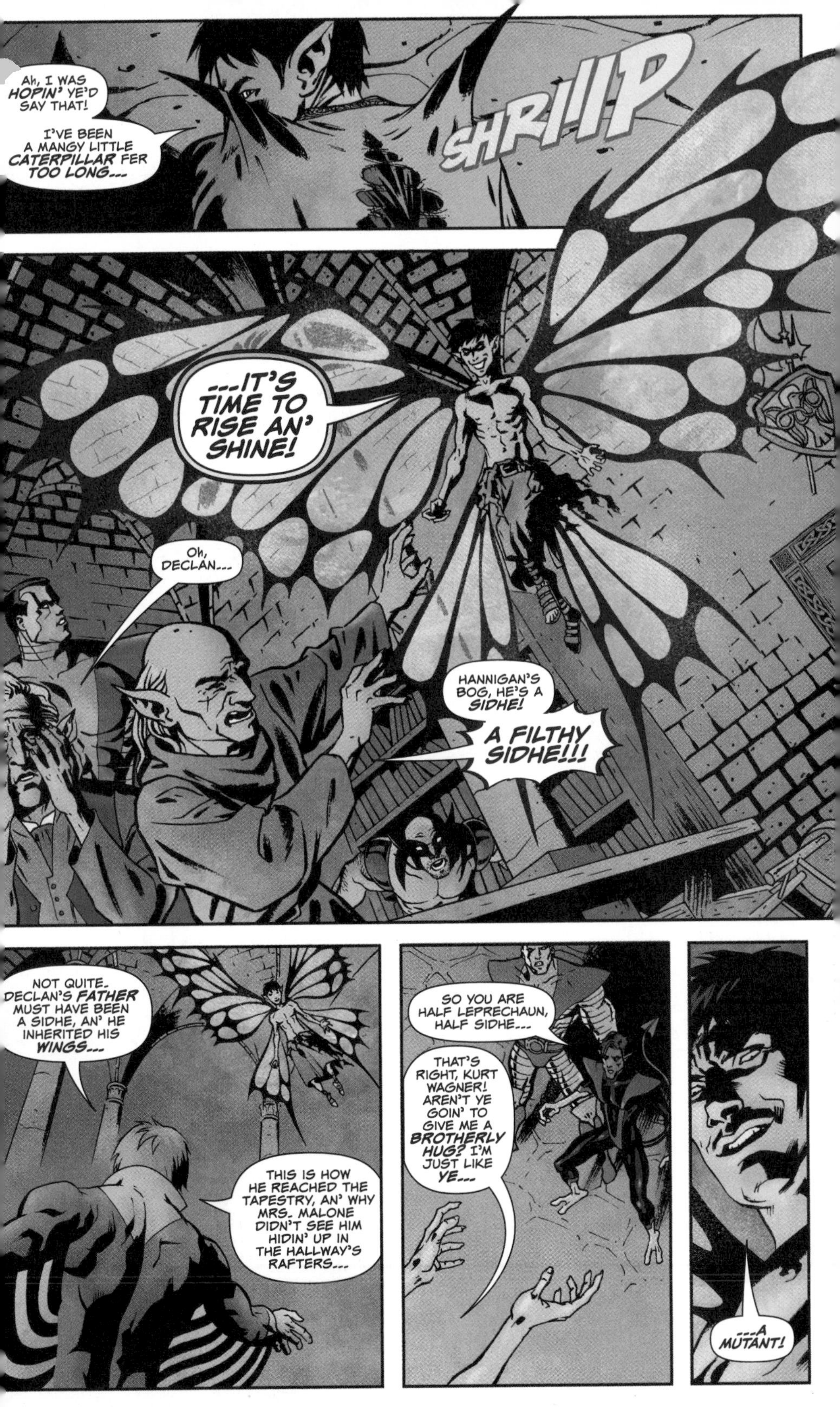

AH, I WAS HOPIN' YE'D SAY THAT!
I'VE BEEN A MANGY LITTLE CATERPILLAR FER TOO LONG---
SHRIIIP
---IT'S TIME TO RISE AN' SHINE!
OH, DECLAN---
HANNIGAN'S BOG, HE'S A SIDHE!
A FILTHY SIDHE!!!
NOT QUITE. DECLAN'S FATHER MUST HAVE BEEN A SIDHE, AN' HE INHERITED HIS WINGS---
THIS IS HOW HE REACHED THE TAPESTRY, AN' WHY MRS. MALONE DIDN'T SEE HIM HIDIN' UP IN THE HALLWAY'S RAFTERS---
SO YOU ARE HALF LEPRECHAUN, HALF SIDHE---
THAT'S RIGHT, KURT WAGNER! AREN'T YE GOIN' TO GIVE ME A BROTHERLY HUG? I'M JUST LIKE YE---
---A MUTANT!

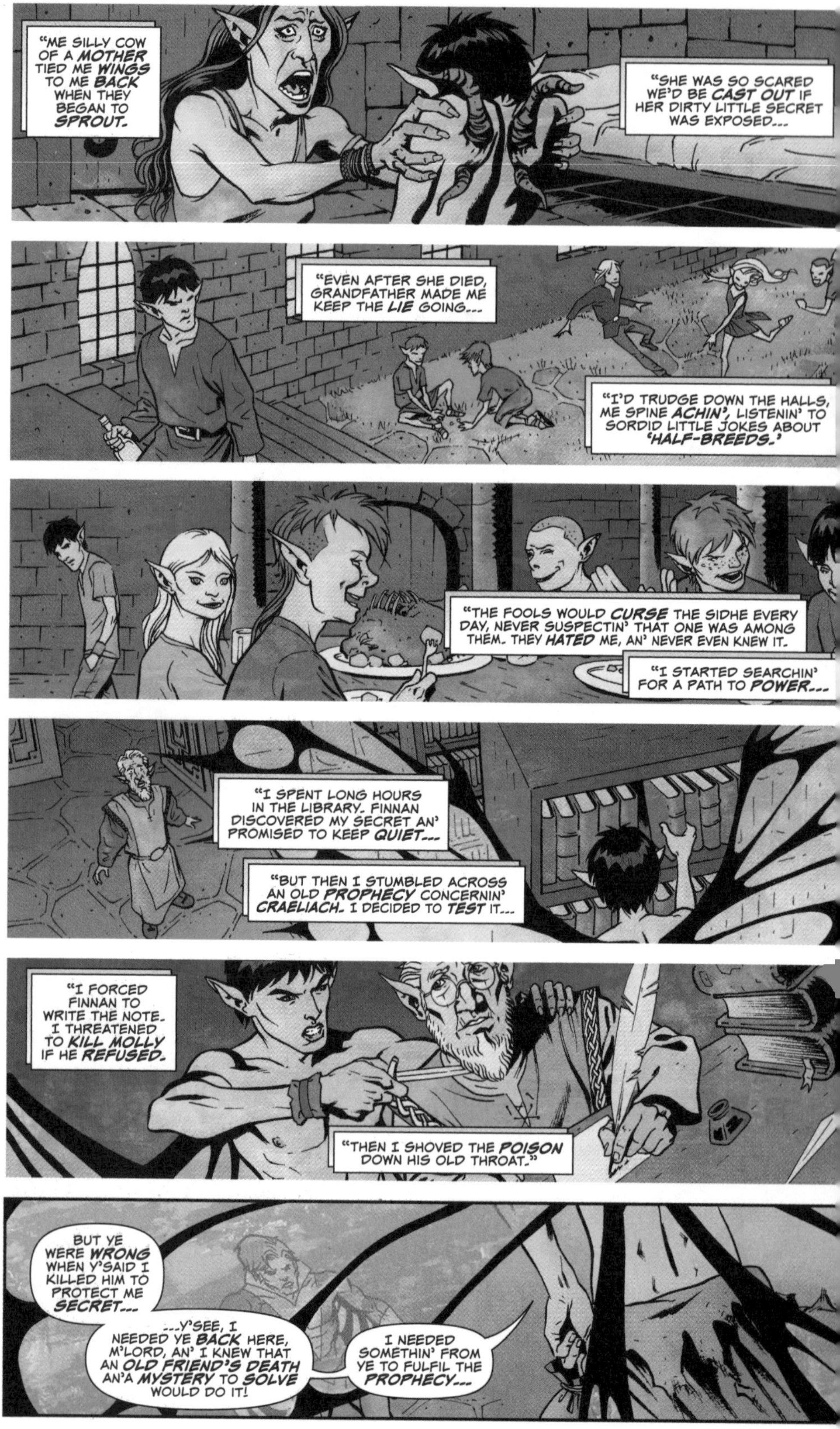

"ME SILLY COW OF A MOTHER TIED ME WINGS TO ME BACK WHEN THEY BEGAN TO SPROUT.
"SHE WAS SO SCARED WE'D BE CAST OUT IF HER DIRTY LITTLE SECRET WAS EXPOSED...
"EVEN AFTER SHE DIED, GRANDFATHER MADE ME KEEP THE LIE GOING...
"I'D TRUDGE DOWN THE HALLS, ME SPINE ACHIN', LISTENIN' TO SORDID LITTLE JOKES ABOUT 'HALF-BREEDS.'
"THE FOOLS WOULD CURSE THE SIDHE EVERY DAY, NEVER SUSPECTIN' THAT ONE WAS AMONG THEM. THEY HATED ME, AN' NEVER EVEN KNEW IT.
"I STARTED SEARCHIN' FOR A PATH TO POWER...
"I SPENT LONG HOURS IN THE LIBRARY. FINNAN DISCOVERED MY SECRET AN' PROMISED TO KEEP QUIET...
"BUT THEN I STUMBLED ACROSS AN OLD PROPHECY CONCERNIN' CRAELIACH. I DECIDED TO TEST IT...
"I FORCED FINNAN TO WRITE THE NOTE. I THREATENED TO KILL MOLLY IF HE REFUSED.
"THEN I SHOVED THE POISON DOWN HIS OLD THROAT."
BUT YE WERE WRONG WHEN Y'SAID I KILLED HIM TO PROTECT ME SECRET...
...Y'SEE, I NEEDED YE BACK HERE, M'LORD, AN' I KNEW THAT AN OLD FRIEND'S DEATH AN'A MYSTERY TO SOLVE WOULD DO IT!
I NEEDED SOMETHIN' FROM YE TO FULFIL THE PROPHECY...

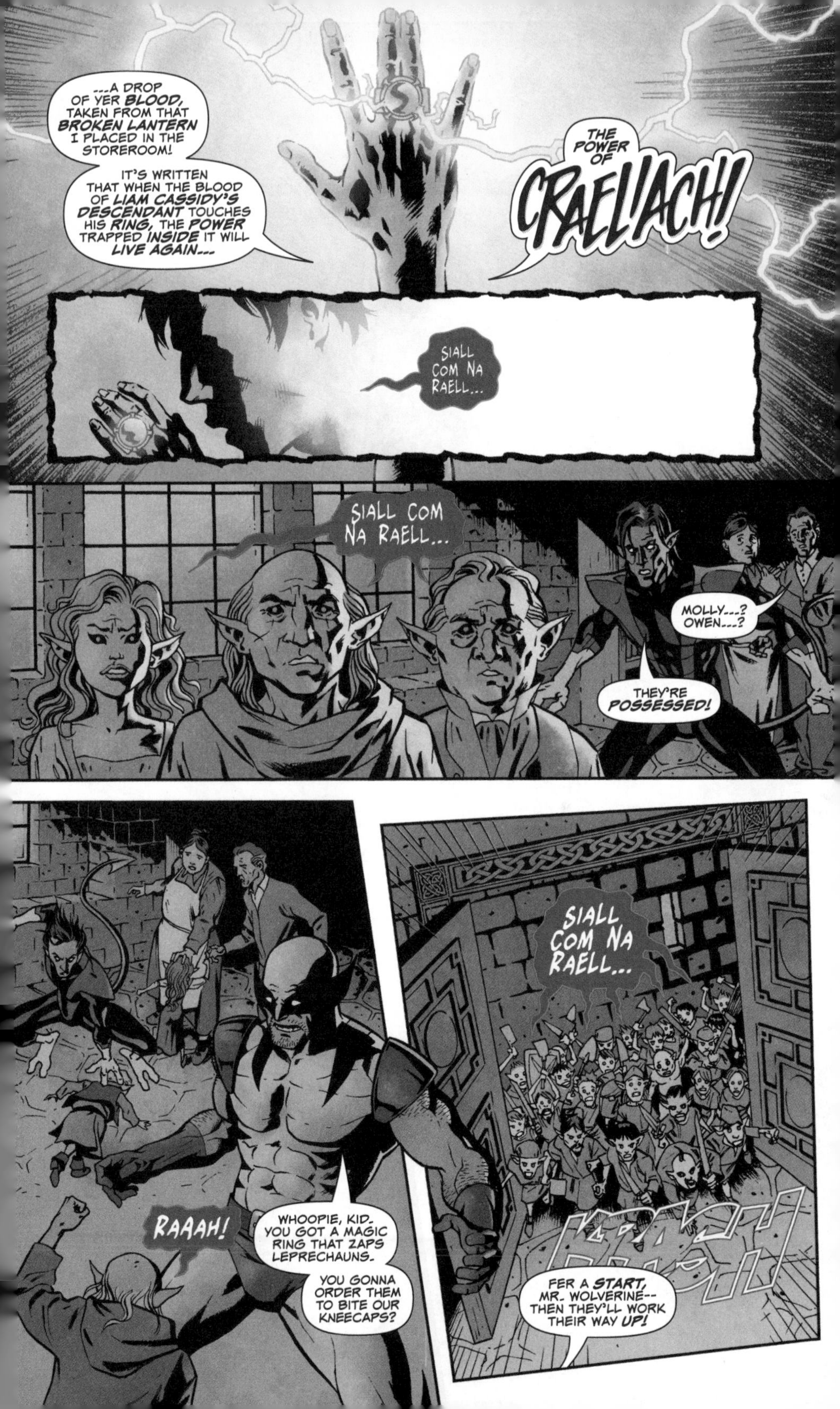
...A DROP OF YER BLOOD, TAKEN FROM THAT BROKEN LANTERN I PLACED IN THE STOREROOM!
IT'S WRITTEN THAT WHEN THE BLOOD OF LIAM CASSIDY'S DESCENDANT TOUCHES HIS RING, THE POWER TRAPPED INSIDE IT WILL LIVE AGAIN...
THE POWER OF CRAELIACH!
SIALL COM NA RAELL...
SIALL COM NA RAELL...
MOLLY...? OWEN...?
THEY'RE POSSESSED!
SIALL COM NA RAELL...
RAAAH!
WHOOPIE, KID. YOU GOT A MAGIC RING THAT ZAPS LEPRECHAUNS.
YOU GONNA ORDER THEM TO BITE OUR KNEECAPS?
FER A START, MR. WOLVERINE-- THEN THEY'LL WORK THEIR WAY UP!

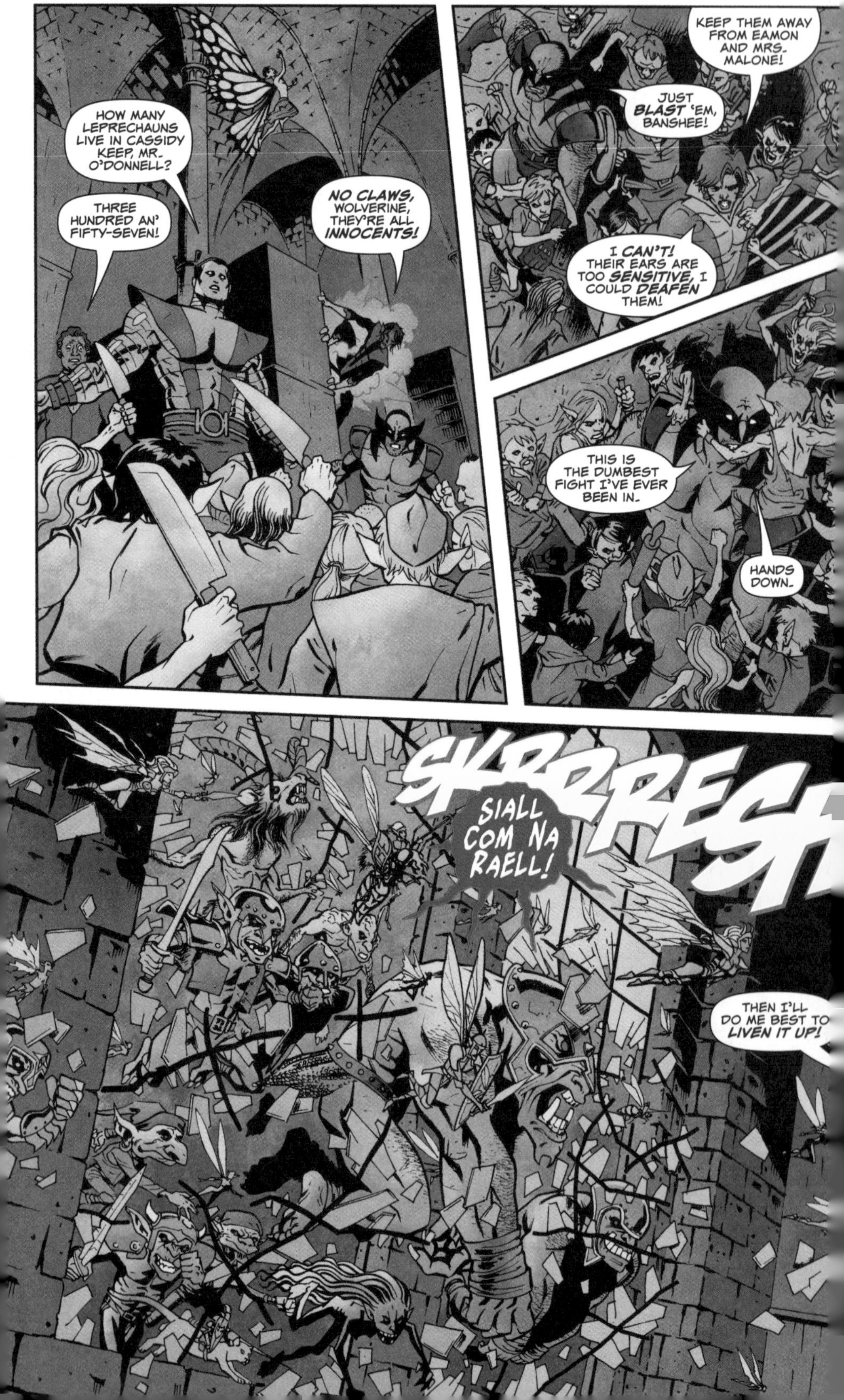
HOW MANY LEPRECHAUNS LIVE IN CASSIDY KEEP, MR. O'DONNELL?
THREE HUNDRED AN' FIFTY-SEVEN!
NO CLAWS, WOLVERINE, THEY'RE ALL INNOCENTS!
KEEP THEM AWAY FROM EAMON AND MRS. MALONE!
JUST BLAST 'EM, BANSHEE!
I CAN'T! THEIR EARS ARE TOO SENSITIVE, I COULD DEAFEN THEM!
THIS IS THE DUMBEST FIGHT I'VE EVER BEEN IN.
HANDS DOWN.
SKRRRESH
SIALL COM NA RAELL!
THEN I'LL DO ME BEST TO LIVEN IT UP!

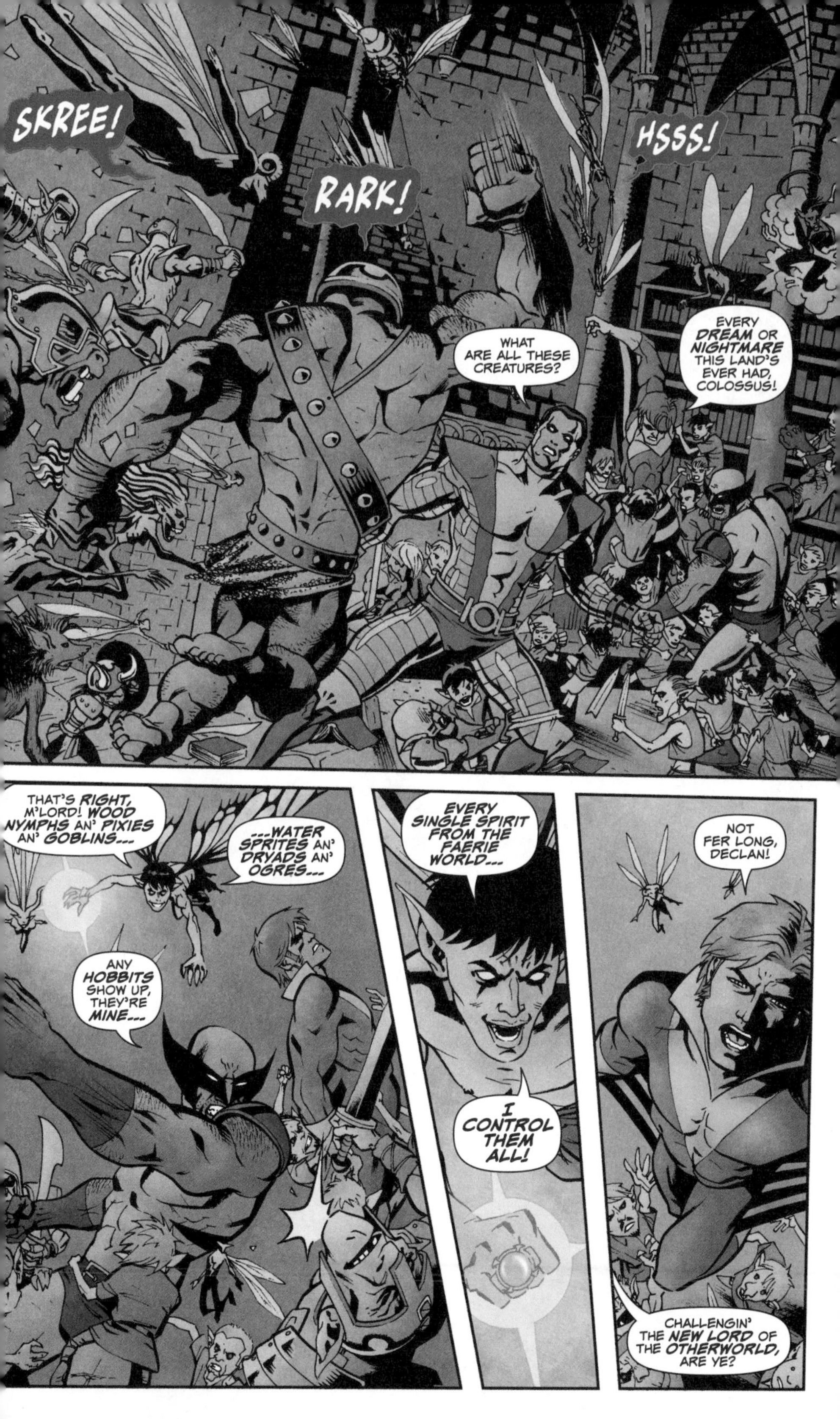
SKREE!
RARK!
HSSS!
WHAT ARE ALL THESE CREATURES?
EVERY DREAM OR NIGHTMARE THIS LAND'S EVER HAD, COLOSSUS!
THAT'S RIGHT, M'LORD! WOOD NYMPHS AN' PIXIES AN' GOBLINS...
...WATER SPRITES AN' DRYADS AN' OGRES...
ANY HOBBITS SHOW UP, THEY'RE MINE...
EVERY SINGLE SPIRIT FROM THE FAERIE WORLD...
I CONTROL THEM ALL!
NOT FER LONG, DECLAN!
CHALLENGIN' THE NEW LORD OF THE OTHERWORLD, ARE YE?

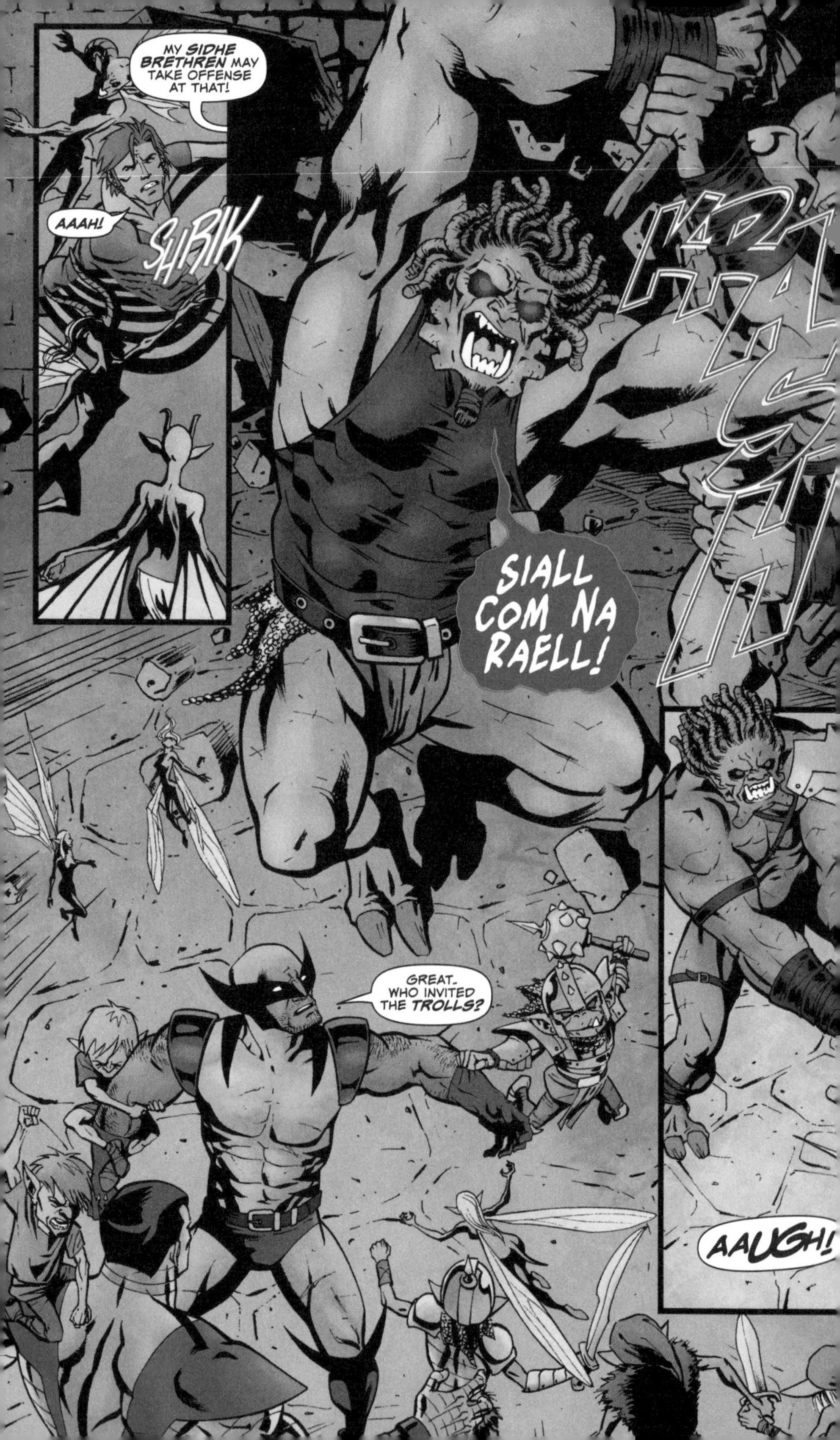
MY SIDHE BRETHREN MAY TAKE OFFENSE AT THAT!
AAAH!
SHIRIK
SIALL COM NA RAELL!
GREAT. WHO INVITED THE TROLLS?
AAUGH!

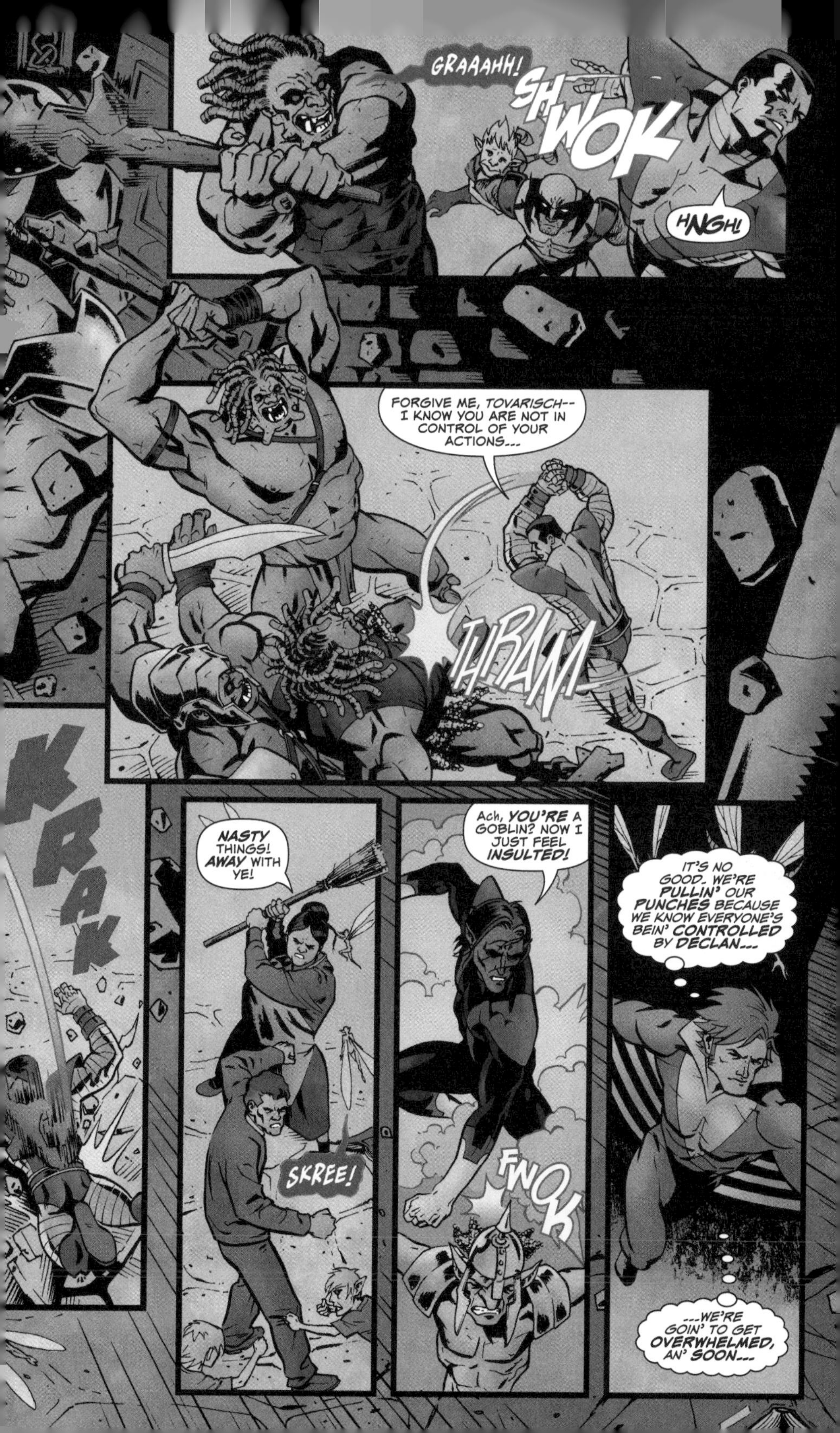
GRAAAHH!
SHWOK
HNGH!
FORGIVE ME, TOVARISCH-- I KNOW YOU ARE NOT IN CONTROL OF YOUR ACTIONS...
THRAM
KRAK
NASTY THINGS! AWAY WITH YE!
SKREE!
Ach, YOU'RE A GOBLIN? NOW I JUST FEEL INSULTED!
FWOK
IT'S NO GOOD. WE'RE PULLIN' OUR PUNCHES BECAUSE WE KNOW EVERYONE'S BEIN' CONTROLLED BY DECLAN...
...WE'RE GOIN' TO GET OVERWHELMED, AN' SOON...

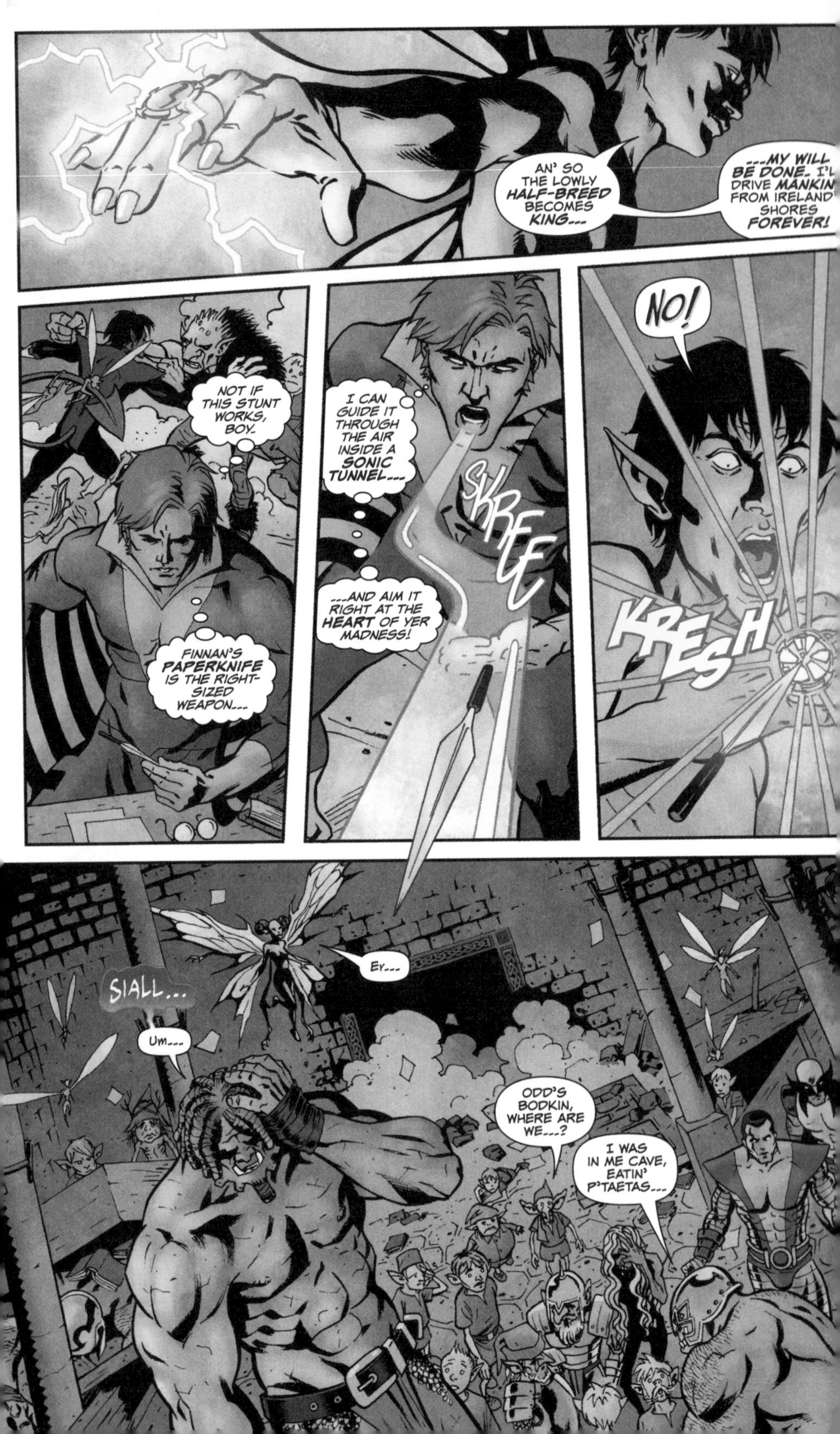
AN' SO THE LOWLY HALF-BREED BECOMES KING---
---MY WILL BE DONE. I'LL DRIVE MANKIND FROM IRELAND'S SHORES FOREVER!
NOT IF THIS STUNT WORKS, BOY.
FINNAN'S PAPERKNIFE IS THE RIGHT-SIZED WEAPON---
I CAN GUIDE IT THROUGH THE AIR INSIDE A SONIC TUNNEL---
---AND AIM IT RIGHT AT THE HEART OF YER MADNESS!
SKREEE
NO!
KRESH
Er---
SIALL...
Um---
ODD'S BODKIN, WHERE ARE WE---?
I WAS IN ME CAVE, EATIN' P'TAETAS---

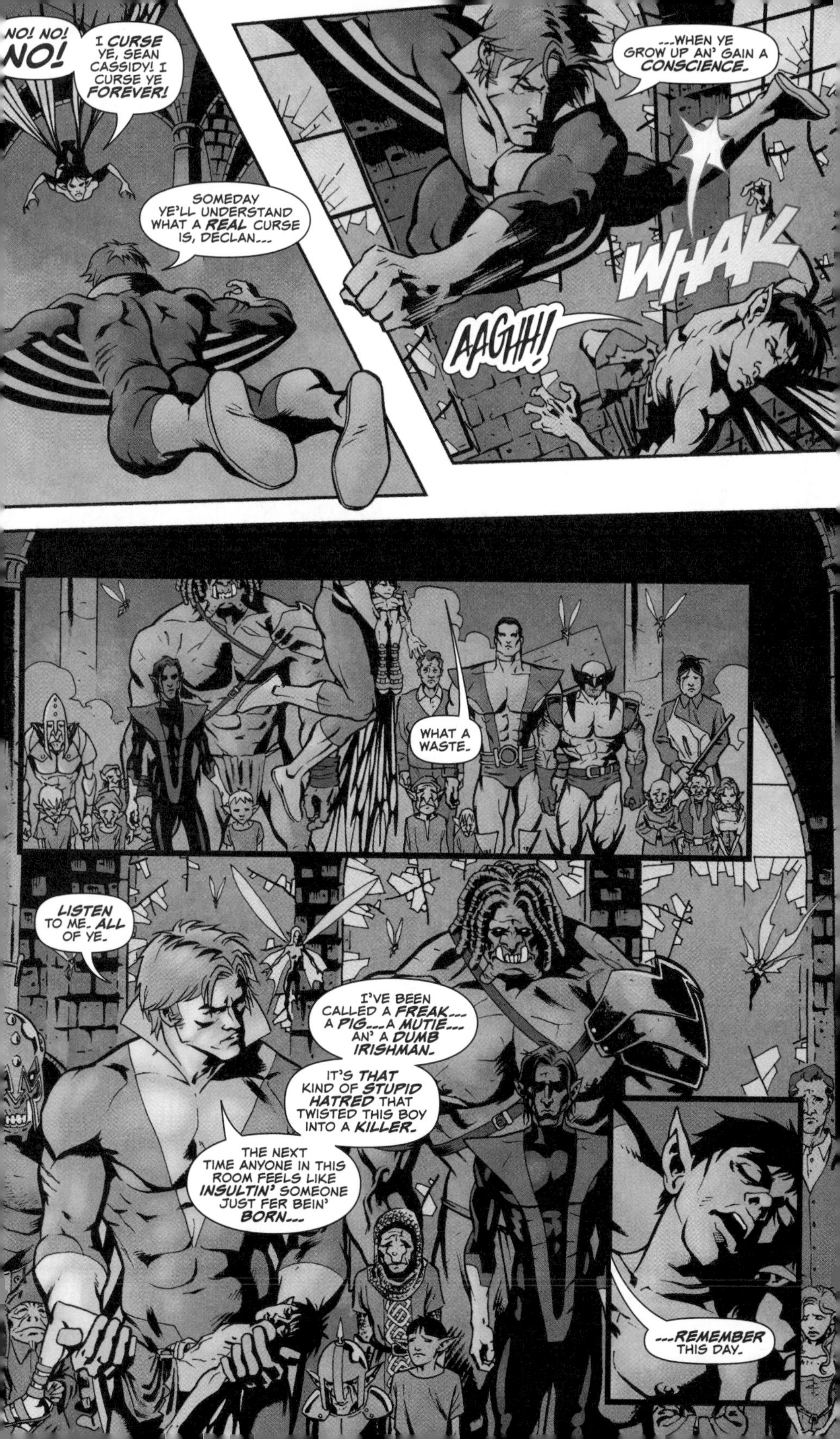

NO! NO! NO!
I CURSE YE, SEAN CASSIDY! I CURSE YE FOREVER!
SOMEDAY YE'LL UNDERSTAND WHAT A REAL CURSE IS, DECLAN...
...WHEN YE GROW UP AN' GAIN A CONSCIENCE.
WHAK
AAGHH!
WHAT A WASTE.
LISTEN TO ME. ALL OF YE.
I'VE BEEN CALLED A FREAK... A PIG... A MUTIE... AN' A DUMB IRISHMAN.
IT'S THAT KIND OF STUPID HATRED THAT TWISTED THIS BOY INTO A KILLER.
THE NEXT TIME ANYONE IN THIS ROOM FEELS LIKE INSULTIN' SOMEONE JUST FER BEIN' BORN...
...REMEMBER THIS DAY.

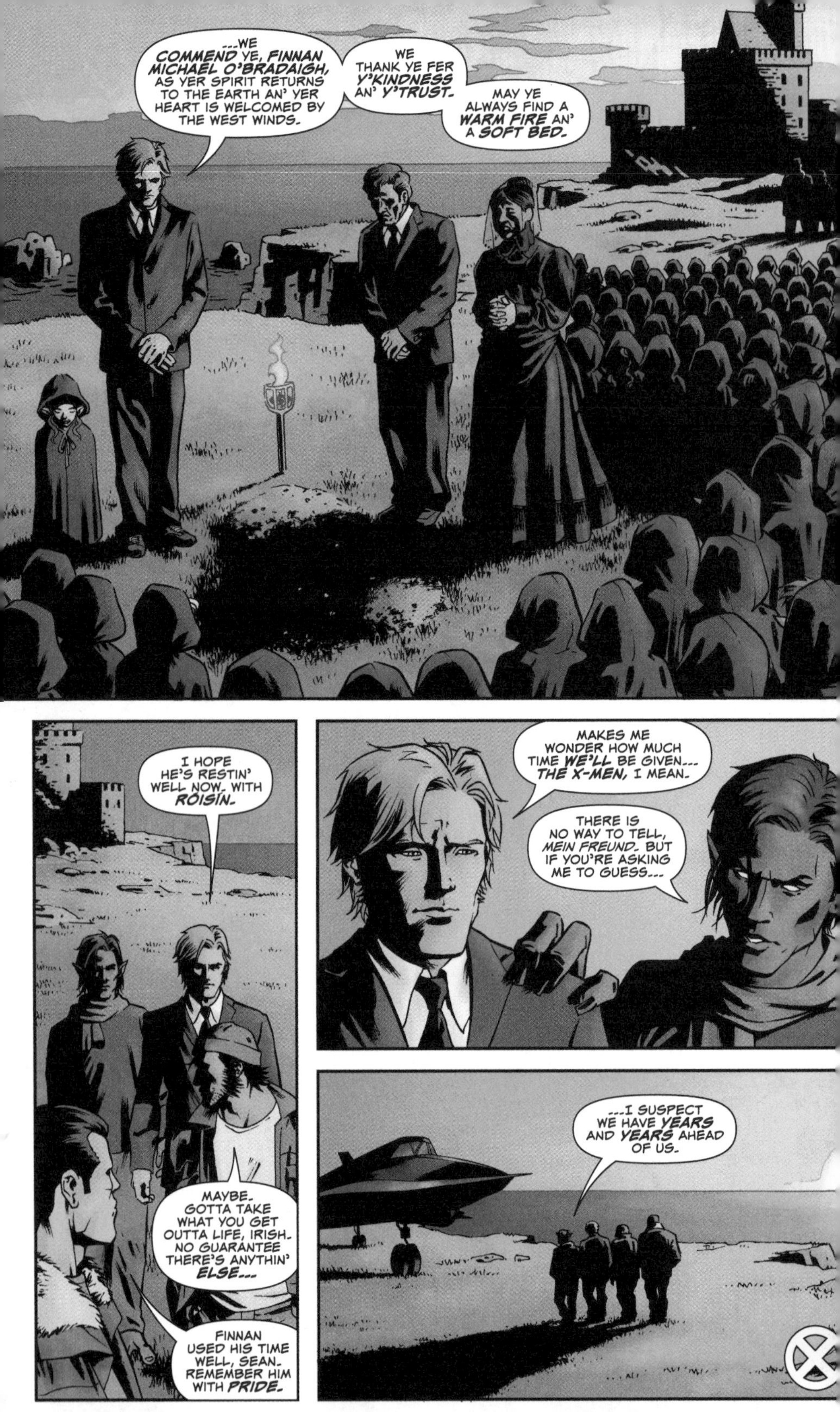
...WE COMMEND YE, FINNAN MICHAEL O'BRADAIGH, AS YER SPIRIT RETURNS TO THE EARTH AN' YER HEART IS WELCOMED BY THE WEST WINDS.
WE THANK YE FER Y'KINDNESS AN' Y'TRUST.
MAY YE ALWAYS FIND A WARM FIRE AN' A SOFT BED.
I HOPE HE'S RESTIN' WELL NOW. WITH ROISÍN.
MAYBE. GOTTA TAKE WHAT YOU GET OUTTA LIFE, IRISH. NO GUARANTEE THERE'S ANYTHIN' ELSE...
FINNAN USED HIS TIME WELL, SEAN. REMEMBER HIM WITH PRIDE.
MAKES ME WONDER HOW MUCH TIME WE'LL BE GIVEN... THE X-MEN, I MEAN.
THERE IS NO WAY TO TELL, MEIN FREUND. BUT IF YOU'RE ASKING ME TO GUESS...
...I SUSPECT WE HAVE YEARS AND YEARS AHEAD OF US.

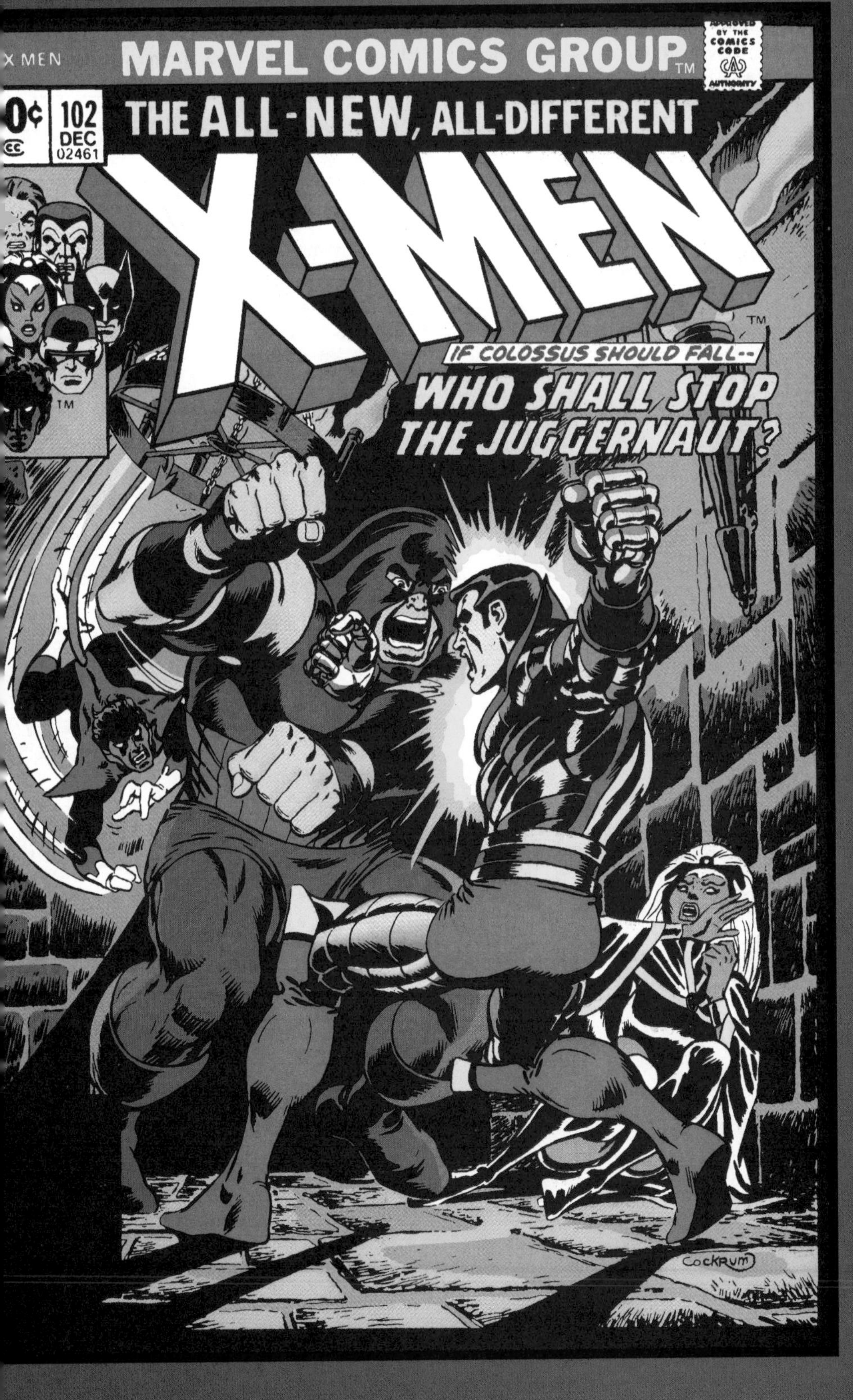

X MEN
MARVEL COMICS GROUP TM
APPROVED BY THE COMICS CODE AUTHORITY
0¢
102
DEC
02461
THE ALL-NEW, ALL-DIFFERENT
X-MEN TM
IF COLOSSUS SHOULD FALL--
WHO SHALL STOP THE JUGGERNAUT?
COCKRUM

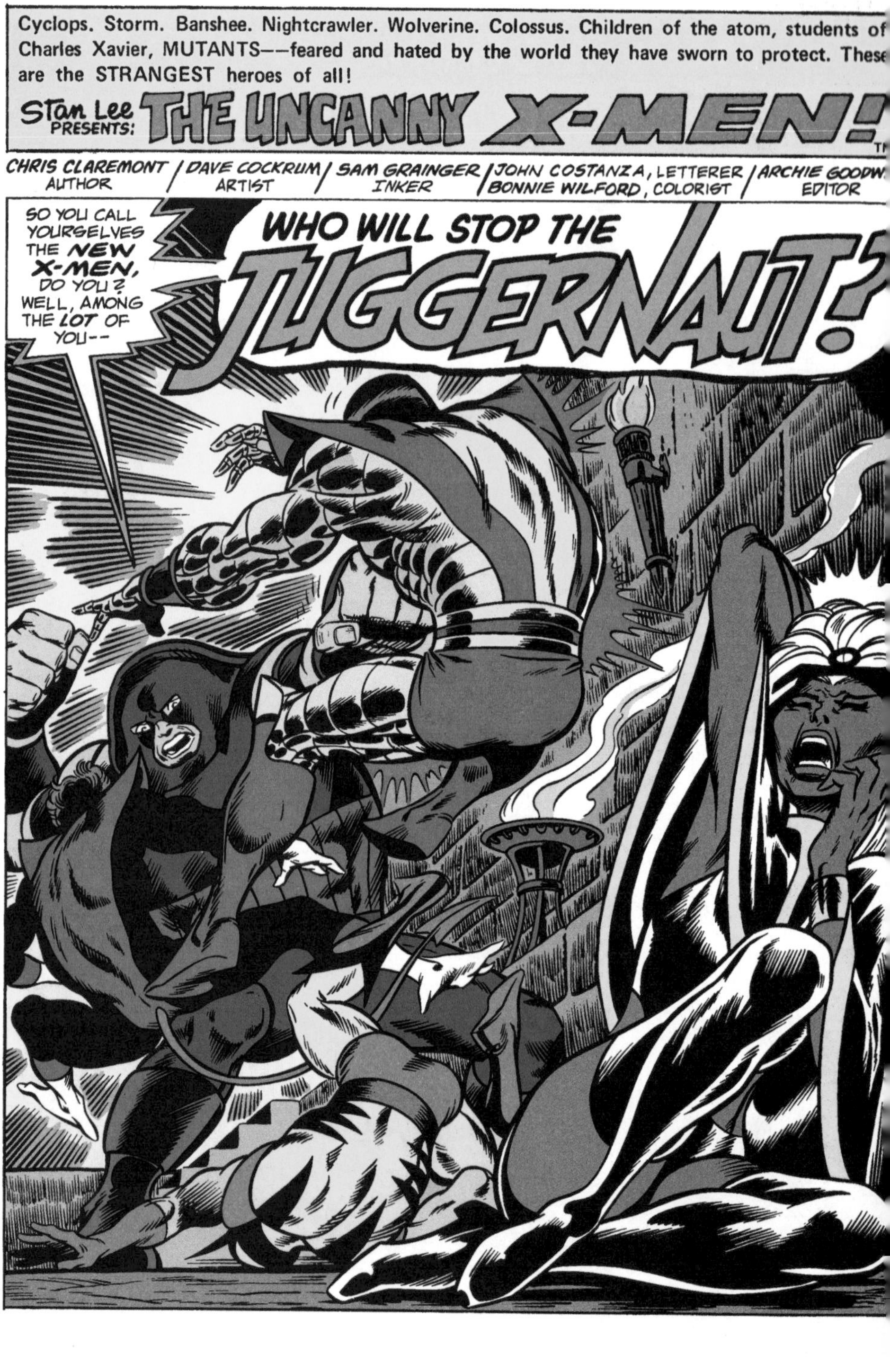

Cyclops. Storm. Banshee. Nightcrawler. Wolverine. Colossus. Children of the atom, students of Charles Xavier, MUTANTS––feared and hated by the world they have sworn to protect. These are the STRANGEST heroes of all!
STAN LEE PRESENTS: THE UNCANNY X-MEN!
CHRIS CLAREMONT AUTHOR / DAVE COCKRUM ARTIST / SAM GRAINGER INKER / JOHN COSTANZA, LETTERER BONNIE WILFORD, COLORIST / ARCHIE GOODW EDITOR
SO YOU CALL YOURSELVES THE NEW X-MEN, DO YOU? WELL, AMONG THE LOT OF YOU--
WHO WILL STOP THE JUGGERNAUT?

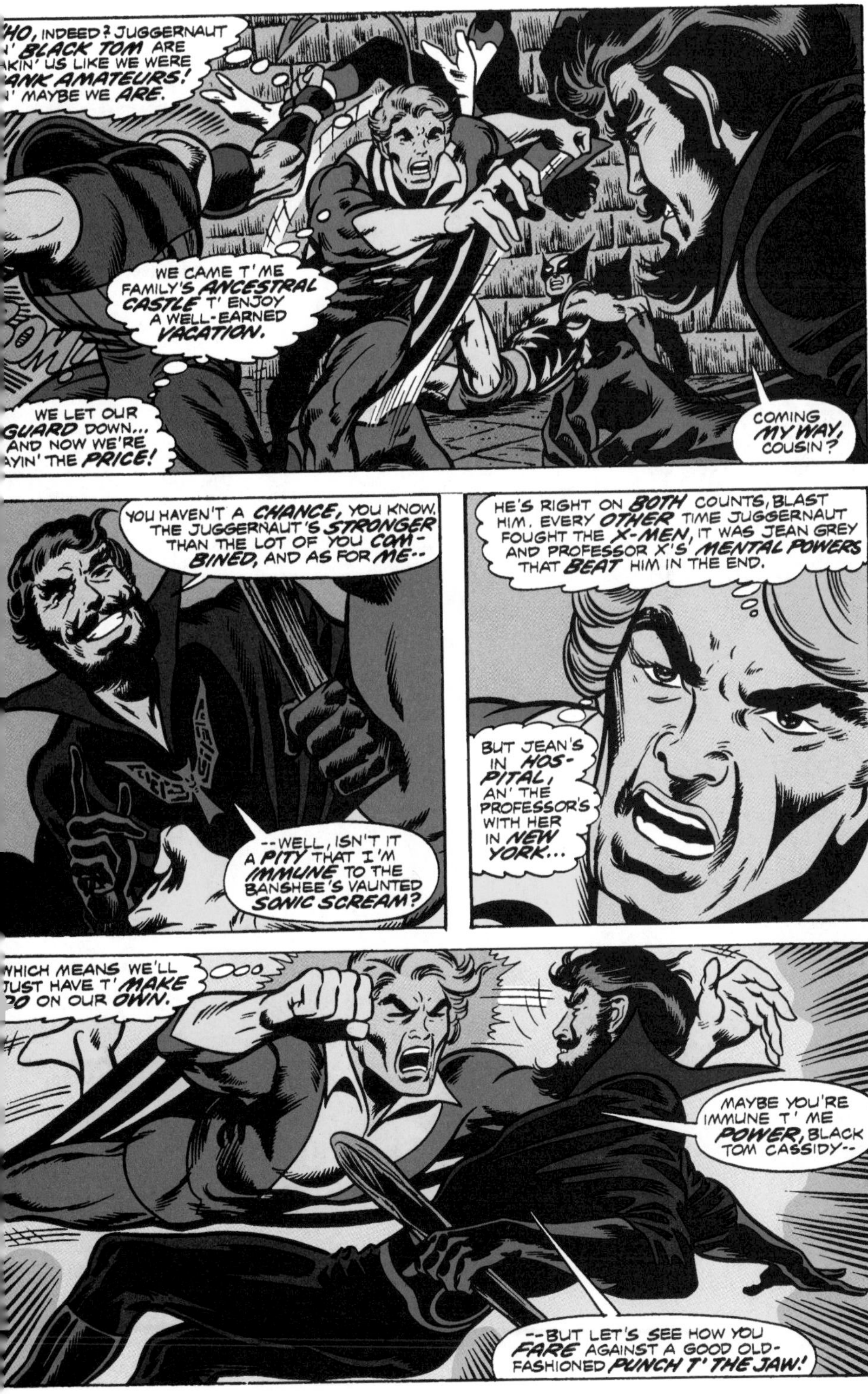
HO, INDEED? JUGGERNAUT N' BLACK TOM ARE AKIN' US LIKE WE WERE ANK AMATEURS! N' MAYBE WE ARE.
WE CAME T'ME FAMILY'S ANCESTRAL CASTLE T' ENJOY A WELL-EARNED VACATION.
WE LET OUR GUARD DOWN... AND NOW WE'RE AYIN' THE PRICE!
COMING MY WAY, COUSIN?
YOU HAVEN'T A CHANCE, YOU KNOW. THE JUGGERNAUT'S STRONGER THAN THE LOT OF YOU COMBINED, AND AS FOR ME--
--WELL, ISN'T IT A PITY THAT I'M IMMUNE TO THE BANSHEE'S VAUNTED SONIC SCREAM?
HE'S RIGHT ON BOTH COUNTS, BLAST HIM. EVERY OTHER TIME JUGGERNAUT FOUGHT THE X-MEN, IT WAS JEAN GREY AND PROFESSOR X'S MENTAL POWERS THAT BEAT HIM IN THE END.
BUT JEAN'S IN HOSPITAL, AN' THE PROFESSOR'S WITH HER IN NEW YORK...
WHICH MEANS WE'LL JUST HAVE T' MAKE DO ON OUR OWN.
MAYBE YOU'RE IMMUNE T' ME POWER, BLACK TOM CASSIDY--
--BUT LET'S SEE HOW YOU FARE AGAINST A GOOD OLD-FASHIONED PUNCH T' THE JAW!

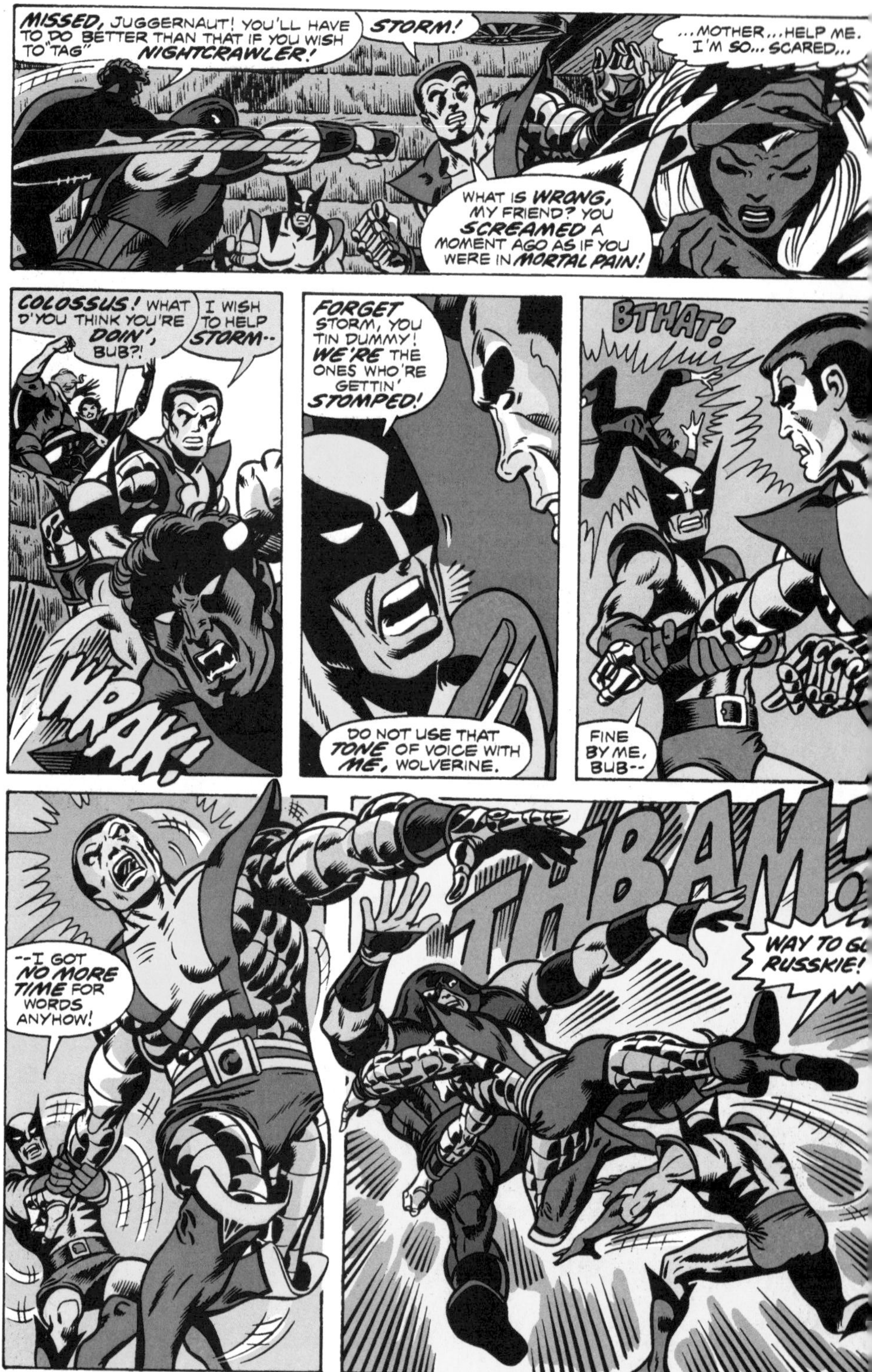
MISSED, JUGGERNAUT! YOU'LL HAVE TO DO BETTER THAN THAT IF YOU WISH TO "TAG" NIGHTCRAWLER!
STORM!
...MOTHER...HELP ME. I'M SO...SCARED...
WHAT IS WRONG, MY FRIEND? YOU SCREAMED A MOMENT AGO AS IF YOU WERE IN MORTAL PAIN!
COLOSSUS! WHAT D'YOU THINK YOU'RE DOIN', BUB?!
I WISH TO HELP STORM--
WRAK!
FORGET STORM, YOU TIN DUMMY! WE'RE THE ONES WHO'RE GETTIN' STOMPED!
DO NOT USE THAT TONE OF VOICE WITH ME, WOLVERINE.
BTHAT!
FINE BY ME, BUB--
--I GOT NO MORE TIME FOR WORDS ANYHOW!
THBAM!
WAY TO GO RUSSKIE!

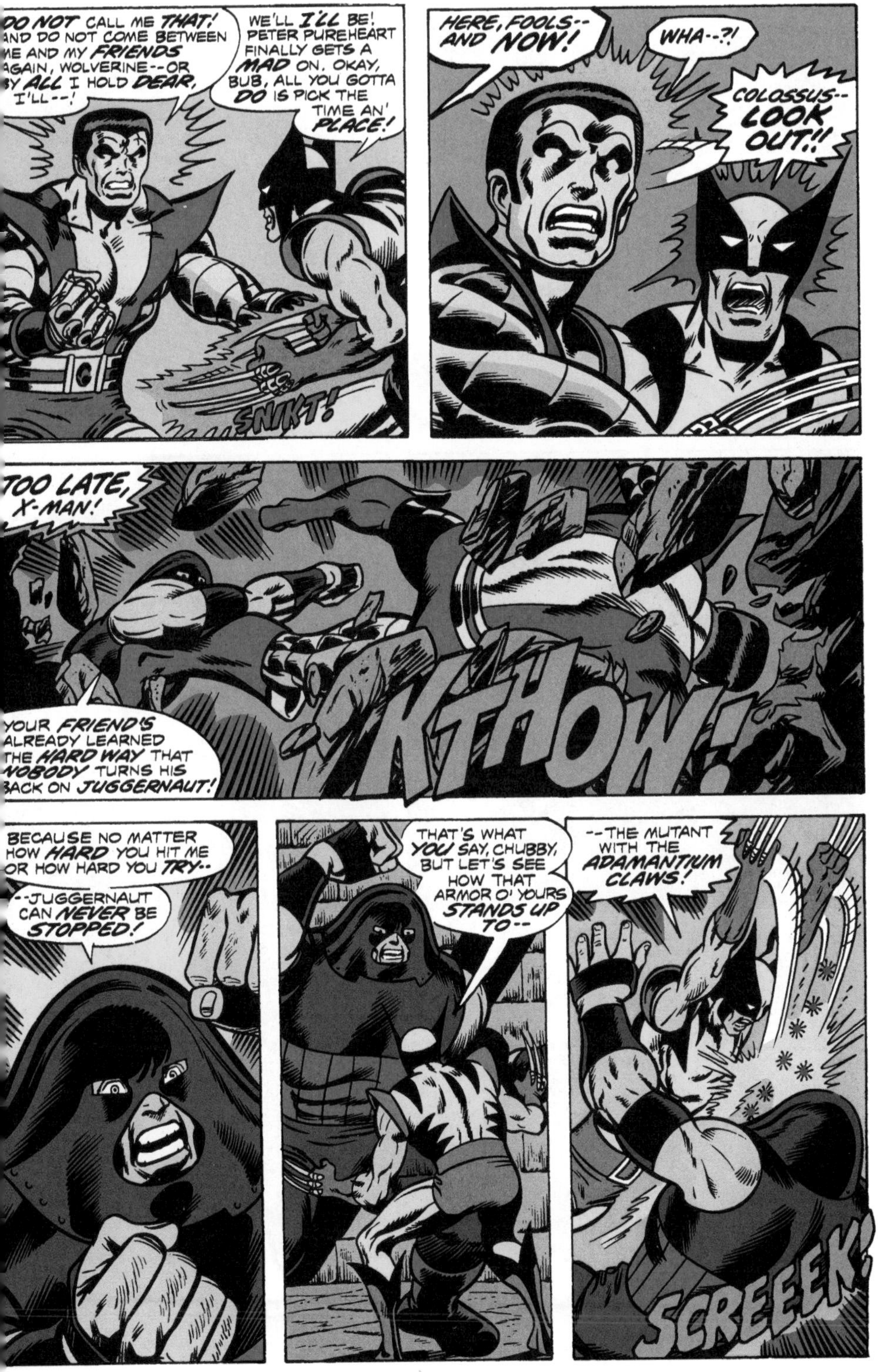
DO NOT CALL ME THAT! AND DO NOT COME BETWEEN ME AND MY FRIENDS AGAIN, WOLVERINE--OR BY ALL I HOLD DEAR, I'LL--!
WE'LL I'LL BE! PETER PUREHEART FINALLY GETS A MAD ON. OKAY, BUB, ALL YOU GOTTA DO IS PICK THE TIME AN' PLACE!
SNIKT!
HERE, FOOLS--AND NOW!
WHA--?!
COLOSSUS--LOOK OUT!!
TOO LATE, X-MAN!
YOUR FRIEND'S ALREADY LEARNED THE HARD WAY THAT NOBODY TURNS HIS BACK ON JUGGERNAUT!
KTHOW!
BECAUSE NO MATTER HOW HARD YOU HIT ME OR HOW HARD YOU TRY--
--JUGGERNAUT CAN NEVER BE STOPPED!
THAT'S WHAT YOU SAY, CHUBBY, BUT LET'S SEE HOW THAT ARMOR O' YOURS STANDS UP TO--
--THE MUTANT WITH THE ADAMANTIUM CLAWS!
SCREEEK!

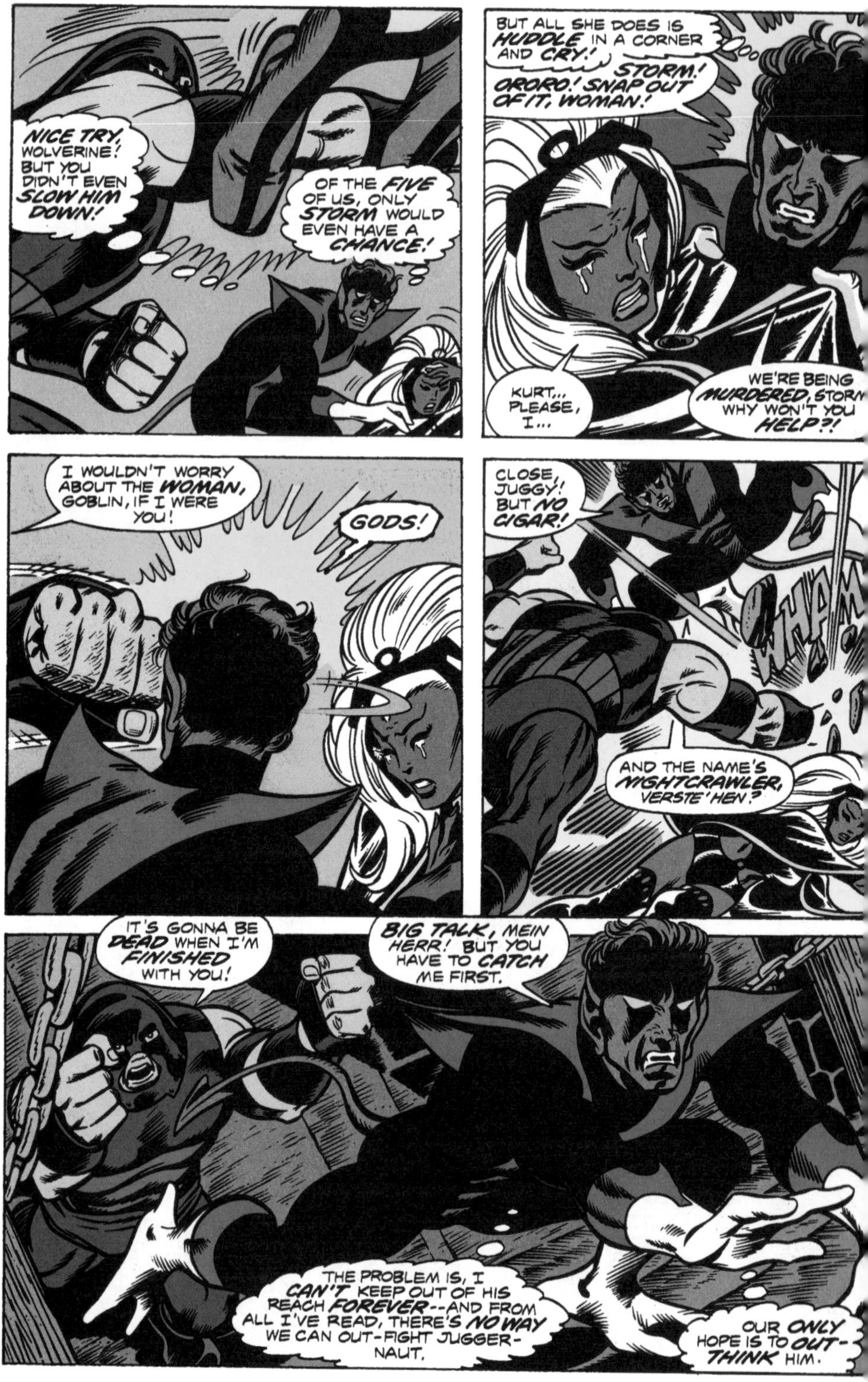
NICE TRY, WOLVERINE! BUT YOU DIDN'T EVEN SLOW HIM DOWN!
OF THE FIVE OF US, ONLY STORM WOULD EVEN HAVE A CHANCE!
BUT ALL SHE DOES IS HUDDLE IN A CORNER AND CRY!
STORM! ORORO! SNAP OUT OF IT, WOMAN!
KURT... PLEASE, I...
WE'RE BEING MURDERED, STORM! WHY WON'T YOU HELP?!
I WOULDN'T WORRY ABOUT THE WOMAN, GOBLIN, IF I WERE YOU!
GODS!
CLOSE, JUGGY! BUT NO CIGAR!
AND THE NAME'S NIGHTCRAWLER, VERSTE'HEN?
IT'S GONNA BE DEAD WHEN I'M FINISHED WITH YOU!
BIG TALK, MEIN HERR! BUT YOU HAVE TO CATCH ME FIRST.
THE PROBLEM IS, I CAN'T KEEP OUT OF HIS REACH FOREVER--AND FROM ALL I'VE READ, THERE'S NO WAY WE CAN OUT-FIGHT JUGGER-NAUT.
OUR ONLY HOPE IS TO OUT-THINK HIM.

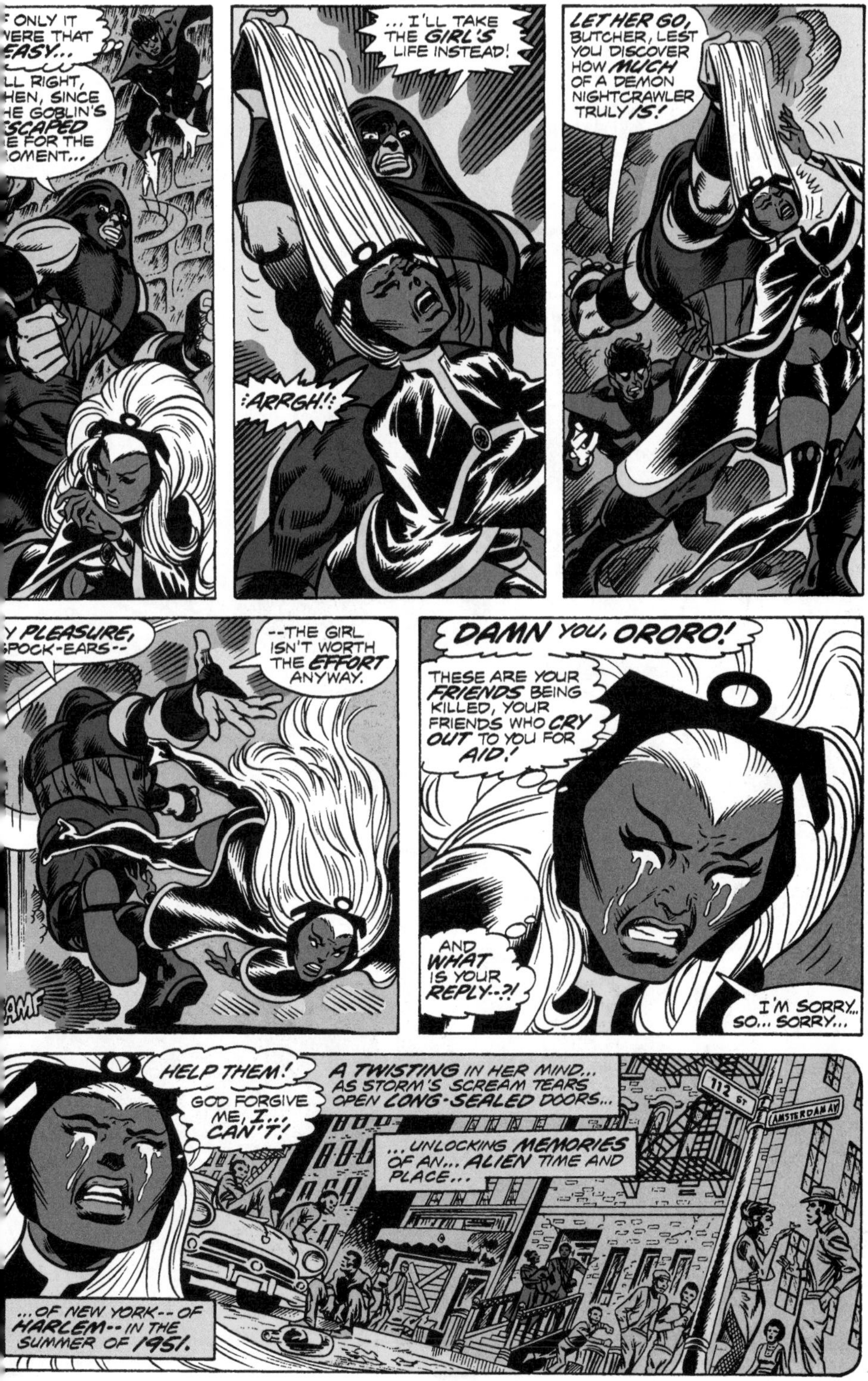
F ONLY IT WERE THAT EASY...
LL RIGHT, HEN, SINCE HE GOBLIN'S ESCAPED E FOR THE OMENT...
... I'LL TAKE THE GIRL'S LIFE INSTEAD!
ARRGH!
LET HER GO, BUTCHER, LEST YOU DISCOVER HOW MUCH OF A DEMON NIGHTCRAWLER TRULY IS!
Y PLEASURE, SPOCK-EARS--
--THE GIRL ISN'T WORTH THE EFFORT ANYWAY.
AMF
DAMN YOU, ORORO!
THESE ARE YOUR FRIENDS BEING KILLED, YOUR FRIENDS WHO CRY OUT TO YOU FOR AID!
AND WHAT IS YOUR REPLY--?!
I'M SORRY... SO... SORRY...
HELP THEM!
GOD FORGIVE ME, I... CAN'T!
A TWISTING IN HER MIND... AS STORM'S SCREAM TEARS OPEN LONG-SEALED DOORS...
... UNLOCKING MEMORIES OF AN... ALIEN TIME AND PLACE...
112 ST
AMSTERDAM AV
...OF NEW YORK-- OF HARLEM-- IN THE SUMMER OF 1951.

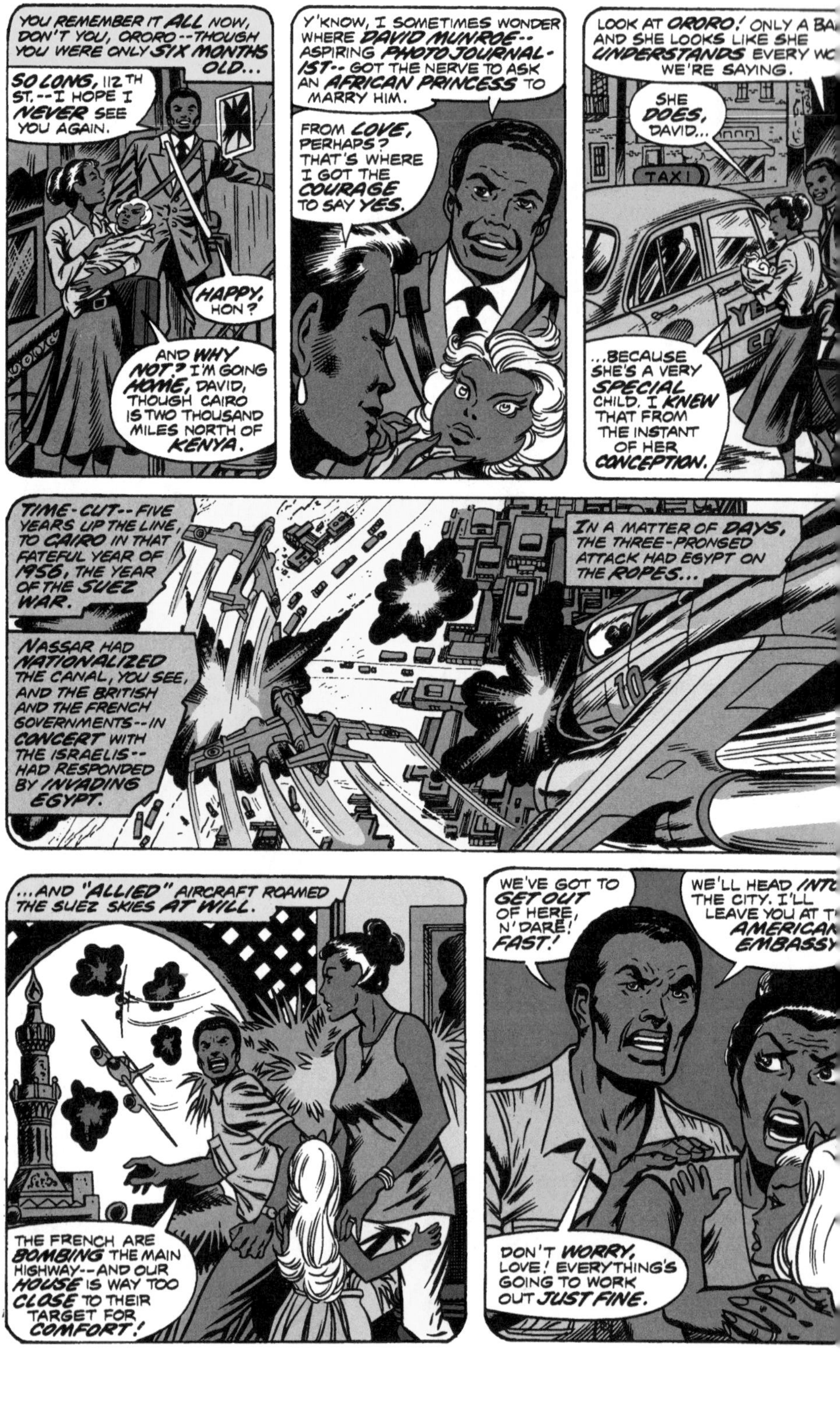
YOU REMEMBER IT ALL NOW, DON'T YOU, ORORO--THOUGH YOU WERE ONLY SIX MONTHS OLD...
SO LONG, 112TH ST.--I HOPE I NEVER SEE YOU AGAIN.
HAPPY, HON?
AND WHY NOT? I'M GOING HOME, DAVID, THOUGH CAIRO IS TWO THOUSAND MILES NORTH OF KENYA.
Y'KNOW, I SOMETIMES WONDER WHERE DAVID MUNROE--ASPIRING PHOTOJOURNAL-IST--GOT THE NERVE TO ASK AN AFRICAN PRINCESS TO MARRY HIM.
FROM LOVE, PERHAPS? THAT'S WHERE I GOT THE COURAGE TO SAY YES.
LOOK AT ORORO! ONLY A BA
AND SHE LOOKS LIKE SHE
UNDERSTANDS EVERY WO
WE'RE SAYING.
SHE DOES, DAVID...
TAXI
...BECAUSE SHE'S A VERY SPECIAL CHILD. I KNEW THAT FROM THE INSTANT OF HER CONCEPTION.
TIME-CUT--FIVE YEARS UP THE LINE, TO CAIRO IN THAT FATEFUL YEAR OF 1956, THE YEAR OF THE SUEZ WAR.
NASSAR HAD NATIONALIZED THE CANAL, YOU SEE, AND THE BRITISH AND THE FRENCH GOVERNMENTS--IN CONCERT WITH THE ISRAELIS--HAD RESPONDED BY INVADING EGYPT.
IN A MATTER OF DAYS, THE THREE-PRONGED ATTACK HAD EGYPT ON THE ROPES...
...AND "ALLIED" AIRCRAFT ROAMED THE SUEZ SKIES AT WILL.
THE FRENCH ARE BOMBING THE MAIN HIGHWAY--AND OUR HOUSE IS WAY TOO CLOSE TO THEIR TARGET FOR COMFORT!
WE'VE GOT TO GET OUT OF HERE, N'DARE! FAST!
WE'LL HEAD INTO
THE CITY. I'LL
LEAVE YOU AT T
AMERICAN
EMBASSY
DON'T WORRY, LOVE! EVERYTHING'S GOING TO WORK OUT JUST FINE.

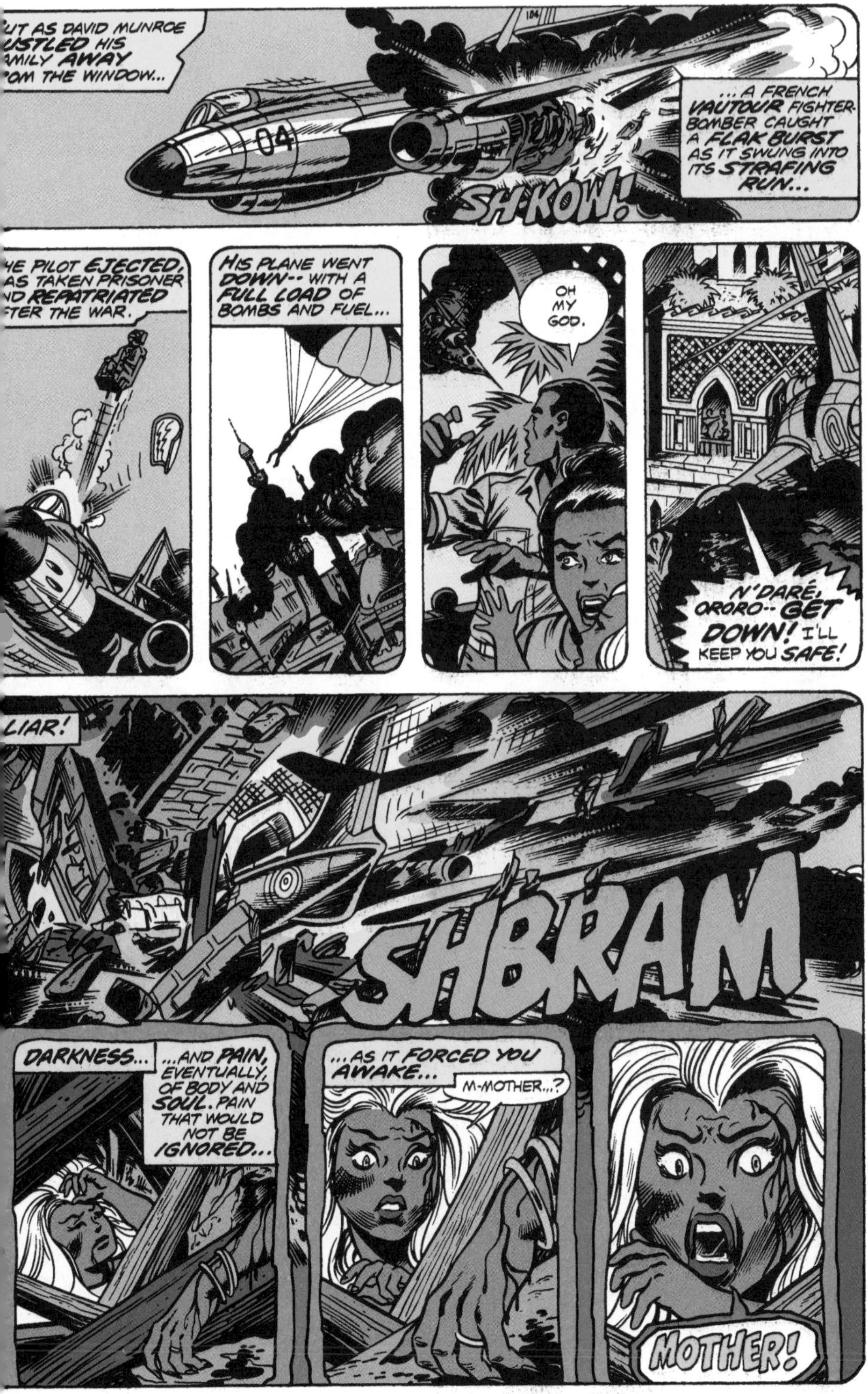
UT AS DAVID MUNROE USTLED HIS AMILY AWAY OM THE WINDOW...
...A FRENCH VAUTOUR FIGHTER-BOMBER CAUGHT A FLAK BURST AS IT SWUNG INTO ITS STRAFING RUN...
SH-KOW!
HE PILOT EJECTED, AS TAKEN PRISONER ND REPATRIATED FTER THE WAR.
HIS PLANE WENT DOWN-- WITH A FULL LOAD OF BOMBS AND FUEL...
OH MY GOD.
N'DARÉ, ORORO-- GET DOWN! I'LL KEEP YOU SAFE!
LIAR!
SHBRAM
DARKNESS...
...AND PAIN, EVENTUALLY, OF BODY AND SOUL. PAIN THAT WOULD NOT BE IGNORED...
...AS IT FORCED YOU AWAKE...
M-MOTHER...?
MOTHER!

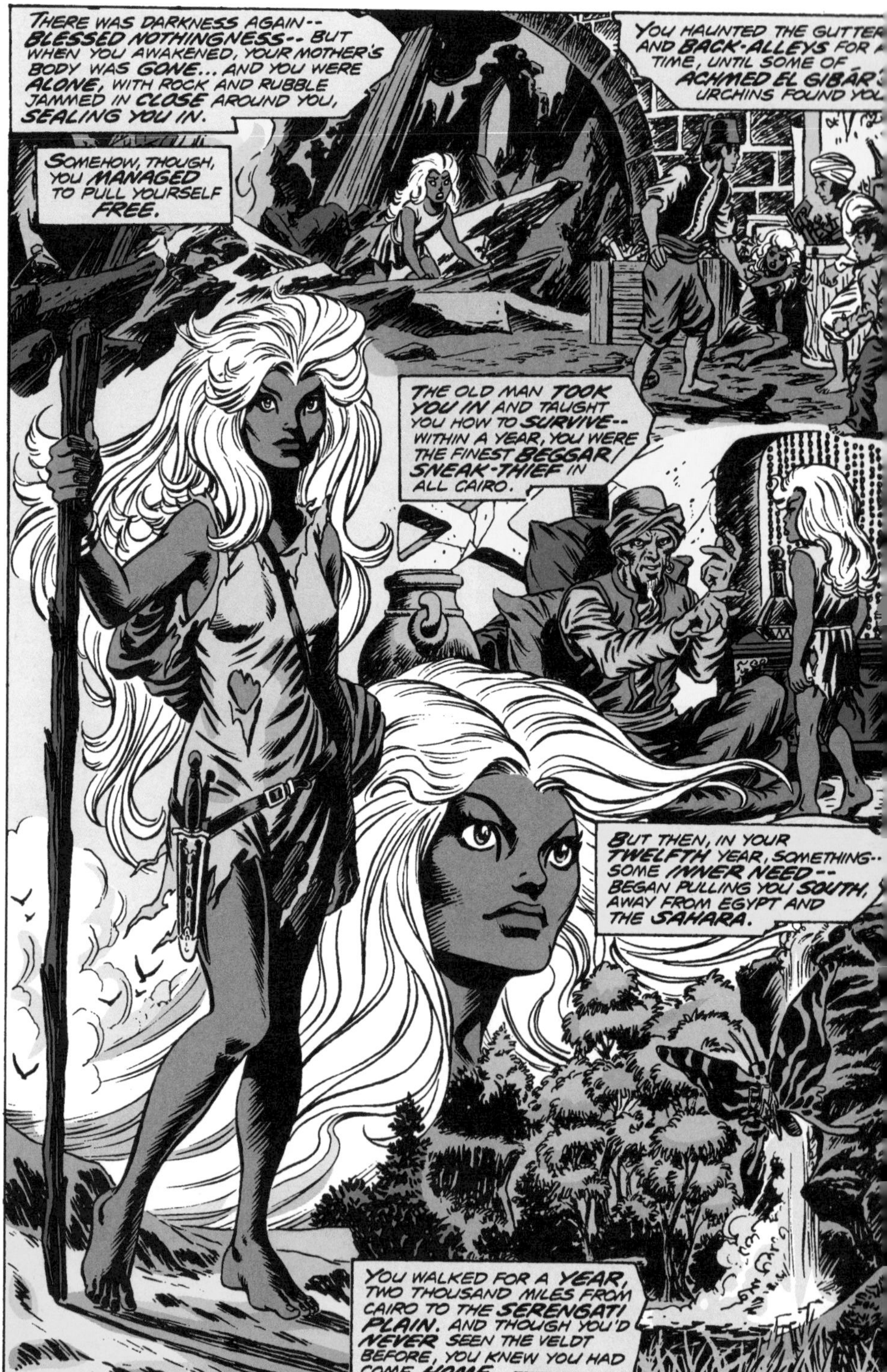
THERE WAS DARKNESS AGAIN-- BLESSED NOTHINGNESS-- BUT WHEN YOU AWAKENED, YOUR MOTHER'S BODY WAS GONE... AND YOU WERE ALONE, WITH ROCK AND RUBBLE JAMMED IN CLOSE AROUND YOU, SEALING YOU IN.
SOMEHOW, THOUGH, YOU MANAGED TO PULL YOURSELF FREE.
YOU HAUNTED THE GUTTER AND BACK-ALLEYS FOR A TIME, UNTIL SOME OF ACHMED EL GIBĀR'S URCHINS FOUND YOU
THE OLD MAN TOOK YOU IN AND TAUGHT YOU HOW TO SURVIVE-- WITHIN A YEAR, YOU WERE THE FINEST BEGGAR/ SNEAK-THIEF IN ALL CAIRO.
BUT THEN, IN YOUR TWELFTH YEAR, SOMETHING-- SOME INNER NEED-- BEGAN PULLING YOU SOUTH, AWAY FROM EGYPT AND THE SAHARA.
YOU WALKED FOR A YEAR, TWO THOUSAND MILES FROM CAIRO TO THE SERENGATI PLAIN. AND THOUGH YOU'D NEVER SEEN THE VELDT BEFORE, YOU KNEW YOU HAD COME HOME.

...ERE YOU HAD REMAINED-- THE GIRL GROWING INTO A WOMAN, ALL MEMORIES OF YOUR PAST LIFE FADING WITH THE PASSAGE OF THE YEARS-- CONTENT IN YOUR SOLITUDE...

...UNTIL CHARLES XAVIER HAD COME TO LEAD THE GODDESS FROM HER NEST...

AN OCEAN AWAY, THAT SELF-SAME PROFESSOR XAVIER STIRS...

WHAT...? I THOUGHT I HEARD SOMEONE CALL MY NAME.... BUT SO FAINT... FAR-AWAY...

IT'S...STORM!

IMAGES FLOODING MY SENSES THROUGH THE TELEPATHIC RAPPORT I SHARE WITH MY STUDENTS-- I-- CAN FEEL HER PAIN... AND.... FEAR! AND... DOMINATING HER EVERY THOUGHT IS THE FACE OF-- CAIN MARKO!

SCOTT, IT'S IMPERATIVE I SPEAK WITH YOU, OUT IN THE CORRIDOR.

HUH--? CERTAINLY, PROFESSOR. I'LL BE RIGHT WITH YOU.

BUT IN THE MEANTIME, THIS IS A PERFECT OPPORTUNITY TO INTRODUCE MY NEW YORK ROOMMATE.

CHARLES XAVIER, MEET MISTY KNIGHT.

MY PLEASURE.

SCOTT, IF YOU PLEASE -- EVERY SECOND IS VITAL.

WELL, I'LL BE--! I'M SORRY FOR THAT, MISTY.

I'VE NEVER SEEN THE PROFESSOR THIS BRUSQUE AND...RUDE BEFORE.

THAT'S OKAY. IT'S YOU I'M WORRIED ABOUT. SOMETHING'S BEEN EATIN' YOU UP INSIDE EVER SINCE THAT SPACE FLIGHT. WHAT IS IT, JEAN? I'D LIKE TO HELP.

I KNOW.

SO TELL ME, MISTY KNIGHT...

...HOW WOULD YOU FEEL IF YOU'D...DIED. THEN BROUGHT YOURSELF BACK TO LIFE?

PLACE-CUT--TO A NEARBY ANTEROOM...

THE X-MEN HAVE BEEN *AMBUSHED* BY *JUGGERNAUT.*

YOU MUST LEAVE FOR IRELAND *IMMEDIATELY* AND GIVE THEM WHAT *ASSISTANCE* YOU CAN.

NO, PROFESSOR, NOT THIS TIME.

I'M STAYING HERE AT THE *HOSPITAL* UNTIL JEAN IS *OUT OF DANGER.*

YOU'RE--*WHAT?!*

YOU'RE PUTTING THE LIFE OF *ONE WOMAN* AHEAD OF THOSE OF YOUR *FELLOW X-MEN?!*

I AM. BECAUSE THAT WOMAN IS THE MOST *IMPORTANT* THING IN MY LIFE.

BESIDES THERE'S *NOTHING* I CAN DO TO HELP THE X-MEN, *NO WAY* I CAN GET TO THEM IN TIME TO MAKE A *DIFFERENCE.*

AND *YOU YOURSELF* HAVE SAID THAT, SOONER OR LATER, THE *NEW* TEAM IS GOING TO HAVE TO LEARN TO FIGHT *ON ITS OWN.*

CALLOUS AS IT SOUNDS, IT LOOKS LIKE THAT TIME IS *NOW.*

HOW-- *DARE--* YOU!?!

YOU *UNGRATEFUL,* UNSPEAKABLE--*CUR* I TOOK YOU *IN!* GAVE YOU-- GAVE --I-- *SCOTT!!*

PROFESSOR, WHAT *IS* IT?!

NO! NOT MY *MIND!* NOT *AGAIN!*

MADNESS. IMAGES / SENSATIONS / EMOTIONS RUNNING *RIOT* IN CHARLES XAVIER'S MIND...

THE FACE IN THE *MIRROR!* OH, MY *GOD,* SCOTT--

--IT'S THE FACE IN MY *DREAM!!*

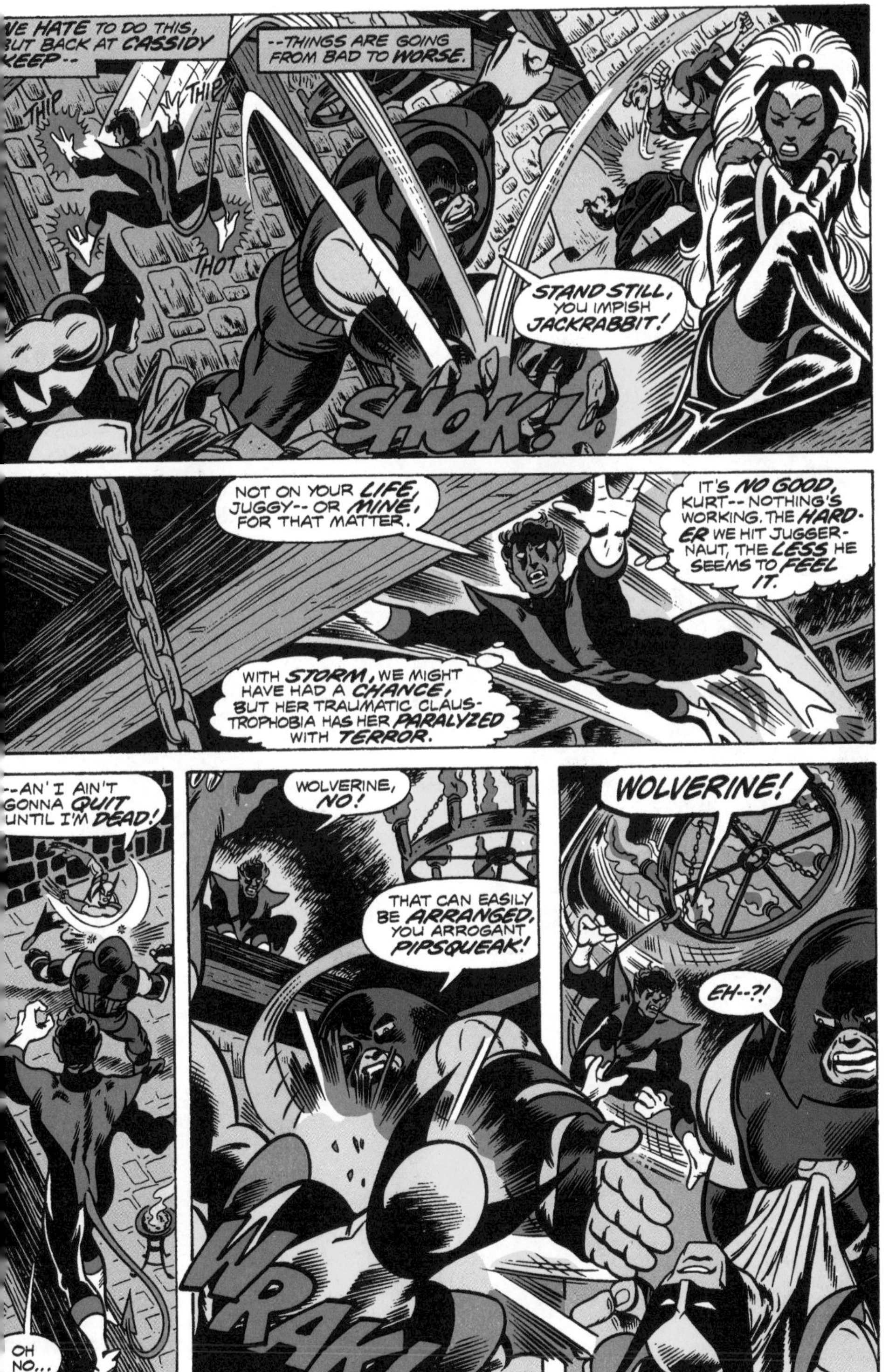
WE HATE TO DO THIS, BUT BACK AT CASSIDY KEEP--
--THINGS ARE GOING FROM BAD TO WORSE.
THIP
THIP
THOT
STAND STILL, YOU IMPISH JACKRABBIT!
SHOK!!
NOT ON YOUR LIFE, JUGGY-- OR MINE, FOR THAT MATTER.
IT'S NO GOOD, KURT-- NOTHING'S WORKING. THE HARDER WE HIT JUGGERNAUT, THE LESS HE SEEMS TO FEEL IT.
WITH STORM, WE MIGHT HAVE HAD A CHANCE, BUT HER TRAUMATIC CLAUSTROPHOBIA HAS HER PARALYZED WITH TERROR.
--AN' I AIN'T GONNA QUIT UNTIL I'M DEAD!
OH NO...
WOLVERINE, NO!
THAT CAN EASILY BE ARRANGED, YOU ARROGANT PIPSQUEAK!
WRAK!
WOLVERINE!
EH--?!

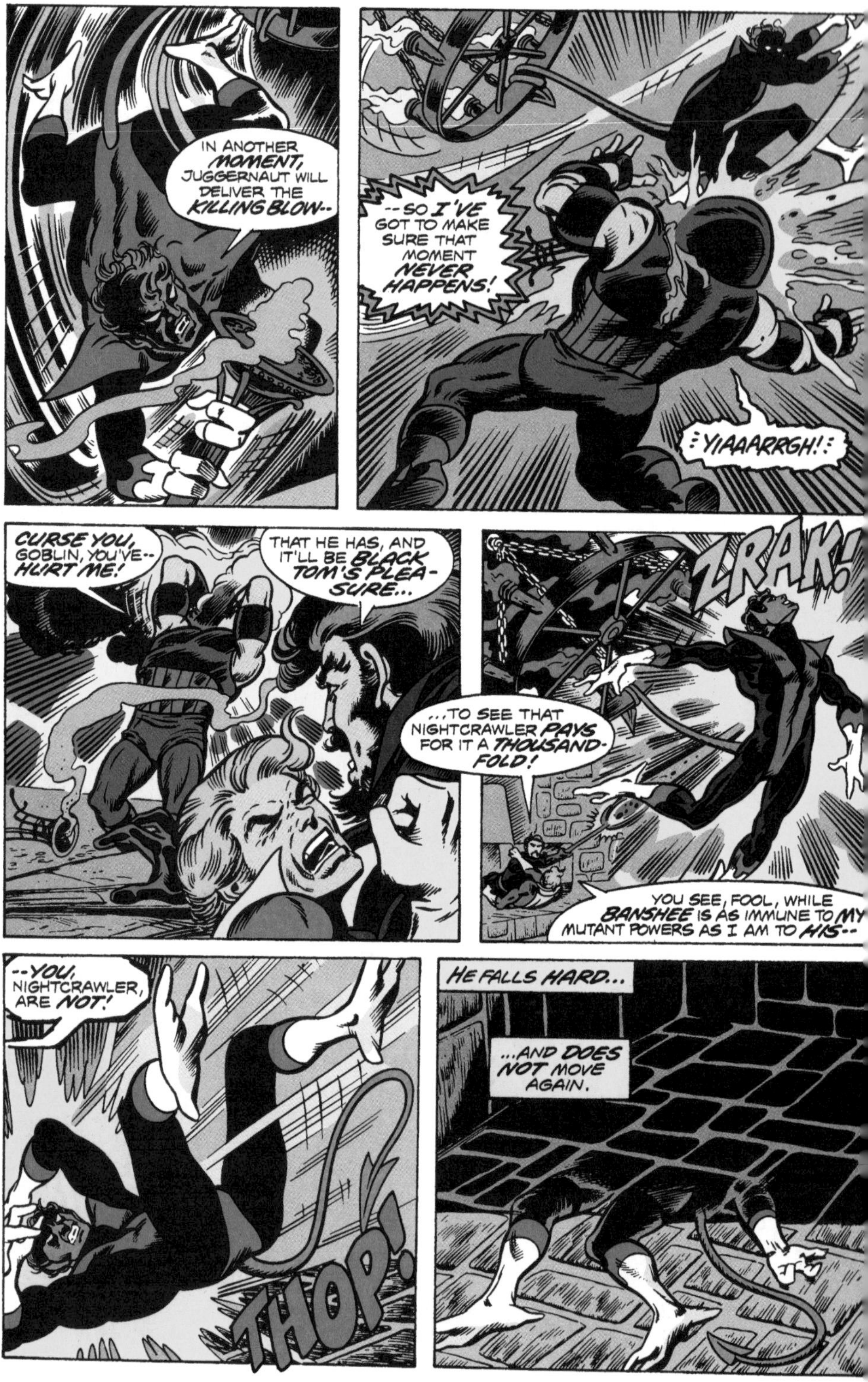
IN ANOTHER MOMENT, JUGGERNAUT WILL DELIVER THE KILLING BLOW--
--SO I'VE GOT TO MAKE SURE THAT MOMENT NEVER HAPPENS!
YIAAARRGH!
CURSE YOU, GOBLIN, YOU'VE-- HURT ME!
THAT HE HAS, AND IT'LL BE BLACK TOM'S PLEASURE...
...TO SEE THAT NIGHTCRAWLER PAYS FOR IT A THOUSAND-FOLD!
ZRAK!
YOU SEE, FOOL, WHILE BANSHEE IS AS IMMUNE TO MY MUTANT POWERS AS I AM TO HIS--
--YOU, NIGHTCRAWLER, ARE NOT!
THOP!
HE FALLS HARD...
...AND DOES NOT MOVE AGAIN.

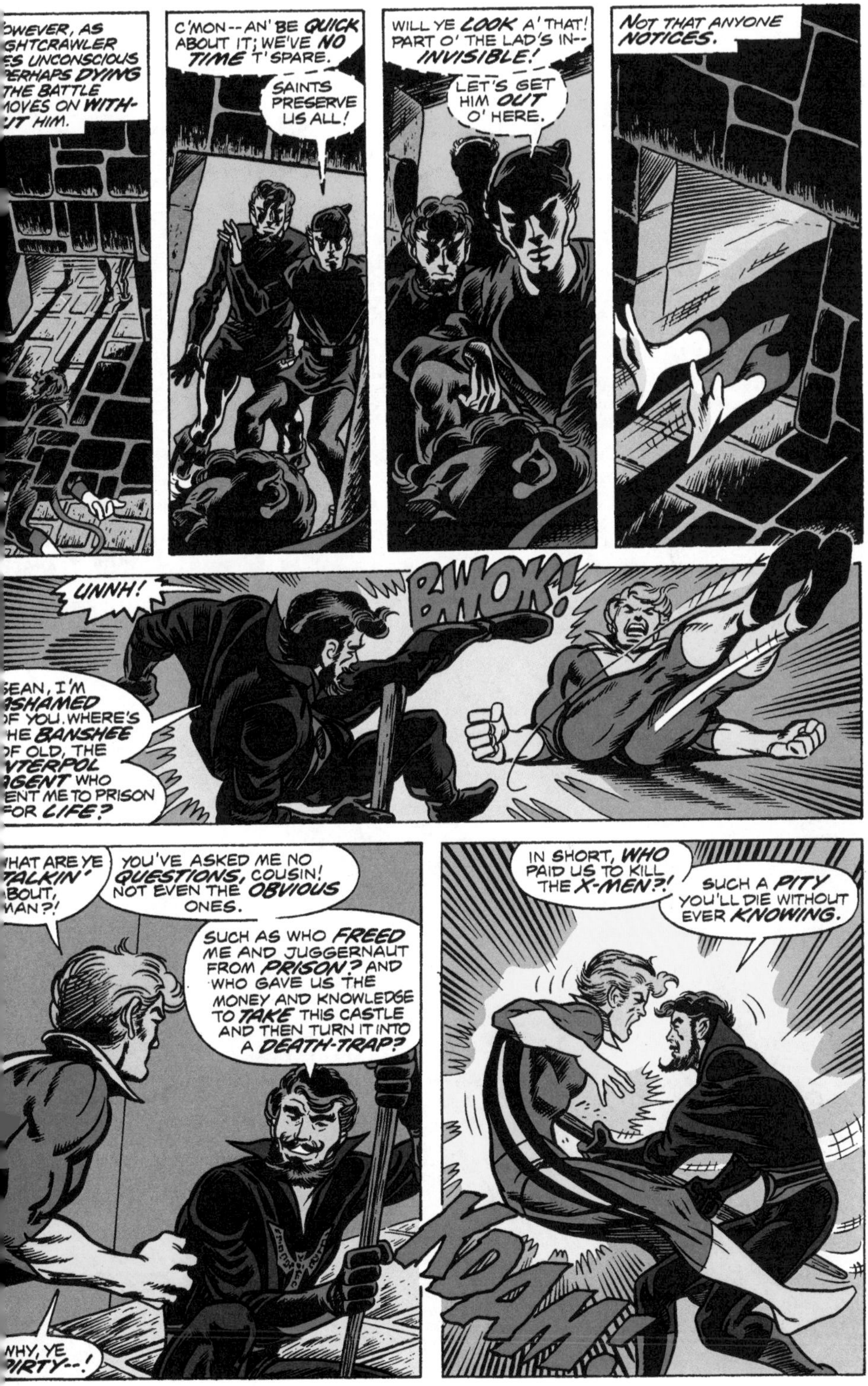
OWEVER, AS GHTCRAWLER ES UNCONSCIOUS ERHAPS DYING THE BATTLE MOVES ON WITH- UT HIM.
C'MON -- AN' BE QUICK ABOUT IT; WE'VE NO TIME T' SPARE.
SAINTS PRESERVE US ALL!
WILL YE LOOK A' THAT! PART O' THE LAD'S IN-- INVISIBLE!
LET'S GET HIM OUT O' HERE.
NOT THAT ANYONE NOTICES.
UNNH!
BWOK!
SEAN, I'M ASHAMED OF YOU. WHERE'S HE BANSHEE OF OLD, THE TERPOL AGENT WHO ENT ME TO PRISON FOR LIFE?
HAT ARE YE TALKIN' BOUT, MAN?!
YOU'VE ASKED ME NO QUESTIONS, COUSIN! NOT EVEN THE OBVIOUS ONES.
SUCH AS WHO FREED ME AND JUGGERNAUT FROM PRISON? AND WHO GAVE US THE MONEY AND KNOWLEDGE TO TAKE THIS CASTLE AND THEN TURN IT INTO A DEATH-TRAP?
WHY, YE DIRTY--!
IN SHORT, WHO PAID US TO KILL THE X-MEN?!
SUCH A PITY YOU'LL DIE WITHOUT EVER KNOWING.
KDAM!

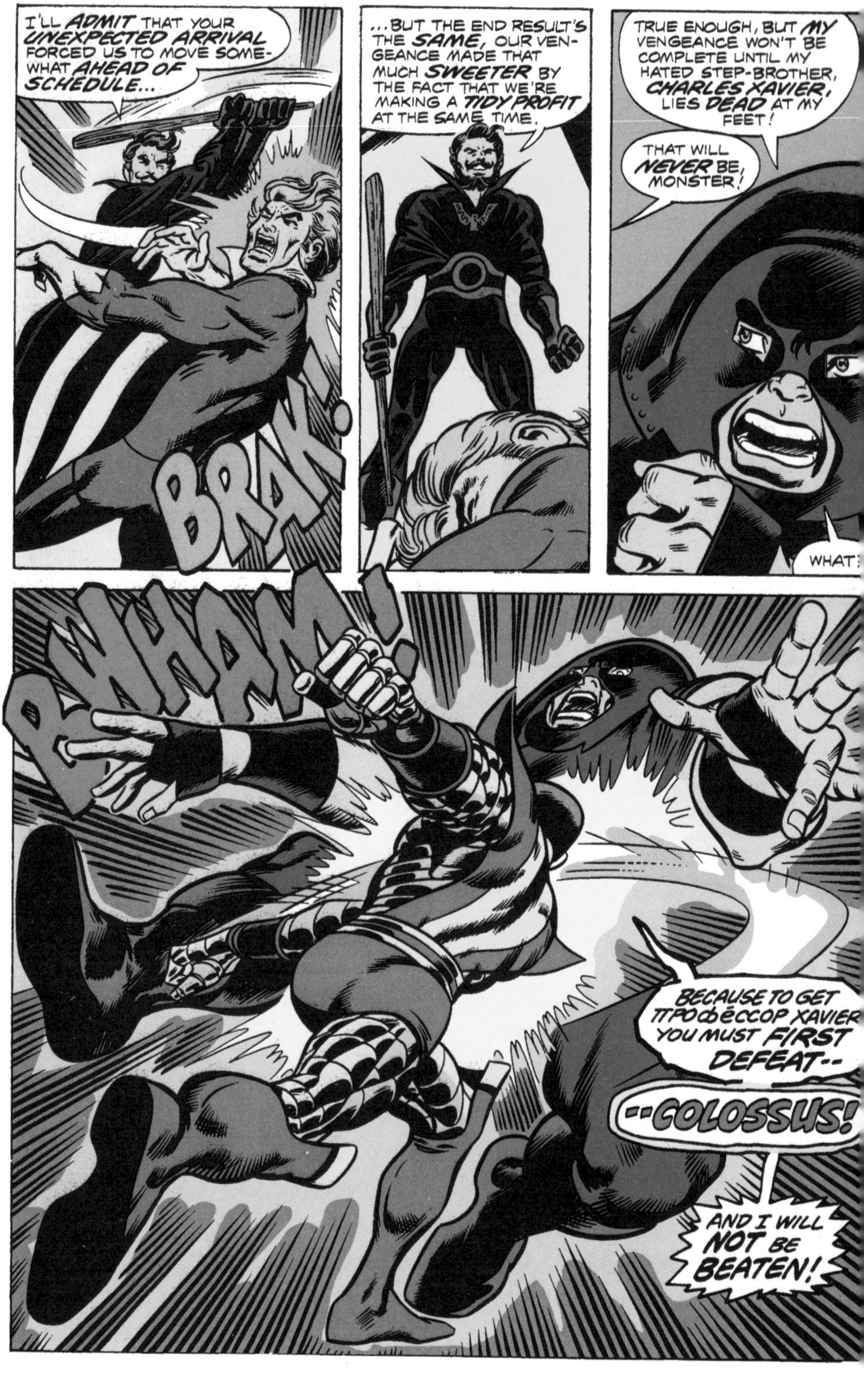
I'LL ADMIT THAT YOUR UNEXPECTED ARRIVAL FORCED US TO MOVE SOMEWHAT AHEAD OF SCHEDULE...
BRAK!
...BUT THE END RESULT'S THE SAME, OUR VENGEANCE MADE THAT MUCH SWEETER BY THE FACT THAT WE'RE MAKING A TIDY PROFIT AT THE SAME TIME.
TRUE ENOUGH, BUT MY VENGEANCE WON'T BE COMPLETE UNTIL MY HATED STEP-BROTHER, CHARLES XAVIER, LIES DEAD AT MY FEET!
THAT WILL NEVER BE, MONSTER!
WHAT?
BWHAM!
BECAUSE TO GET ПРОФЕССОР XAVIER YOU MUST FIRST DEFEAT--
--COLOSSUS!
AND I WILL NOT BE BEATEN!

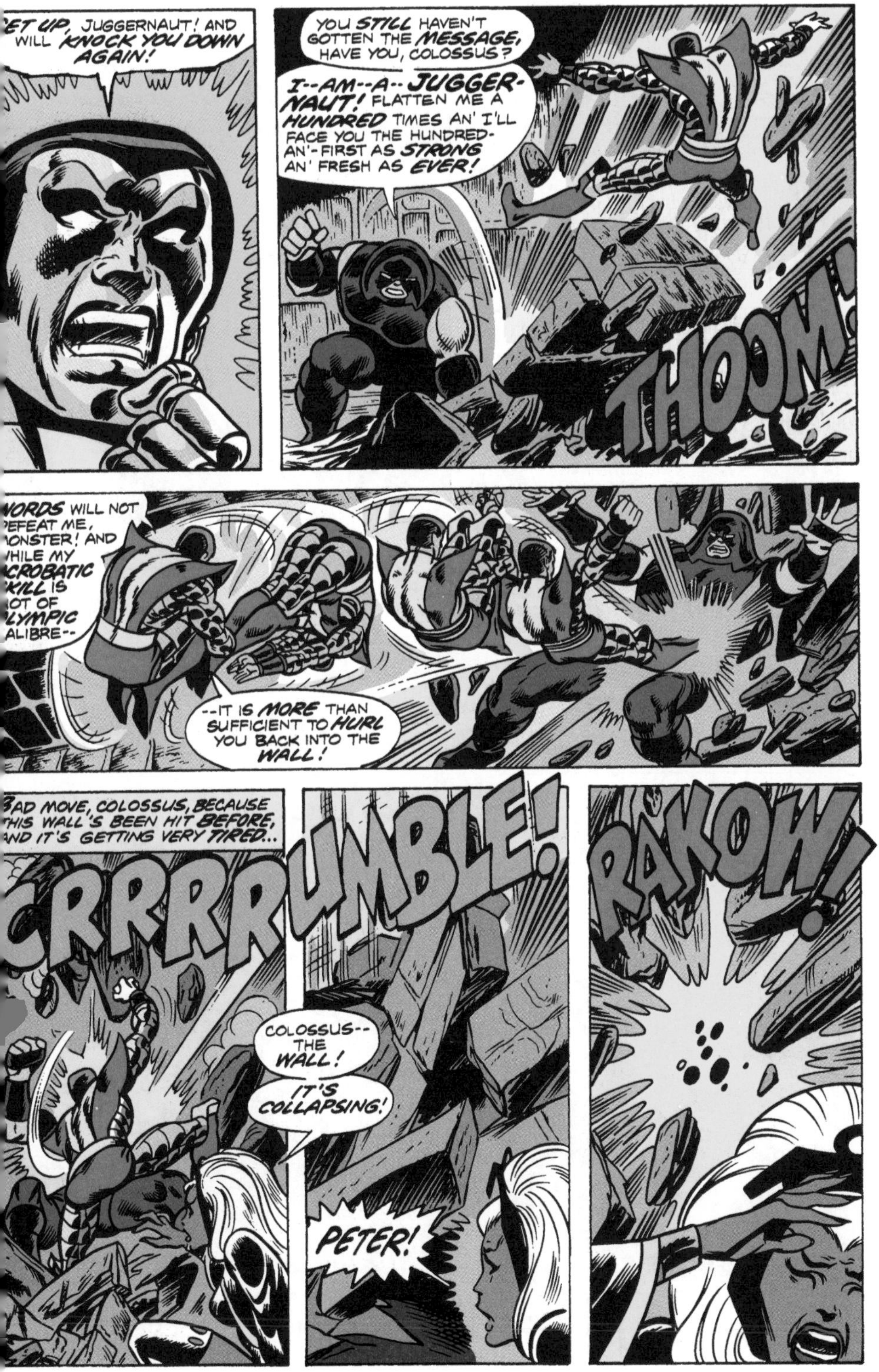
ET UP, JUGGERNAUT! AND WILL KNOCK YOU DOWN AGAIN!
YOU STILL HAVEN'T GOTTEN THE MESSAGE, HAVE YOU, COLOSSUS?
I--AM--A--JUGGERNAUT! FLATTEN ME A HUNDRED TIMES AN' I'LL FACE YOU THE HUNDRED-AN'-FIRST AS STRONG AN' FRESH AS EVER!
THOOM!
ORDS WILL NOT EFEAT ME, ONSTER! AND HILE MY CROBATIC KILL IS OT OF LYMPIC ALIBRE--
--IT IS MORE THAN SUFFICIENT TO HURL YOU BACK INTO THE WALL!
AD MOVE, COLOSSUS, BECAUSE THIS WALL'S BEEN HIT BEFORE, AND IT'S GETTING VERY TIRED...
CRRRRRUMBLE!
COLOSSUS--THE WALL!
IT'S COLLAPSING!
PETER!
RAKOW!

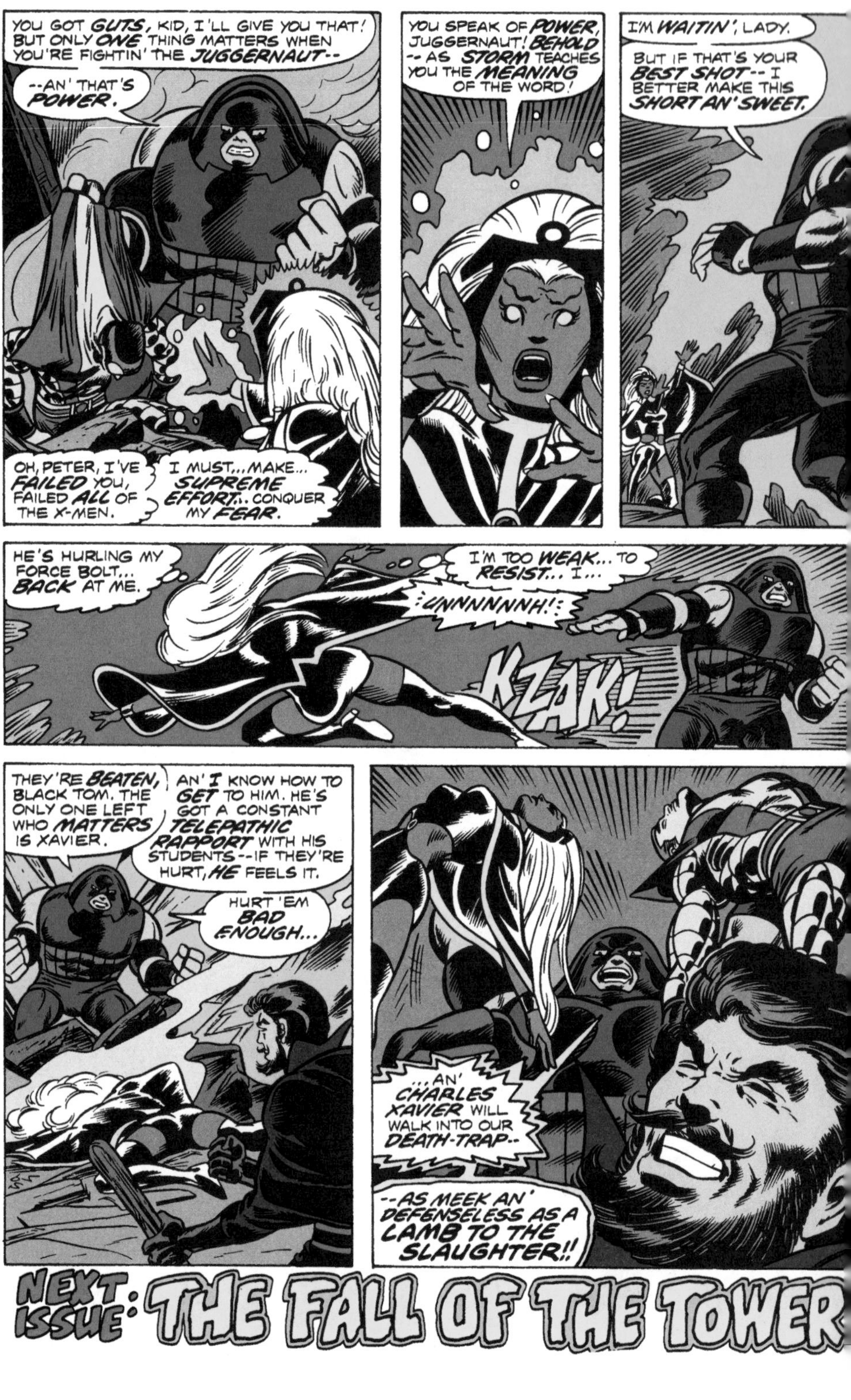
YOU GOT GUTS, KID, I'LL GIVE YOU THAT! BUT ONLY ONE THING MATTERS WHEN YOU'RE FIGHTIN' THE JUGGERNAUT--
--AN' THAT'S POWER.
OH, PETER, I'VE FAILED YOU, FAILED ALL OF THE X-MEN.
I MUST... MAKE... SUPREME EFFORT.. CONQUER MY FEAR.
YOU SPEAK OF POWER, JUGGERNAUT! BEHOLD -- AS STORM TEACHES YOU THE MEANING OF THE WORD!
I'M WAITIN', LADY.
BUT IF THAT'S YOUR BEST SHOT-- I BETTER MAKE THIS SHORT AN' SWEET.
HE'S HURLING MY FORCE BOLT... BACK AT ME.
I'M TOO WEAK... TO RESIST... I...
UNNNNNNH!
KZAK!
THEY'RE BEATEN, BLACK TOM. THE ONLY ONE LEFT WHO MATTERS IS XAVIER.
AN' I KNOW HOW TO GET TO HIM. HE'S GOT A CONSTANT TELEPATHIC RAPPORT WITH HIS STUDENTS--IF THEY'RE HURT, HE FEELS IT.
HURT 'EM BAD ENOUGH...
...AN' CHARLES XAVIER WILL WALK INTO OUR DEATH-TRAP--
--AS MEEK AN' DEFENSELESS AS A LAMB TO THE SLAUGHTER!!
NEXT ISSUE: THE FALL OF THE TOWER

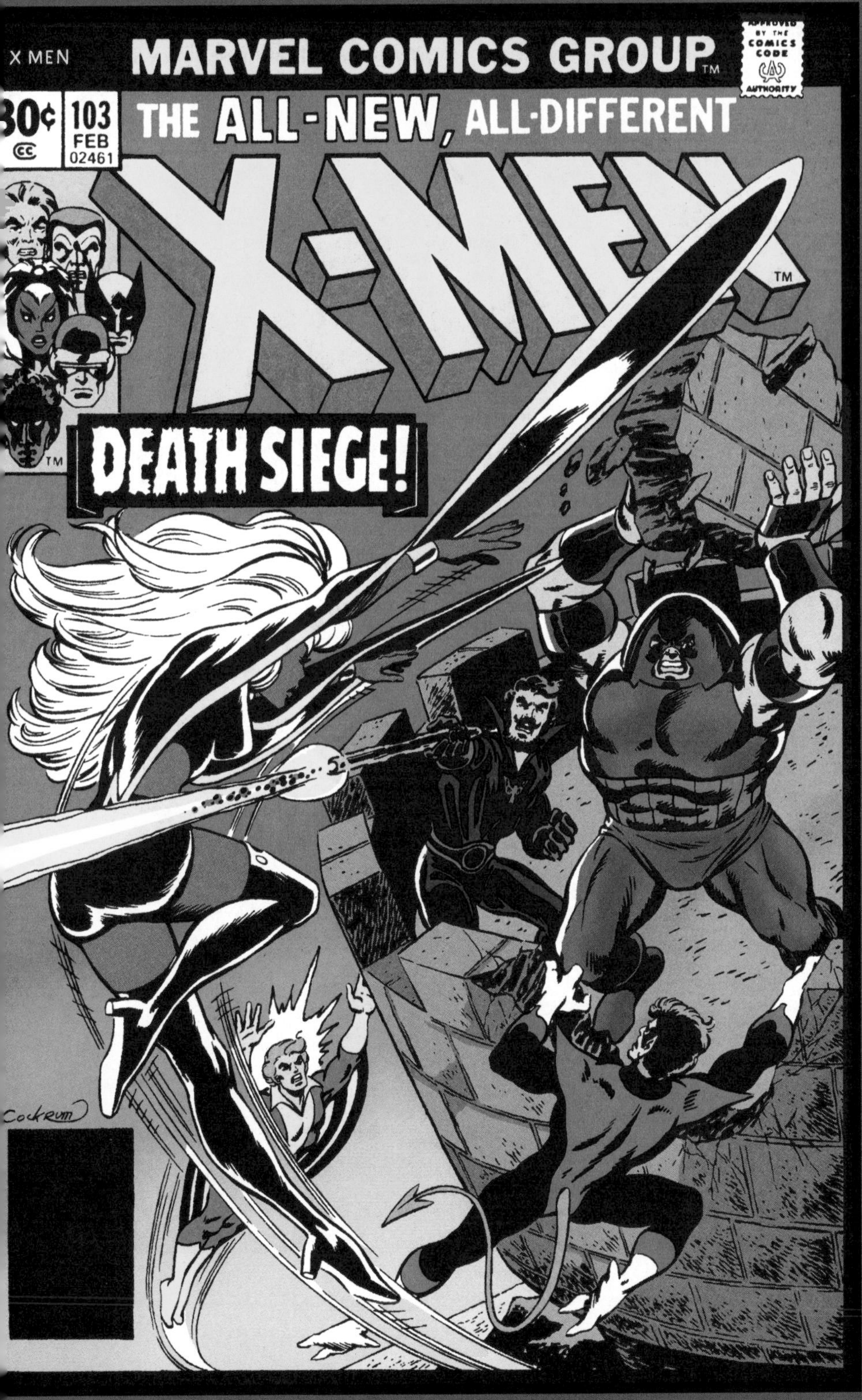
X MEN
MARVEL COMICS GROUP
APPROVED BY THE COMICS CODE AUTHORITY
30¢
CC
103
FEB
02461
THE ALL-NEW, ALL-DIFFERENT
X-MEN
DEATH SIEGE!
COCKRUM

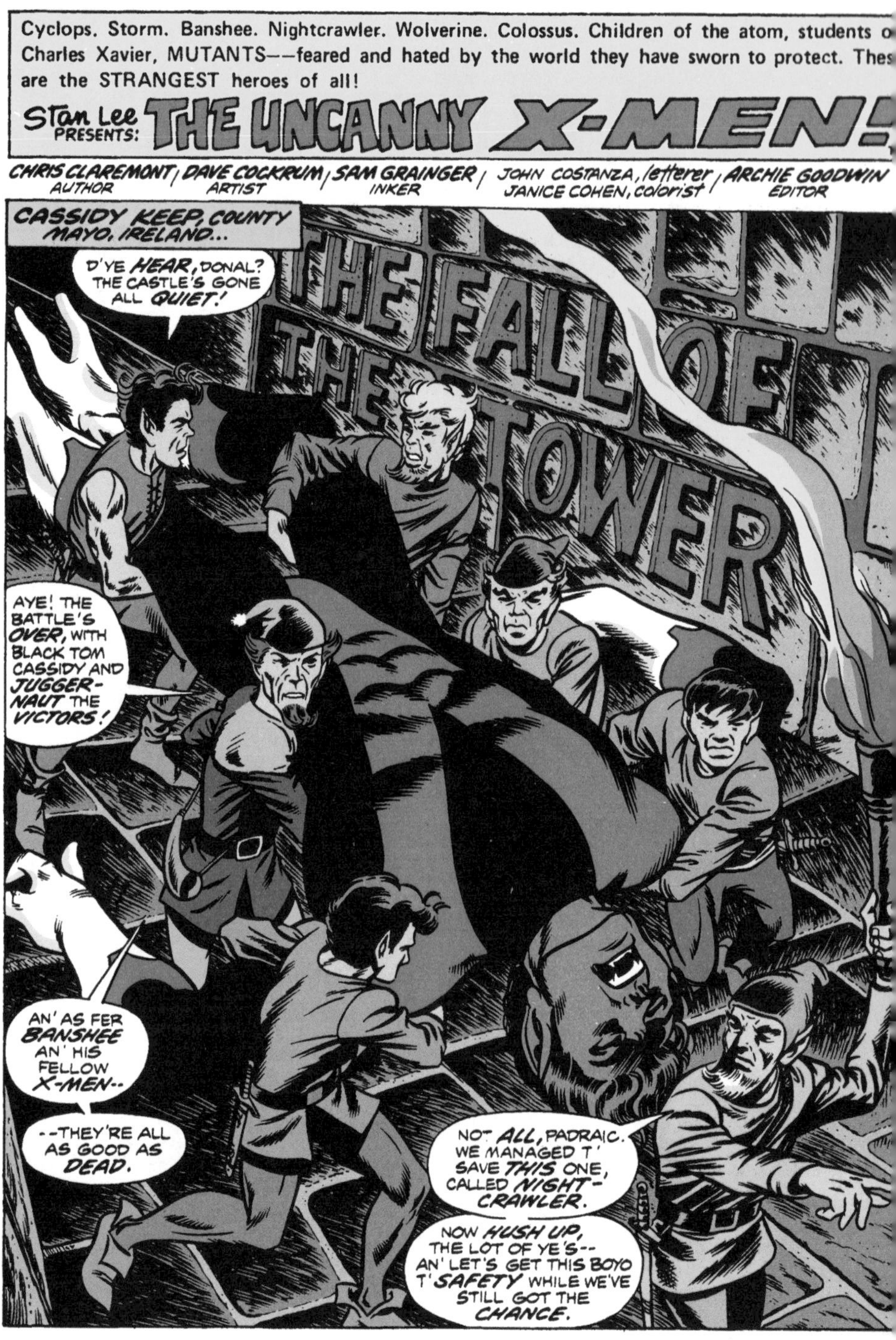

Cyclops. Storm. Banshee. Nightcrawler. Wolverine. Colossus. Children of the atom, students o
Charles Xavier, MUTANTS——feared and hated by the world they have sworn to protect. Thes
are the STRANGEST heroes of all!
Stan Lee PRESENTS: THE UNCANNY X-MEN!
CHRIS CLAREMONT / AUTHOR
DAVE COCKRUM / ARTIST
SAM GRAINGER / INKER
JOHN COSTANZA, letterer / JANICE COHEN, colorist
ARCHIE GOODWIN / EDITOR
CASSIDY KEEP, COUNTY MAYO, IRELAND...
D'YE HEAR, DONAL? THE CASTLE'S GONE ALL QUIET!
THE FALL OF THE TOWER
AYE! THE BATTLE'S OVER, WITH BLACK TOM CASSIDY AND JUGGER-NAUT THE VICTORS!
AN' AS FER BANSHEE AN' HIS FELLOW X-MEN--
--THEY'RE ALL AS GOOD AS DEAD.
NOT ALL, PADRAIC. WE MANAGED T' SAVE THIS ONE, CALLED NIGHT-CRAWLER.
NOW HUSH UP, THE LOT OF YE'S-- AN' LET'S GET THIS BOYO T' SAFETY WHILE WE'VE STILL GOT THE CHANCE.

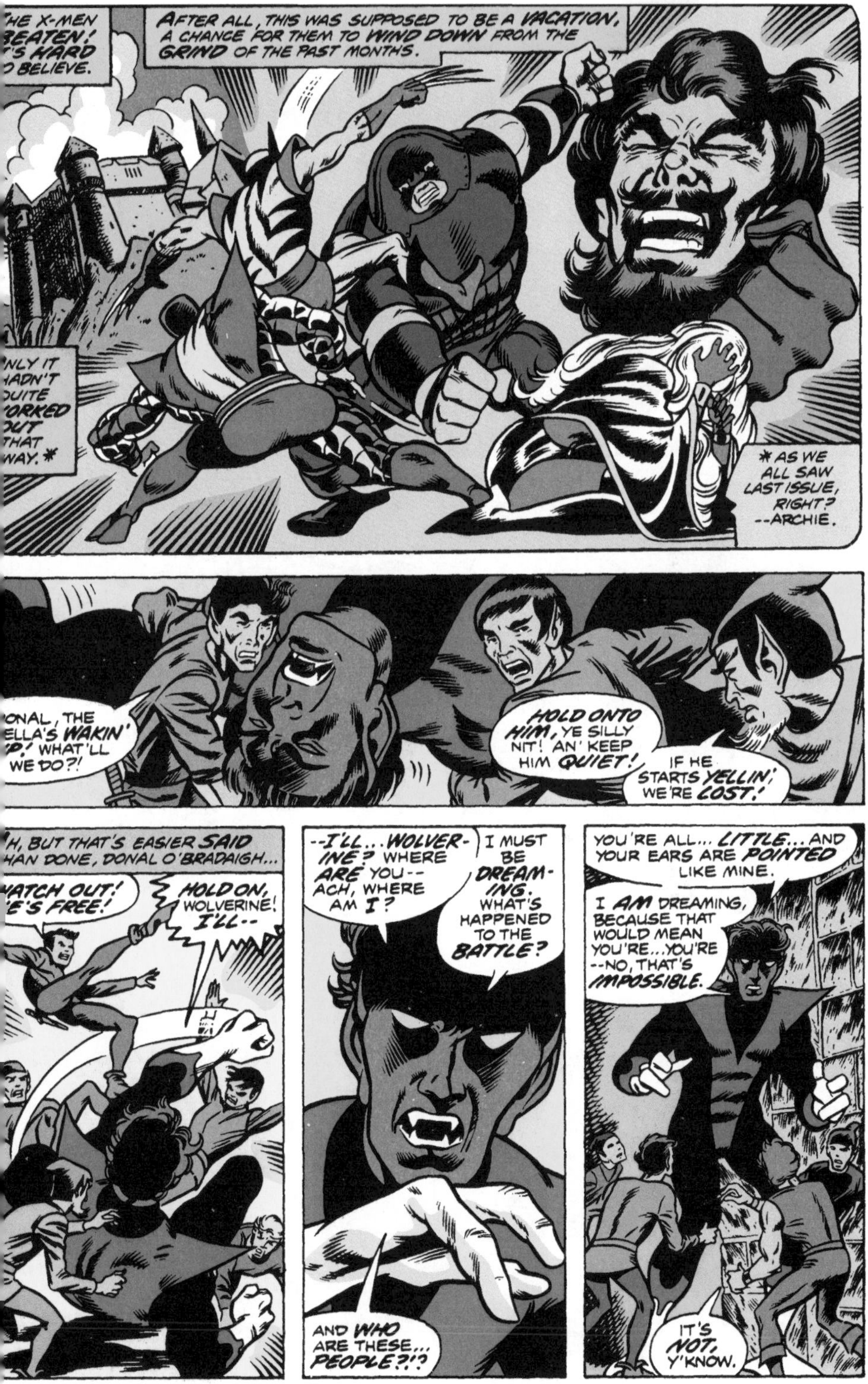
HE X-MEN BEATEN! 'S HARD O BELIEVE.
AFTER ALL, THIS WAS SUPPOSED TO BE A VACATION, A CHANCE FOR THEM TO WIND DOWN FROM THE GRIND OF THE PAST MONTHS.
NLY IT HADN'T UITE ORKED OUT THAT WAY. *
* AS WE ALL SAW LAST ISSUE, RIGHT? --ARCHIE.
ONAL, THE ELLA'S WAKIN' P! WHAT'LL WE DO?!
HOLD ONTO HIM, YE SILLY NIT! AN' KEEP HIM QUIET!
IF HE STARTS YELLIN', WE'RE LOST!
H, BUT THAT'S EASIER SAID HAN DONE, DONAL O'BRADAIGH...
ATCH OUT! E'S FREE!
HOLD ON, WOLVERINE! I'LL--
--I'LL... WOLVERINE? WHERE ARE YOU-- ACH, WHERE AM I?
I MUST BE DREAMING. WHAT'S HAPPENED TO THE BATTLE?
AND WHO ARE THESE... PEOPLE?!?
YOU'RE ALL... LITTLE... AND YOUR EARS ARE POINTED LIKE MINE.
I AM DREAMING, BECAUSE THAT WOULD MEAN YOU'RE... YOU'RE --NO, THAT'S IMPOSSIBLE.
IT'S NOT, Y'KNOW.

LEPRECHAUNS?! *PHANTASTISCH!* I'M TALKING TO *REAL* -- OH, WAIT UNTIL I TELL MY *FRIENDS!*

MEIN GOTT! MY *FRIENDS!* THE BATTLE! WHAT'S *HAPPENED* TO THEM?!

THEY'VE BEEN *CAPTURED*, NIGHTCRAWLER, BY BLACK TOM AND JUGGERNAUT.

WHO--?! OH, IT'S--

EAMON O'DONNELL, MY FRIEND--

--THE *SENESCHAL* O' CASSIDY KEEP, AND-- 'TIL BLACK TOM CAME--THE MAN WHO KEPT THE *FAMILIES* SAFE FROM *HARM.* Y'SEE, YOUR FRIENDS ARE IN *DEADLY DANGER*, IT'S TRUE...

...BUT SO ARE *MINE.*

"IT BEGAN ABOUT A *MONTH* AGO, WHEN BLACK TOM CASSIDY *TRICKED* HIS WAY BACK INTO THIS CASTLE THAT HAD ONCE BEEN HIS *HOME.*

"HE BROUGHT *JUGGERNAUT* WITH HIM! YE CAN *GUESS* WHAT HAPPENED *NEXT.*

"THAT FIRST NIGHT, THEY TOOK *MOST* OF THE FAMILIES PRIS- ONER--

"--AND HELD THEIR LIVES *HOSTAGE* AGAINST MY *GOOD BEHAVIOR.*

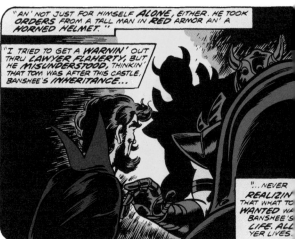

"AN' NOT JUST FOR HIMSELF *ALONE*, EITHER. HE TOOK *ORDERS* FROM A TALL MAN IN *RED* ARMOR AN' A *HORNED HELMET.*"

"I TRIED TO GET A *WARNIN'* OUT THRU *LAWYER FLAHERTY*, BUT HE *MISUNDERSTOOD*, THINKIN' THAT TOM WAS AFTER THIS CASTLE, BANSHEE'S *INHERITANCE*...

"...NEVER *REALIZIN* TH WANTED W BANSHEE'S LIFE. ALL YER LIVES.

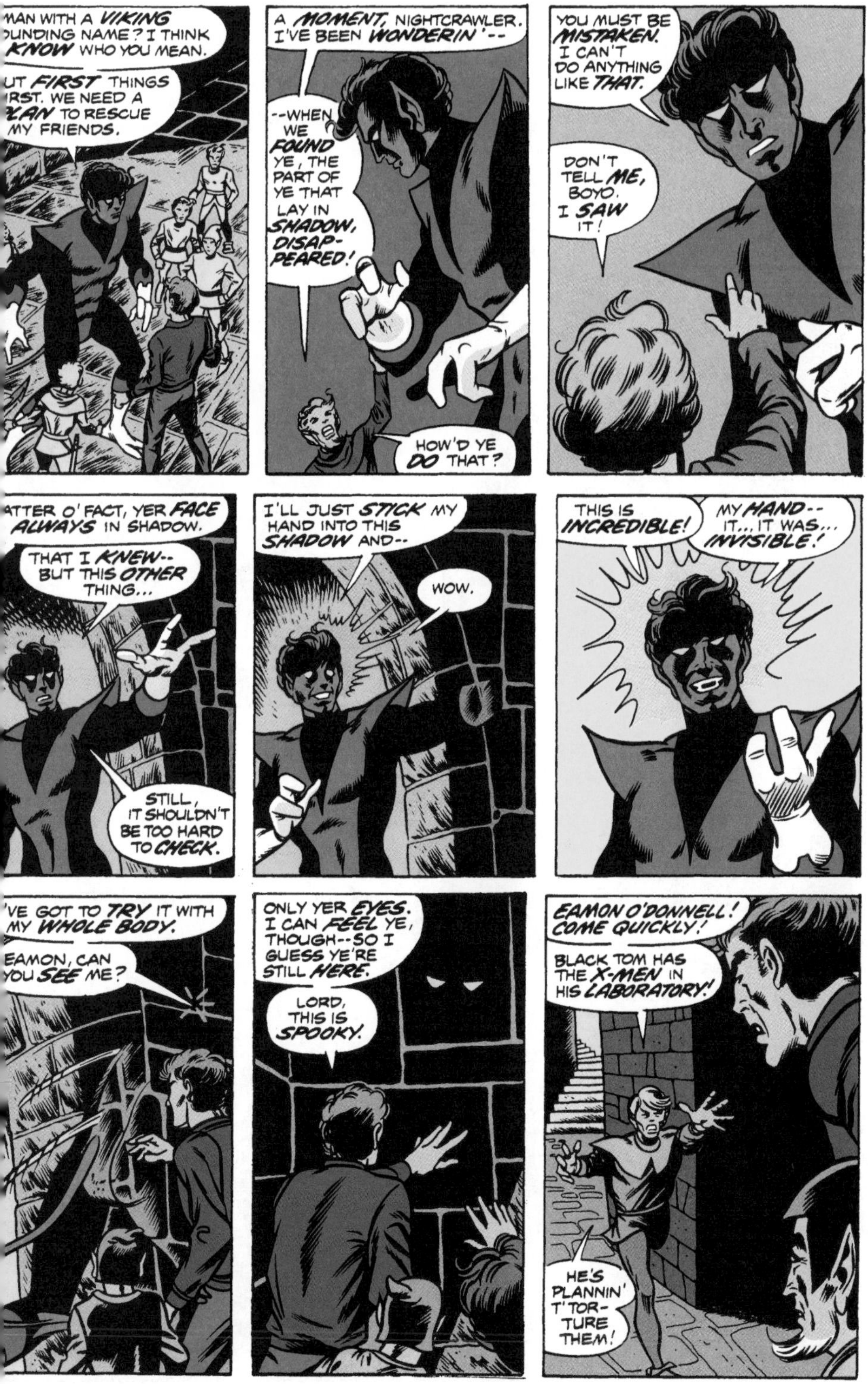
MAN WITH A VIKING OUNDING NAME? I THINK KNOW WHO YOU MEAN.
UT FIRST THINGS IRST. WE NEED A AN TO RESCUE MY FRIENDS.
A MOMENT, NIGHTCRAWLER. I'VE BEEN WONDERIN'--
--WHEN WE FOUND YE, THE PART OF YE THAT LAY IN SHADOW, DISAP-PEARED!
HOW'D YE DO THAT?
YOU MUST BE MISTAKEN. I CAN'T DO ANYTHING LIKE THAT.
DON'T TELL ME, BOYO. I SAW IT!
ATTER O' FACT, YER FACE ALWAYS IN SHADOW.
THAT I KNEW-- BUT THIS OTHER THING...
STILL, IT SHOULDN'T BE TOO HARD TO CHECK.
I'LL JUST STICK MY HAND INTO THIS SHADOW AND--
WOW.
THIS IS INCREDIBLE!
MY HAND-- IT... IT WAS... INVISIBLE!
'VE GOT TO TRY IT WITH MY WHOLE BODY.
EAMON, CAN YOU SEE ME?
ONLY YER EYES. I CAN FEEL YE, THOUGH--SO I GUESS YE'RE STILL HERE.
LORD, THIS IS SPOOKY.
EAMON O'DONNELL! COME QUICKLY!
BLACK TOM HAS THE X-MEN IN HIS LABORATORY!
HE'S PLANNIN' T'TOR-TURE THEM!

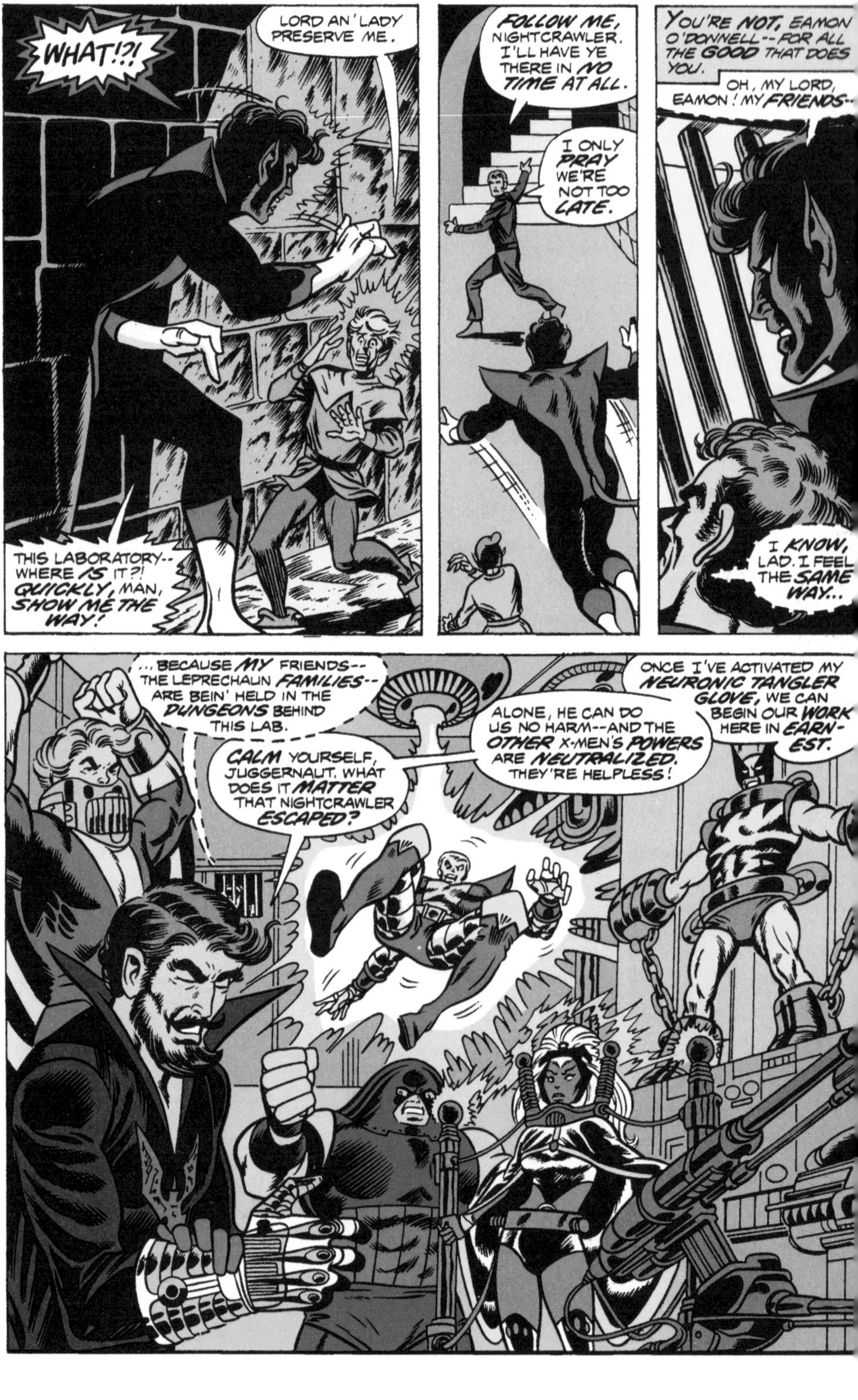
WHAT!?!
LORD AN' LADY PRESERVE ME.
THIS LABORATORY-- WHERE IS IT?! QUICKLY, MAN, SHOW ME THE WAY!
FOLLOW ME, NIGHTCRAWLER. I'LL HAVE YE THERE IN NO TIME AT ALL.
I ONLY PRAY WE'RE NOT TOO LATE.
YOU'RE NOT, EAMON O'DONNELL--FOR ALL THE GOOD THAT DOES YOU.
OH, MY LORD, EAMON! MY FRIENDS--
I KNOW, LAD. I FEEL THE SAME WAY...
...BECAUSE MY FRIENDS-- THE LEPRECHAUN FAMILIES-- ARE BEIN' HELD IN THE DUNGEONS BEHIND THIS LAB.
CALM YOURSELF, JUGGERNAUT. WHAT DOES IT MATTER THAT NIGHTCRAWLER ESCAPED?
ALONE, HE CAN DO US NO HARM--AND THE OTHER X-MEN'S POWERS ARE NEUTRALIZED. THEY'RE HELPLESS!
ONCE I'VE ACTIVATED MY NEURONIC TANGLER GLOVE, WE CAN BEGIN OUR WORK HERE IN EARN-EST.

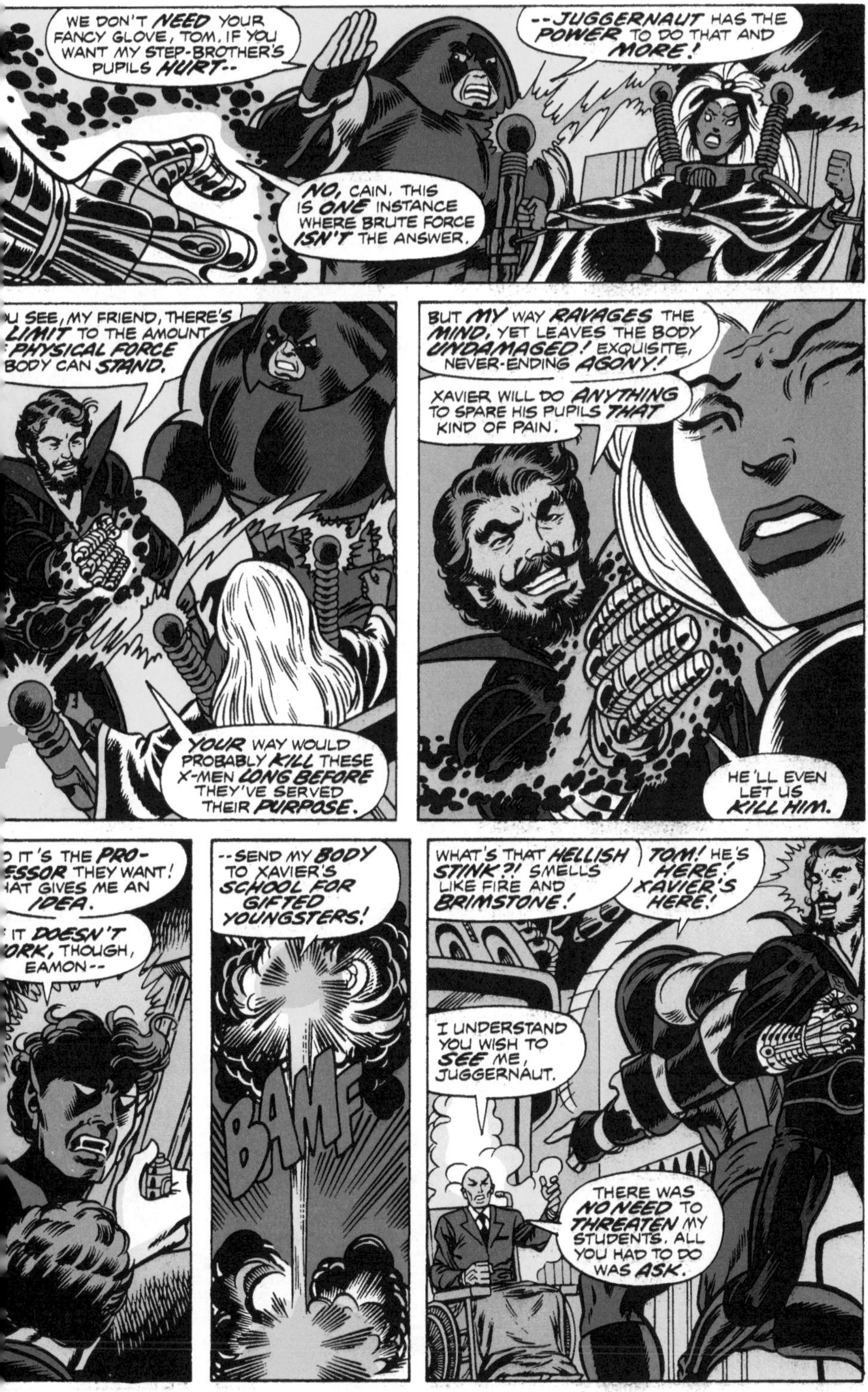

WE DON'T NEED YOUR FANCY GLOVE, TOM. IF YOU WANT MY STEP-BROTHER'S PUPILS HURT--
--JUGGERNAUT HAS THE POWER TO DO THAT AND MORE!
NO, CAIN. THIS IS ONE INSTANCE WHERE BRUTE FORCE ISN'T THE ANSWER.
U SEE, MY FRIEND, THERE'S LIMIT TO THE AMOUNT PHYSICAL FORCE BODY CAN STAND.
YOUR WAY WOULD PROBABLY KILL THESE X-MEN LONG BEFORE THEY'VE SERVED THEIR PURPOSE.
BUT MY WAY RAVAGES THE MIND, YET LEAVES THE BODY UNDAMAGED! EXQUISITE, NEVER-ENDING AGONY!
XAVIER WILL DO ANYTHING TO SPARE HIS PUPILS THAT KIND OF PAIN.
HE'LL EVEN LET US KILL HIM.
O IT'S THE PRO-ESSOR THEY WANT! HAT GIVES ME AN IDEA.
IT DOESN'T ORK, THOUGH, EAMON--
--SEND MY BODY TO XAVIER'S SCHOOL FOR GIFTED YOUNGSTERS!
BAMF
WHAT'S THAT HELLISH STINK?! SMELLS LIKE FIRE AND BRIMSTONE!
TOM! HE'S HERE! XAVIER'S HERE!
I UNDERSTAND YOU WISH TO SEE ME, JUGGERNAUT.
THERE WAS NO NEED TO THREATEN MY STUDENTS. ALL YOU HAD TO DO WAS ASK.

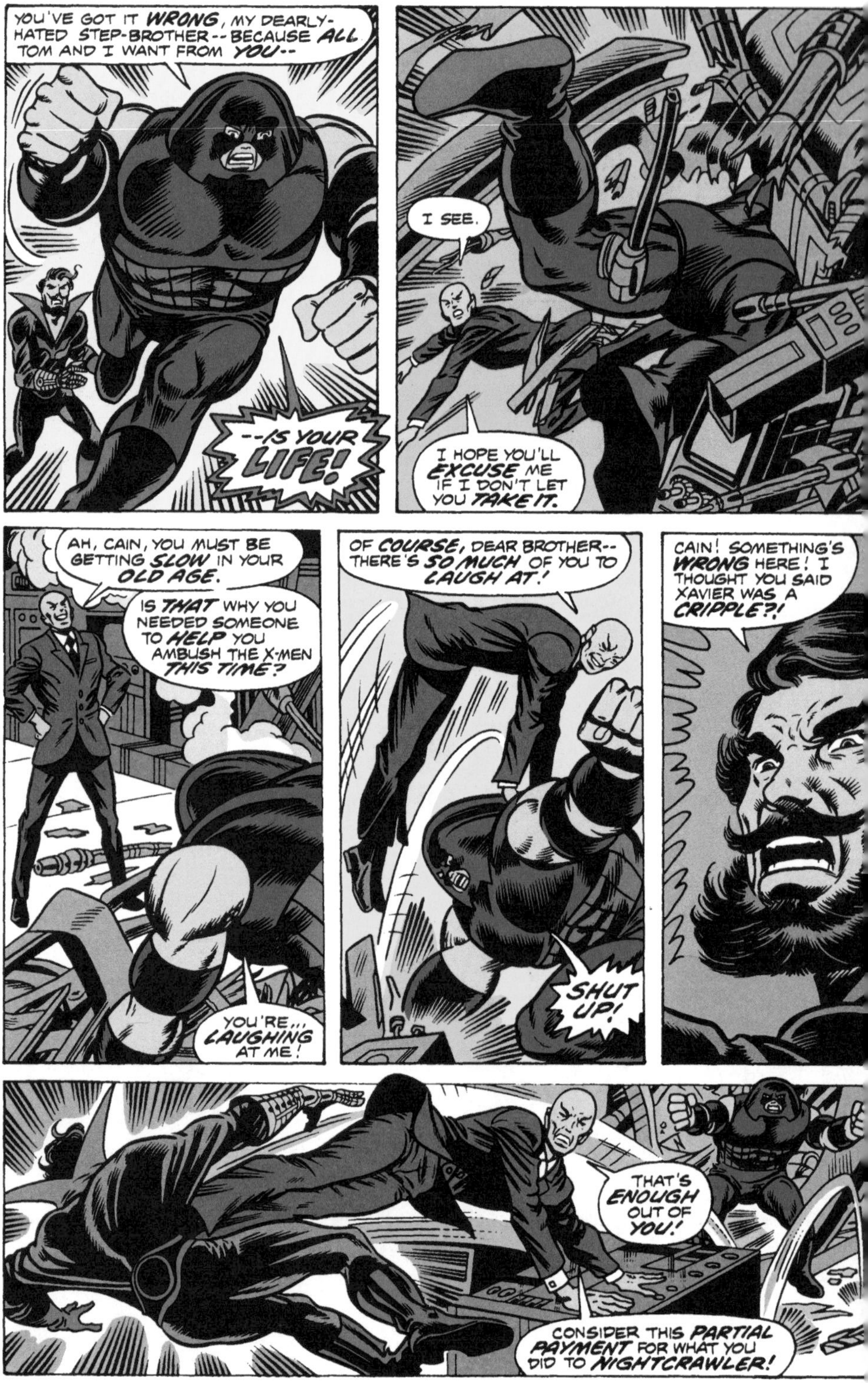
YOU'VE GOT IT WRONG, MY DEARLY-HATED STEP-BROTHER--BECAUSE ALL TOM AND I WANT FROM YOU--
--IS YOUR LIFE!
I SEE.
I HOPE YOU'LL EXCUSE ME IF I DON'T LET YOU TAKE IT.
AH, CAIN, YOU MUST BE GETTING SLOW IN YOUR OLD AGE.
IS THAT WHY YOU NEEDED SOMEONE TO HELP YOU AMBUSH THE X-MEN THIS TIME?
YOU'RE... LAUGHING AT ME!
OF COURSE, DEAR BROTHER-- THERE'S SO MUCH OF YOU TO LAUGH AT!
SHUT UP!
CAIN! SOMETHING'S WRONG HERE! I THOUGHT YOU SAID XAVIER WAS A CRIPPLE?!
THAT'S ENOUGH OUT OF YOU!
CONSIDER THIS PARTIAL PAYMENT FOR WHAT YOU DID TO NIGHTCRAWLER!

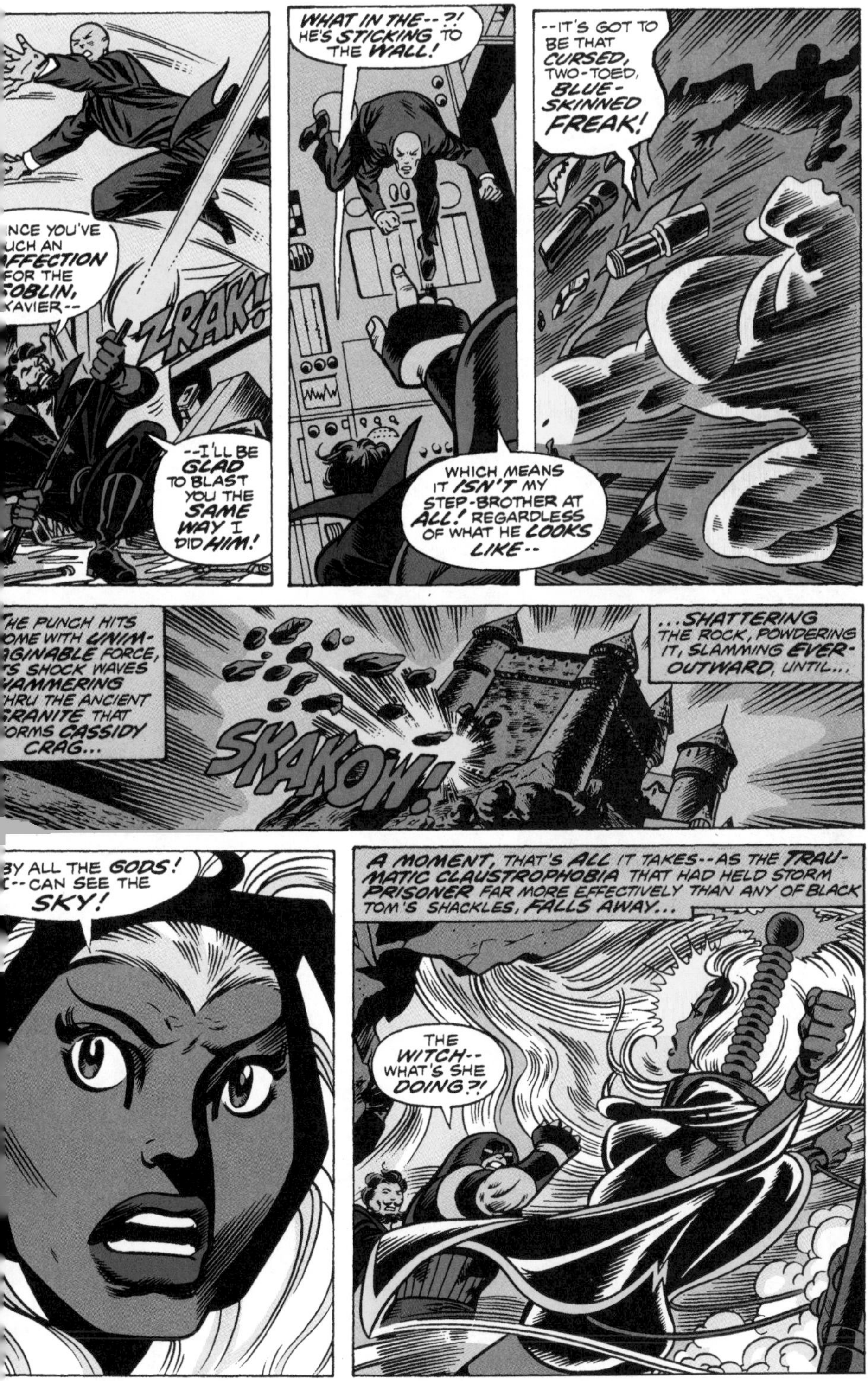
INCE YOU'VE UCH AN AFFECTION FOR THE GOBLIN, XAVIER--
ZRAK!
--I'LL BE GLAD TO BLAST YOU THE SAME WAY I DID HIM!
WHAT IN THE--?! HE'S STICKING TO THE WALL!
WHICH MEANS IT ISN'T MY STEP-BROTHER AT ALL! REGARDLESS OF WHAT HE LOOKS LIKE--
--IT'S GOT TO BE THAT CURSED, TWO-TOED, BLUE-SKINNED FREAK!
THE PUNCH HITS OME WITH UNIM-AGINABLE FORCE, TS SHOCK WAVES HAMMERING THRU THE ANCIENT GRANITE THAT FORMS CASSIDY CRAG...
SKAKOW!
...SHATTERING THE ROCK, POWDERING IT, SLAMMING EVER-OUTWARD, UNTIL...
BY ALL THE GODS! I--CAN SEE THE SKY!
A MOMENT, THAT'S ALL IT TAKES--AS THE TRAUMATIC CLAUSTROPHOBIA THAT HAD HELD STORM PRISONER FAR MORE EFFECTIVELY THAN ANY OF BLACK TOM'S SHACKLES, FALLS AWAY...
THE WITCH--WHAT'S SHE DOING?!

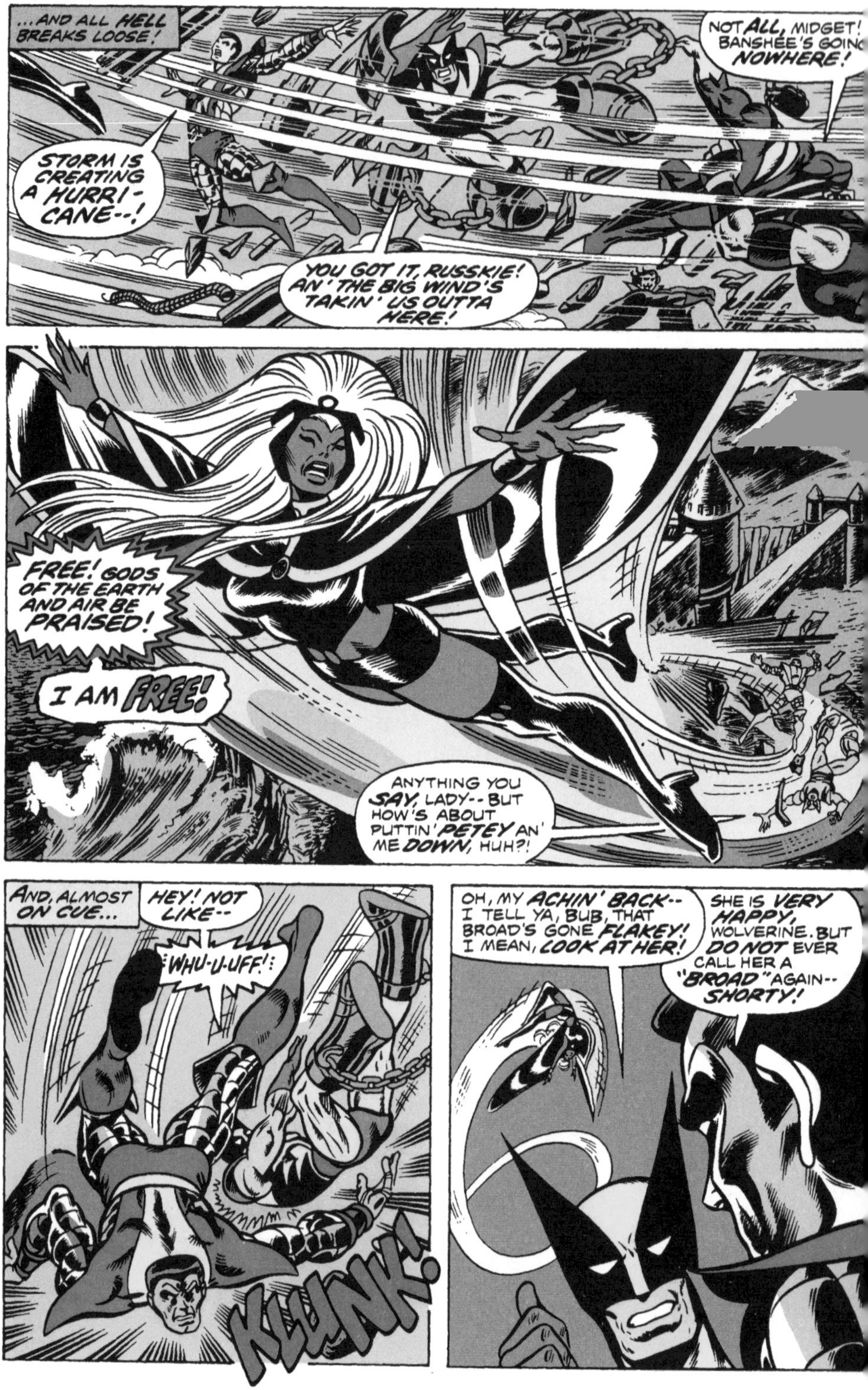
...AND ALL HELL BREAKS LOOSE!
NOT ALL, MIDGET! BANSHEE'S GOING NOWHERE!
STORM IS CREATING A HURRI-CANE--!
YOU GOT IT, RUSSKIE! AN' THE BIG WIND'S TAKIN' US OUTTA HERE!
FREE! GODS OF THE EARTH AND AIR BE PRAISED!
I AM FREE!
ANYTHING YOU SAY, LADY-- BUT HOW'S ABOUT PUTTIN' PETEY AN' ME DOWN, HUH?!
AND, ALMOST ON CUE...
HEY! NOT LIKE--
WHU-U-UFF!
KLUNK!
OH, MY ACHIN' BACK-- I TELL YA, BUB, THAT BROAD'S GONE FLAKEY! I MEAN, LOOK AT HER!
SHE IS VERY HAPPY, WOLVERINE. BUT DO NOT EVER CALL HER A "BROAD" AGAIN-- SHORTY!

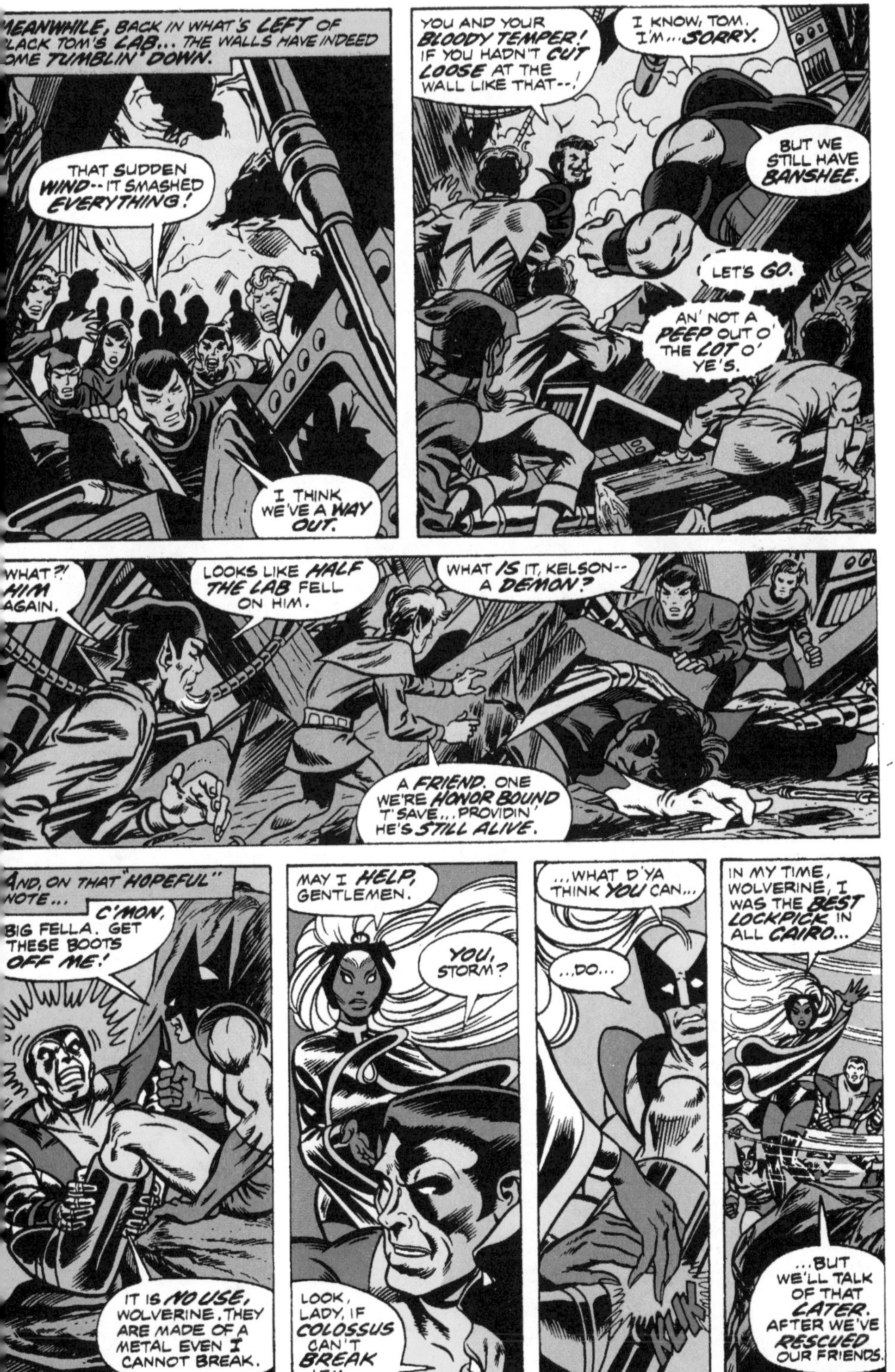
MEANWHILE, BACK IN WHAT'S LEFT OF BLACK TOM'S LAB... THE WALLS HAVE INDEED COME TUMBLIN' DOWN.
THAT SUDDEN WIND-- IT SMASHED EVERYTHING!
I THINK WE'VE A WAY OUT.
YOU AND YOUR BLOODY TEMPER! IF YOU HADN'T CUT LOOSE AT THE WALL LIKE THAT--!
I KNOW, TOM. I'M... SORRY.
BUT WE STILL HAVE BANSHEE.
LET'S GO.
AN' NOT A PEEP OUT O' THE LOT O' YE'S.
WHAT?! HIM AGAIN.
LOOKS LIKE HALF THE LAB FELL ON HIM.
WHAT IS IT, KELSON-- A DEMON?
A FRIEND. ONE WE'RE HONOR BOUND T'SAVE... PROVIDIN' HE'S STILL ALIVE.
AND, ON THAT "HOPEFUL" NOTE...
C'MON, BIG FELLA. GET THESE BOOTS OFF ME!
IT IS NO USE, WOLVERINE. THEY ARE MADE OF A METAL EVEN I CANNOT BREAK.
MAY I HELP, GENTLEMEN.
YOU, STORM?
LOOK, LADY, IF COLOSSUS CAN'T BREAK 'EM...
...WHAT D'YA THINK YOU CAN...
...DO...
KLIK
IN MY TIME, WOLVERINE, I WAS THE BEST LOCKPICK IN ALL CAIRO...
...BUT WE'LL TALK OF THAT LATER. AFTER WE'VE RESCUED OUR FRIENDS.

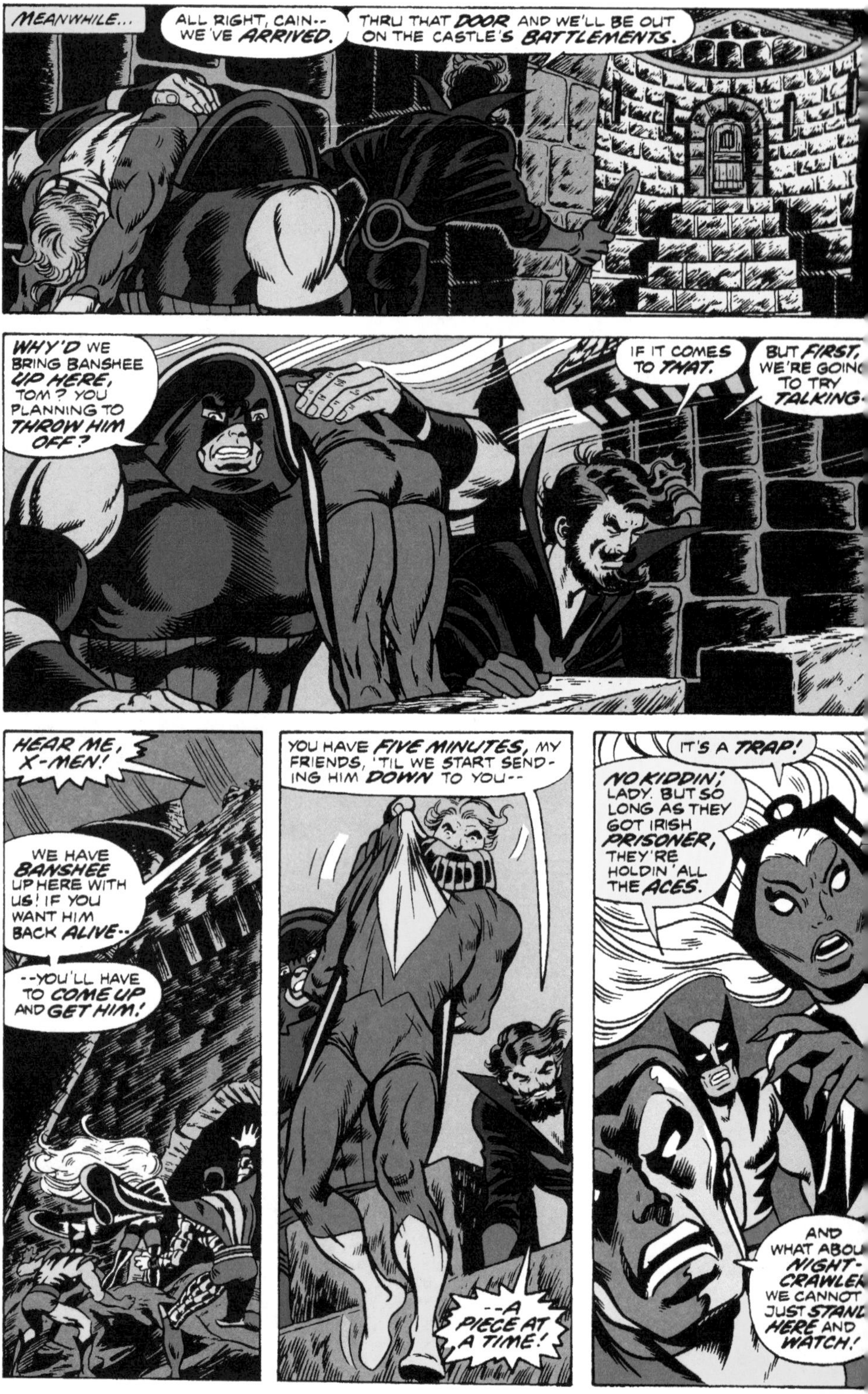
MEANWHILE...
ALL RIGHT, CAIN-- WE'VE ARRIVED.
THRU THAT DOOR AND WE'LL BE OUT ON THE CASTLE'S BATTLEMENTS.
WHY'D WE BRING BANSHEE UP HERE, TOM? YOU PLANNING TO THROW HIM OFF?
IF IT COMES TO THAT.
BUT FIRST, WE'RE GOING TO TRY TALKING--
HEAR ME, X-MEN!
WE HAVE BANSHEE UP HERE WITH US! IF YOU WANT HIM BACK ALIVE--
--YOU'LL HAVE TO COME UP AND GET HIM!
YOU HAVE FIVE MINUTES, MY FRIENDS, 'TIL WE START SENDING HIM DOWN TO YOU--
--A PIECE AT A TIME!
IT'S A TRAP!
NO KIDDIN', LADY. BUT SO LONG AS THEY GOT IRISH PRISONER, THEY'RE HOLDIN' ALL THE ACES.
AND WHAT ABOU NIGHT-CRAWLER WE CANNOT JUST STAND HERE AND WATCH!

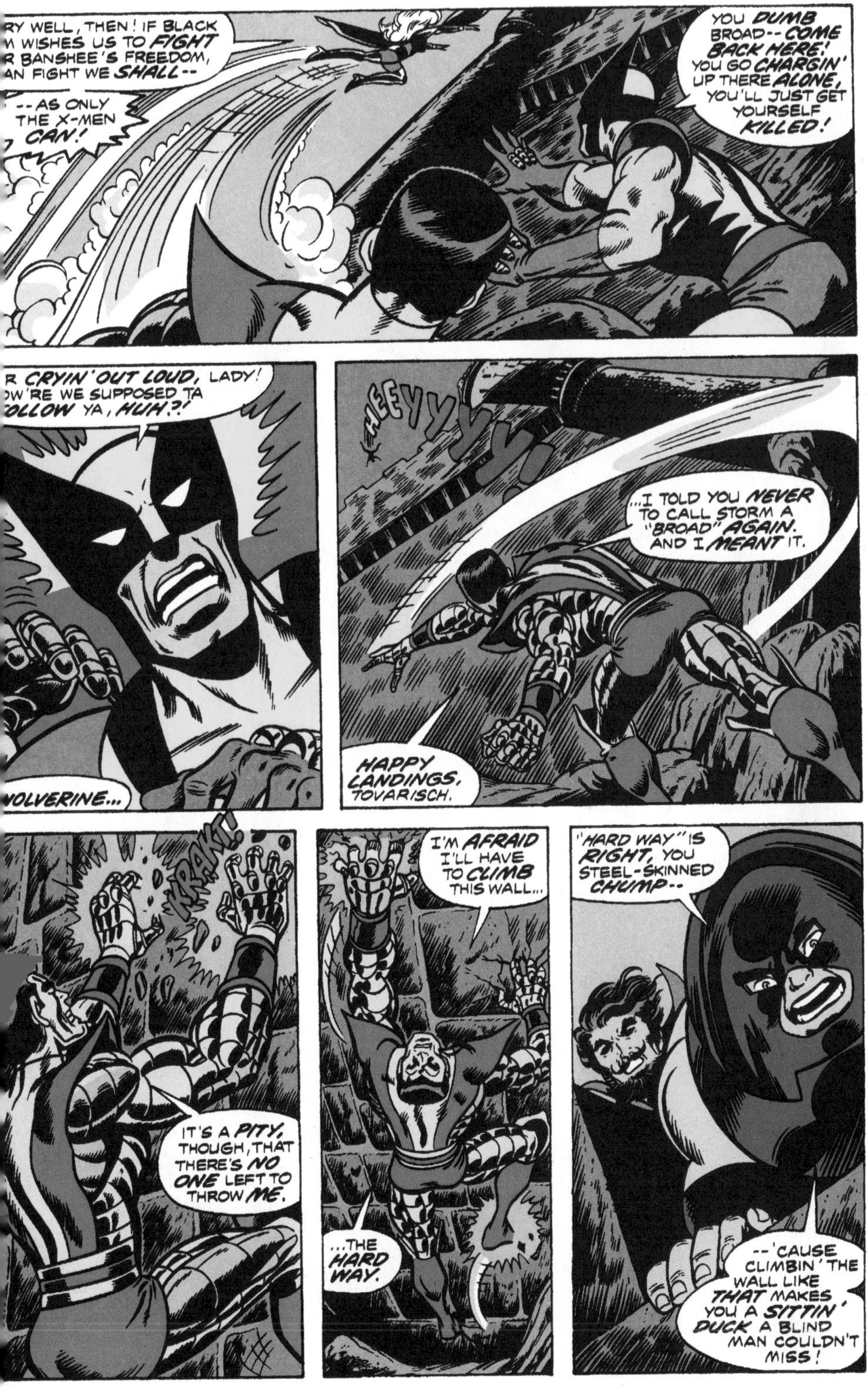

RY WELL, THEN! IF BLACK M WISHES US TO FIGHT R BANSHEE'S FREEDOM, AN FIGHT WE SHALL--
--AS ONLY THE X-MEN CAN!
YOU DUMB BROAD--COME BACK HERE! YOU GO CHARGIN' UP THERE ALONE, YOU'LL JUST GET YOURSELF KILLED!
R CRYIN' OUT LOUD, LADY! W'RE WE SUPPOSED TA FOLLOW YA, HUH?!
HEEYYYYY!
...I TOLD YOU NEVER TO CALL STORM A "BROAD" AGAIN. AND I MEANT IT.
WOLVERINE...
HAPPY LANDINGS, TOVARISCH.
KRAKT!
IT'S A PITY, THOUGH, THAT THERE'S NO ONE LEFT TO THROW ME.
I'M AFRAID I'LL HAVE TO CLIMB THIS WALL...
...THE HARD WAY.
"HARD WAY" IS RIGHT, YOU STEEL-SKINNED CHUMP--
--'CAUSE CLIMBIN' THE WALL LIKE THAT MAKES YOU A SITTIN' DUCK A BLIND MAN COULDN'T MISS!

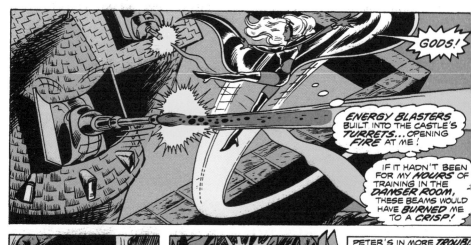

GODS!

ENERGY BLASTERS BUILT INTO THE CASTLE'S *TURRETS*...OPENING *FIRE* AT ME!

IF IT HADN'T BEEN FOR MY *HOURS* OF TRAINING IN THE *DANGER ROOM*, THESE BEAMS WOULD HAVE *BURNED* ME TO A *CRISP!*

WHAT DOES IT *TAKE* TO *KILL YOU,* MUTANT?!

KB

RAK!

PETER'S IN MORE *TROUBLE* THAN HE WILL ADMIT!

BUT I *DARE NOT* STOP TO AID HIM UNTIL THESE BLASTERS ARE *SILENCED!*

A FEW *MINUTES* AGO, THIS HAD BEEN A CALM, *CLEAR* NIGHT, WITH HARDLY A *CLOUD* TO MASK THE *STARS*...

...BUT THAT'S *CHANGED*...

...AS THE *FURY* OF STORM'S *ATTACK* TWISTS WEATHER PATTERNS FOR *MILES* AROUND, CREATING --IN AN INSTANT-- THE *WORST* ATLANTIC GALE IN *LIVING MEMORY.*

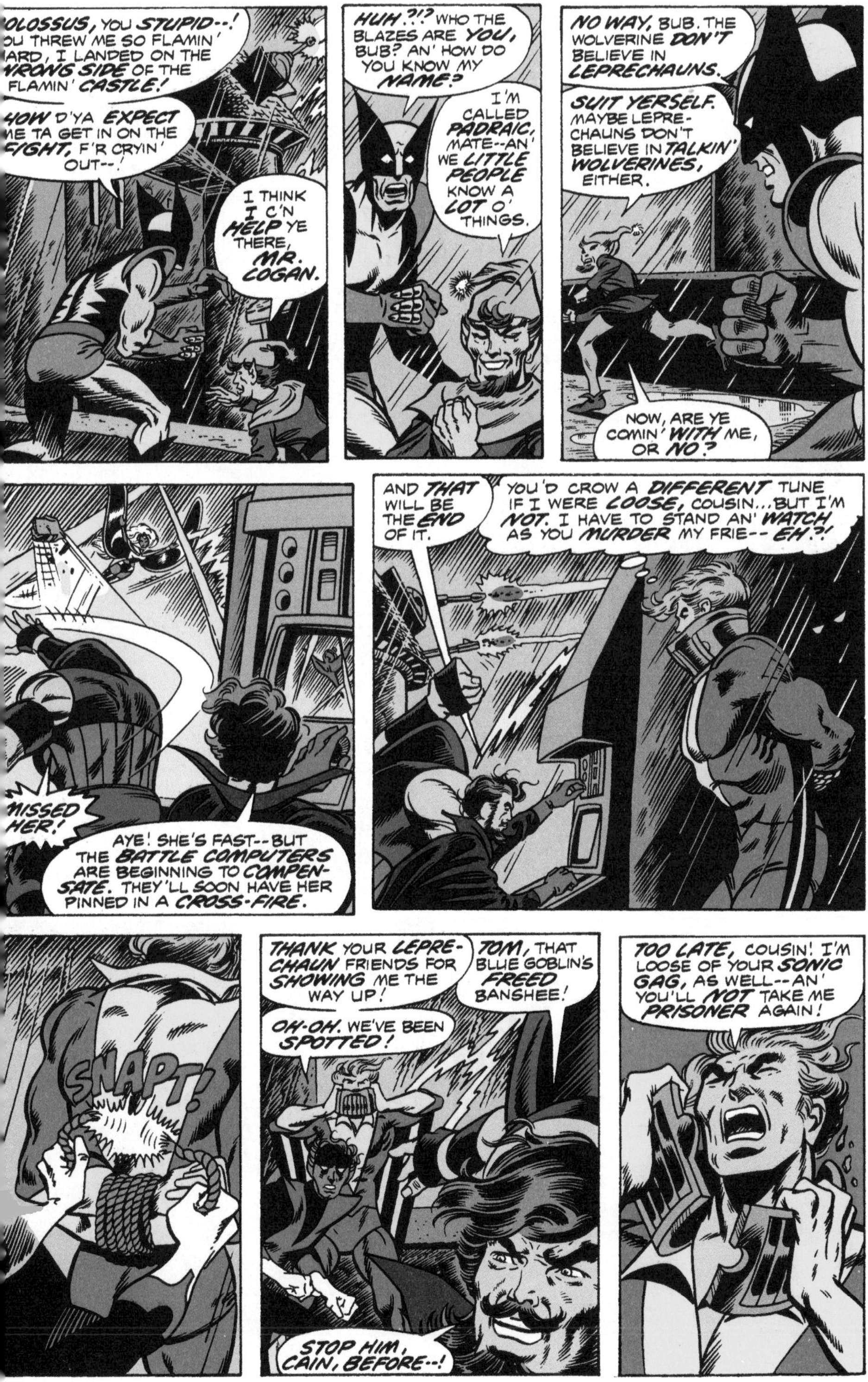
OLOSSUS, YOU STUPID--! OU THREW ME SO FLAMIN' ARD, I LANDED ON THE RONG SIDE OF THE FLAMIN' CASTLE!
HOW D'YA EXPECT ME TA GET IN ON THE FIGHT, F'R CRYIN' OUT--!
I THINK I C'N HELP YE THERE, MR. COGAN.
HUH?!? WHO THE BLAZES ARE YOU, BUB? AN' HOW DO YOU KNOW MY NAME?
I'M CALLED PADRAIC, MATE--AN' WE LITTLE PEOPLE KNOW A LOT O' THINGS.
NO WAY, BUB. THE WOLVERINE DON'T BELIEVE IN LEPRECHAUNS.
SUIT YERSELF. MAYBE LEPRECHAUNS DON'T BELIEVE IN TALKIN' WOLVERINES, EITHER.
NOW, ARE YE COMIN' WITH ME, OR NO?
MISSED HER!
AYE! SHE'S FAST--BUT THE BATTLE COMPUTERS ARE BEGINNING TO COMPENSATE. THEY'LL SOON HAVE HER PINNED IN A CROSS-FIRE.
AND THAT WILL BE THE END OF IT.
YOU'D CROW A DIFFERENT TUNE IF I WERE LOOSE, COUSIN... BUT I'M NOT. I HAVE TO STAND AN' WATCH AS YOU MURDER MY FRIE-- EH?!
SNAPT!
THANK YOUR LEPRECHAUN FRIENDS FOR SHOWING ME THE WAY UP!
TOM, THAT BLUE GOBLIN'S FREED BANSHEE!
OH-OH. WE'VE BEEN SPOTTED!
STOP HIM, CAIN, BEFORE--!
TOO LATE, COUSIN! I'M LOOSE OF YOUR SONIC GAG, AS WELL--AN' YOU'LL NOT TAKE ME PRISONER AGAIN!

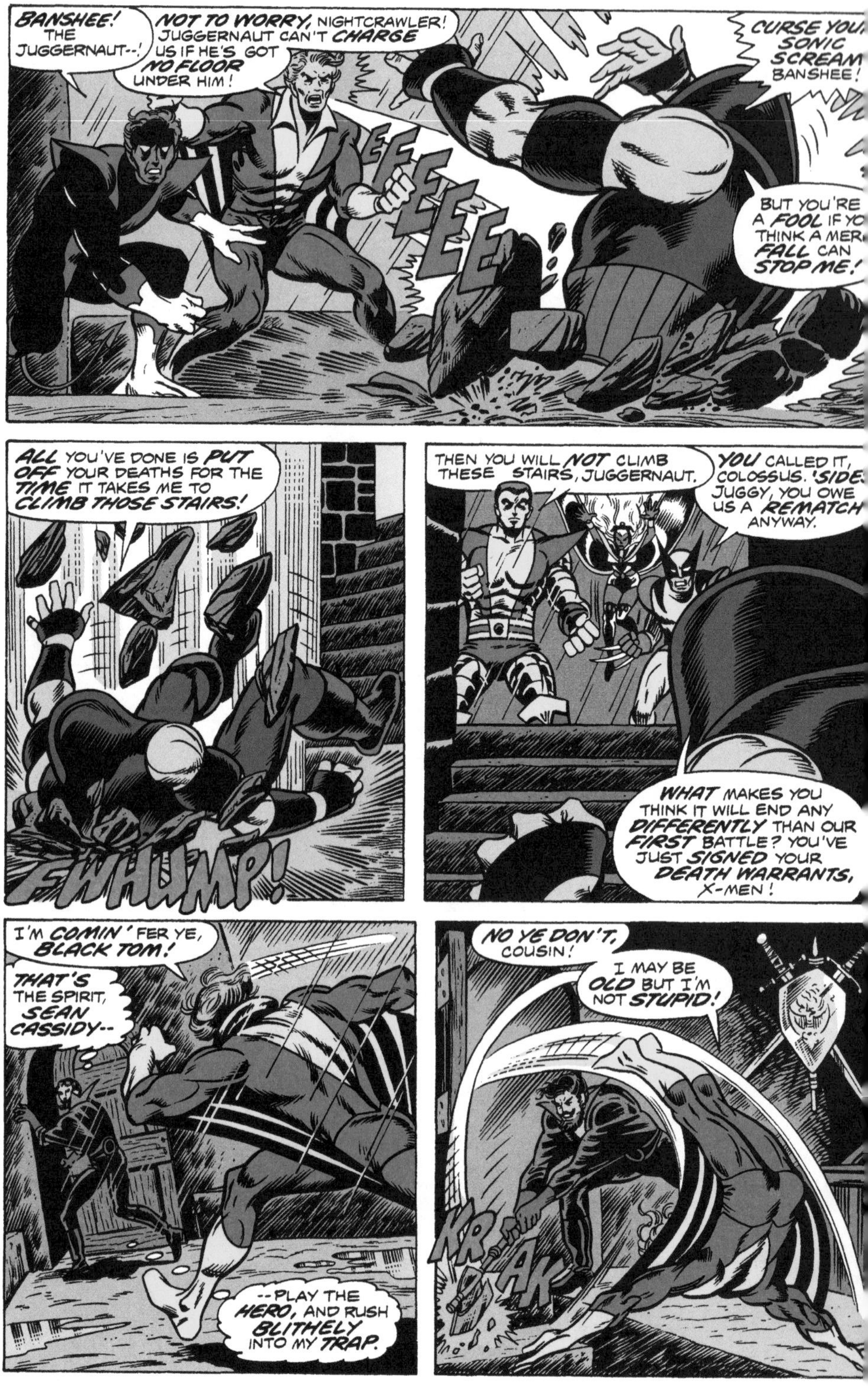
BANSHEE! THE JUGGERNAUT--!
NOT TO WORRY, NIGHTCRAWLER! JUGGERNAUT CAN'T CHARGE US IF HE'S GOT NO FLOOR UNDER HIM!
EEEEEE
CURSE YOU SONIC SCREAM BANSHEE!
BUT YOU'RE A FOOL IF YO THINK A MER FALL CAN STOP ME!
ALL YOU'VE DONE IS PUT OFF YOUR DEATHS FOR THE TIME IT TAKES ME TO CLIMB THOSE STAIRS!
FWHUMP!
THEN YOU WILL NOT CLIMB THESE STAIRS, JUGGERNAUT.
YOU CALLED IT, COLOSSUS. 'SIDE JUGGY, YOU OWE US A REMATCH ANYWAY.
WHAT MAKES YOU THINK IT WILL END ANY DIFFERENTLY THAN OUR FIRST BATTLE? YOU'VE JUST SIGNED YOUR DEATH WARRANTS, X-MEN!
I'M COMIN' FER YE, BLACK TOM!
THAT'S THE SPIRIT, SEAN CASSIDY--
--PLAY THE HERO, AND RUSH BLITHELY INTO MY TRAP.
NO YE DON'T, COUSIN!
I MAY BE OLD BUT I'M NOT STUPID!
KRAK

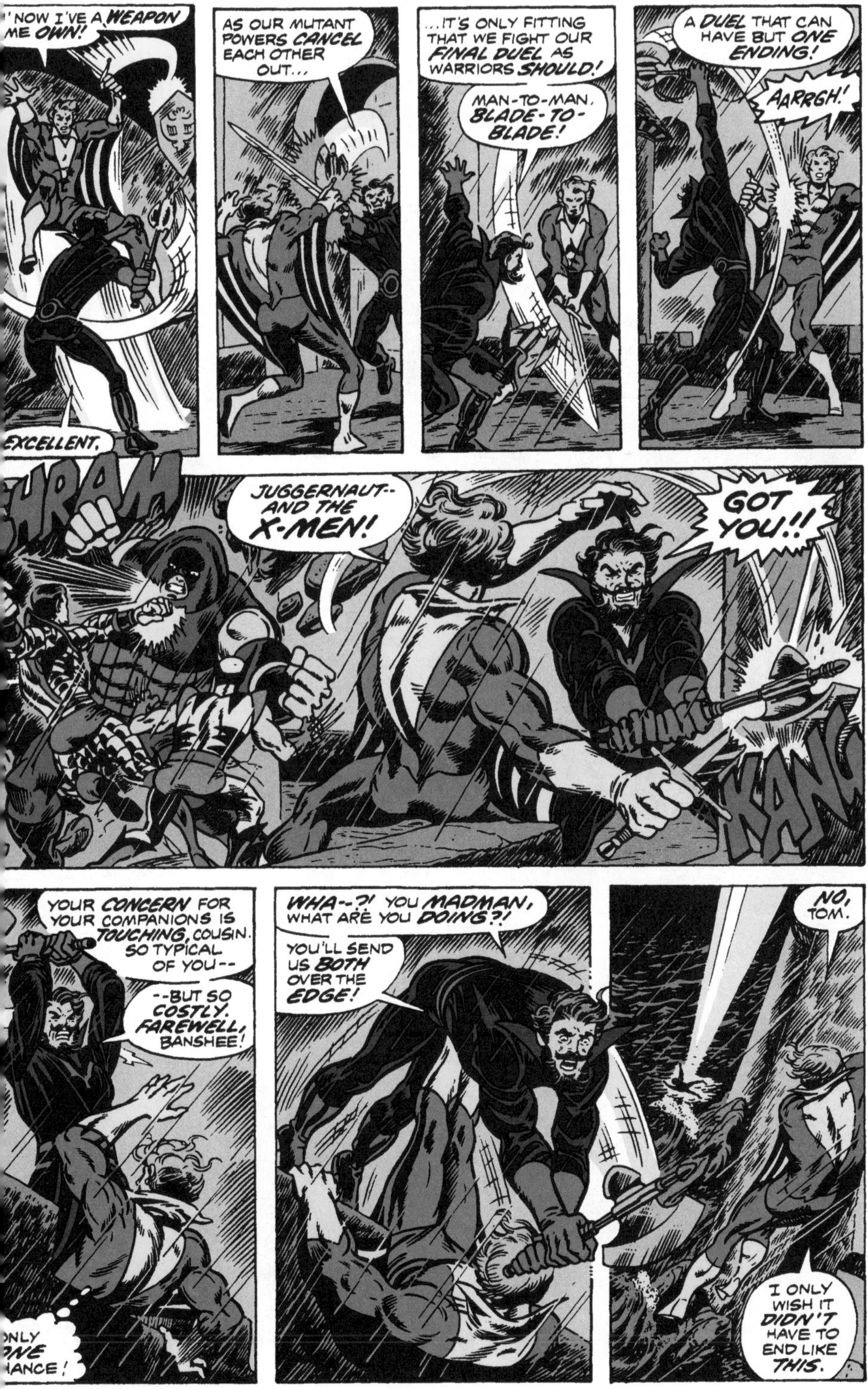'NOW I'VE A WEAPON ME OWN!
EXCELLENT.
AS OUR MUTANT POWERS CANCEL EACH OTHER OUT...
...IT'S ONLY FITTING THAT WE FIGHT OUR FINAL DUEL AS WARRIORS SHOULD!
MAN-TO-MAN, BLADE-TO-BLADE!
A DUEL THAT CAN HAVE BUT ONE ENDING!
AARRGH!
JUGGERNAUT-- AND THE X-MEN!
GOT YOU!!
YOUR CONCERN FOR YOUR COMPANIONS IS TOUCHING, COUSIN. SO TYPICAL OF YOU--
--BUT SO COSTLY. FAREWELL, BANSHEE!
WHA--?! YOU MADMAN, WHAT ARE YOU DOING?!
YOU'LL SEND US BOTH OVER THE EDGE!
NO, TOM.
I ONLY WISH IT DIDN'T HAVE TO END LIKE THIS.

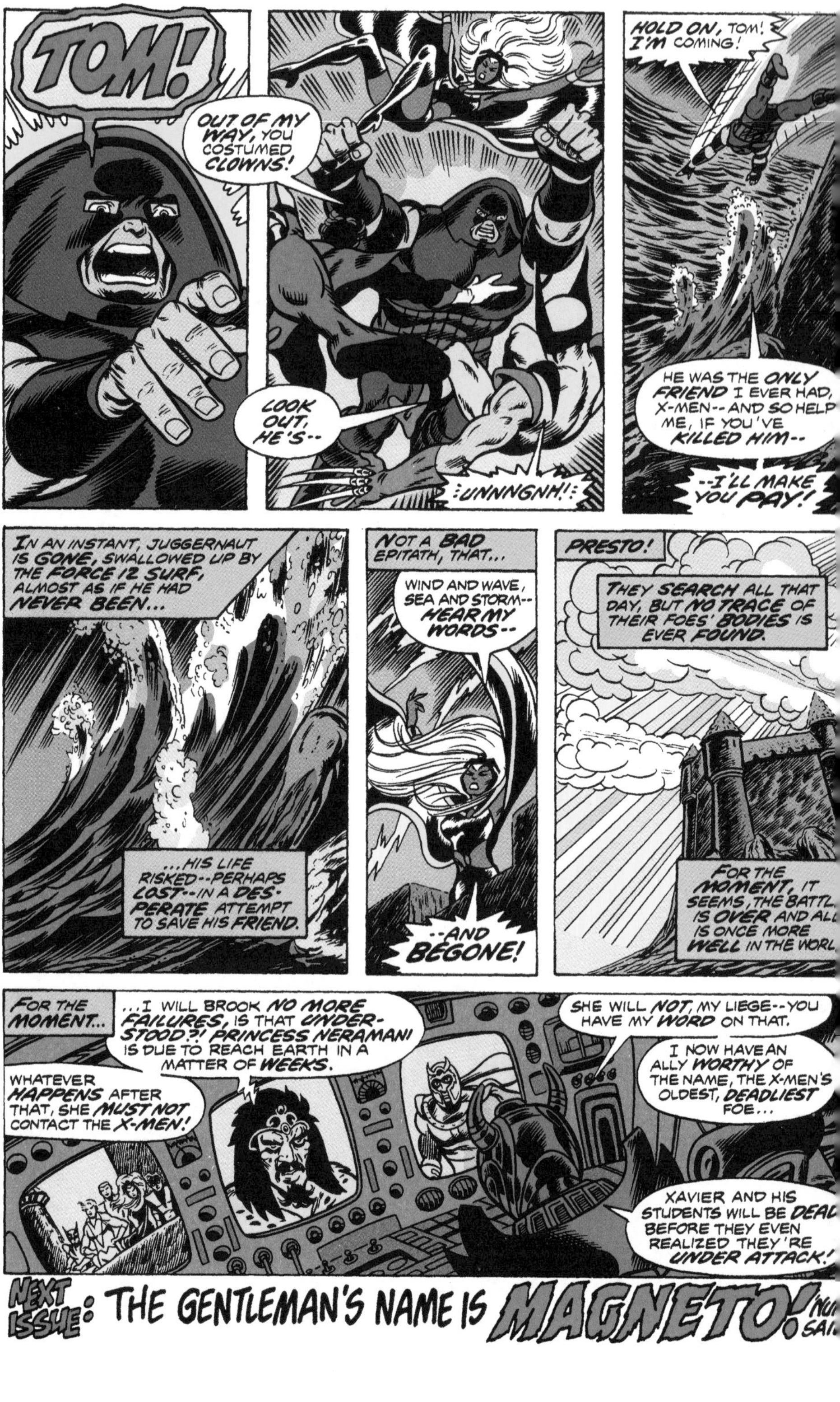
TOM!
OUT OF MY WAY, YOU COSTUMED CLOWNS!
LOOK OUT, HE'S--
UNNNGNH!!
HOLD ON, TOM! I'M COMING!
HE WAS THE ONLY FRIEND I EVER HAD, X-MEN--AND SO HELP ME, IF YOU'VE KILLED HIM--
--I'LL MAKE YOU PAY!
IN AN INSTANT, JUGGERNAUT IS GONE, SWALLOWED UP BY THE FORCE 12 SURF, ALMOST AS IF HE HAD NEVER BEEN...
...HIS LIFE RISKED--PERHAPS LOST--IN A DESPERATE ATTEMPT TO SAVE HIS FRIEND.
NOT A BAD EPITATH, THAT...
WIND AND WAVE, SEA AND STORM--HEAR MY WORDS--
--AND BEGONE!
PRESTO!
THEY SEARCH ALL THAT DAY, BUT NO TRACE OF THEIR FOES' BODIES IS EVER FOUND.
FOR THE MOMENT, IT SEEMS, THE BATTL IS OVER AND ALL IS ONCE MORE WELL IN THE WORL
FOR THE MOMENT...
...I WILL BROOK NO MORE FAILURES, IS THAT UNDERSTOOD?! PRINCESS NERAMANI IS DUE TO REACH EARTH IN A MATTER OF WEEKS.
WHATEVER HAPPENS AFTER THAT, SHE MUST NOT CONTACT THE X-MEN!
SHE WILL NOT, MY LIEGE--YOU HAVE MY WORD ON THAT.
I NOW HAVE AN ALLY WORTHY OF THE NAME, THE X-MEN'S OLDEST, DEADLIEST FOE...
XAVIER AND HIS STUDENTS WILL BE DEAD BEFORE THEY EVEN REALIZED THEY'RE UNDER ATTACK!
NEXT ISSUE: THE GENTLEMAN'S NAME IS MAGNETO!

KNIGHTS OF THE HYKON CHARACTER SKETCHES BY SCOTT KOBLISH

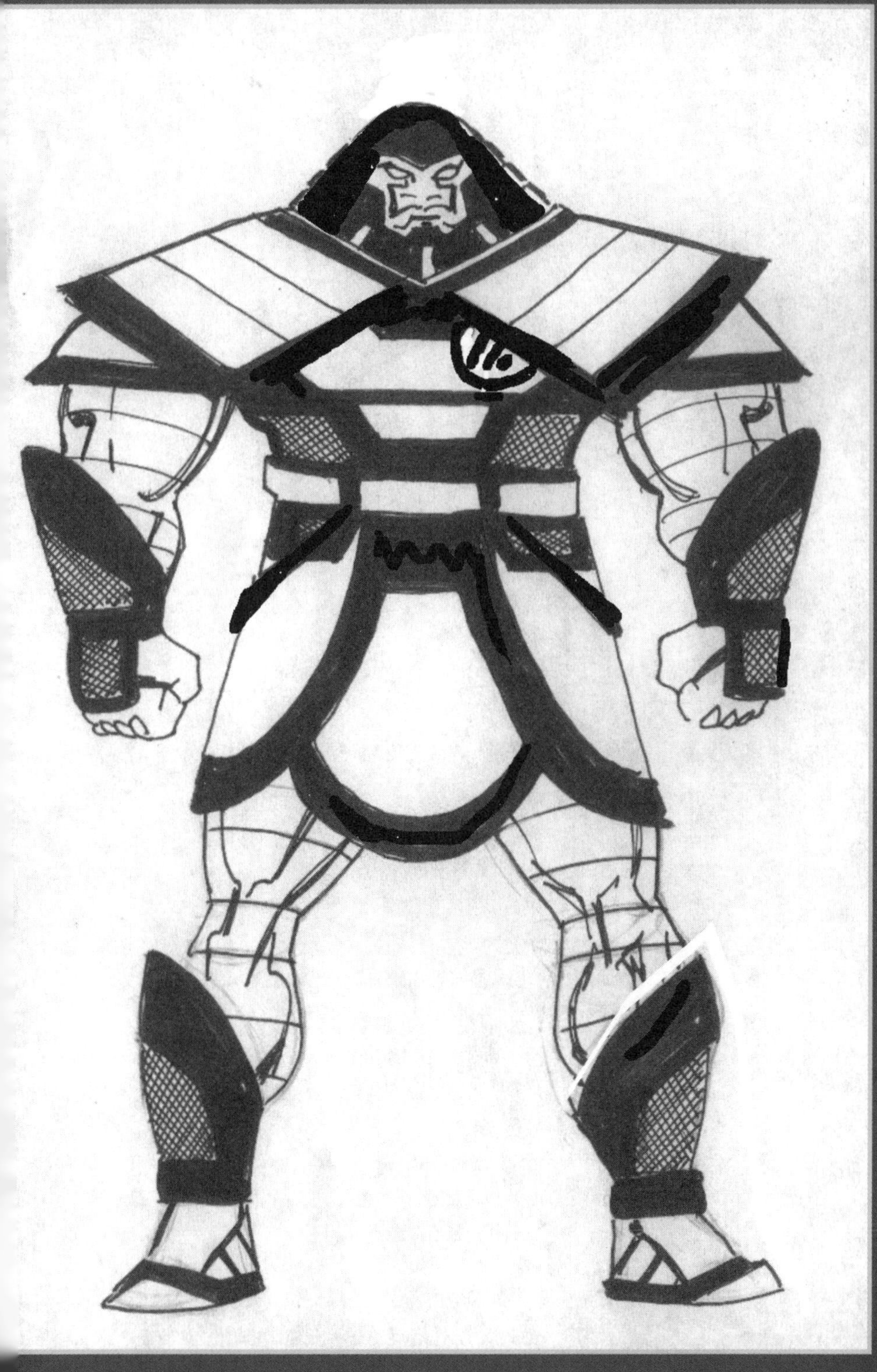

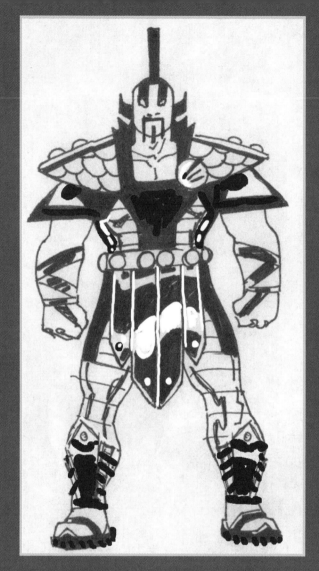

SLEEPING MIST

SKY SONG

BURNING MOON

CLOUD RUNNER

DROWNING SHADOW

BONE D

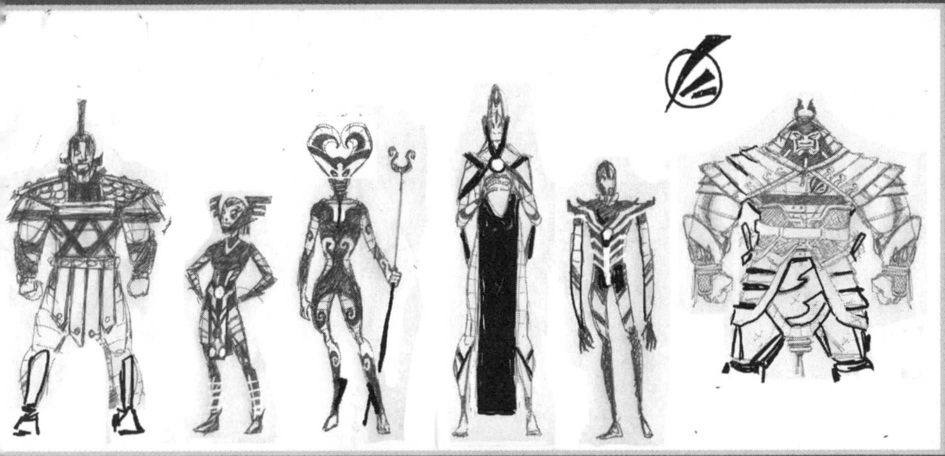

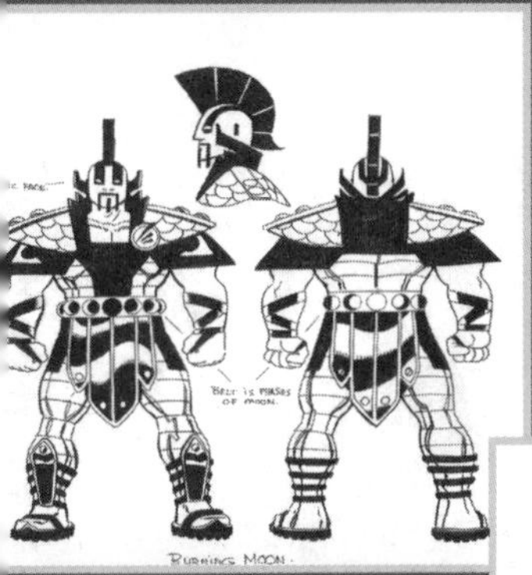
BELT IS PHASES OF MOON.
BURNING MOON.

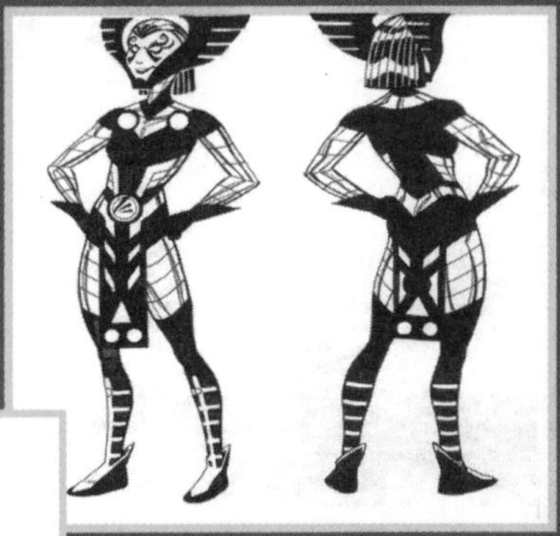

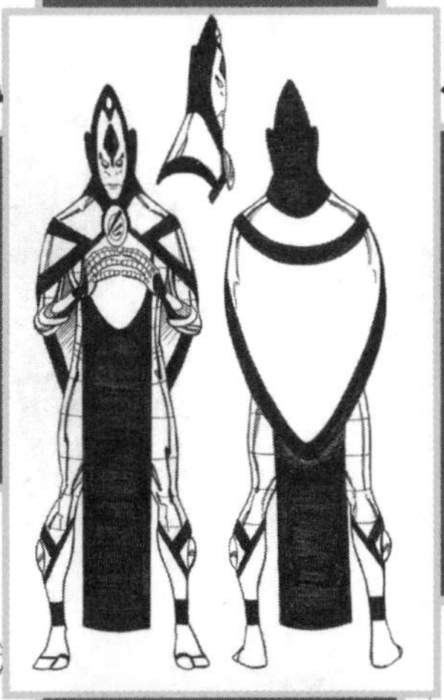

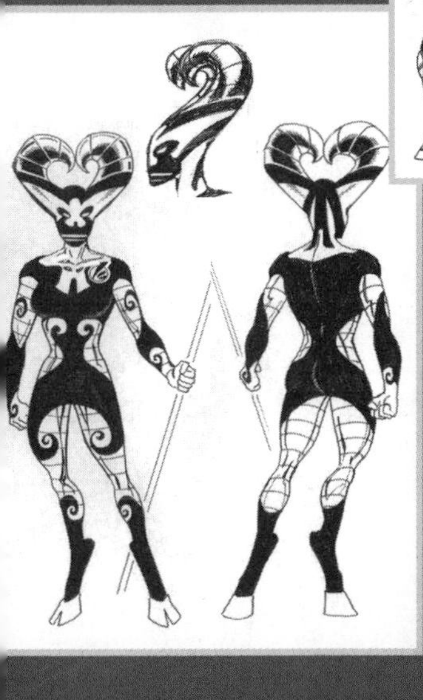

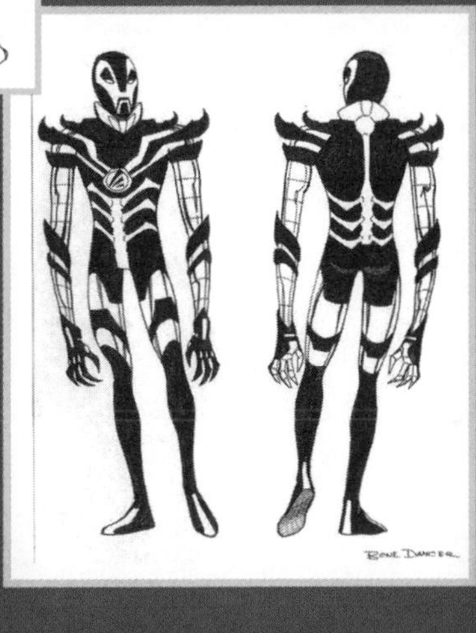
BONE DANCER

UNCANNY
X-MEN
FIRST CLASS